Ecological Integrity and Global Governance

It is increasingly argued that a focus on environmental sustainability is fundamental to effective and equitable governance, and ultimately for the good of mankind. This book argues that, in the face of increasing environmental challenges, it is essential to recognize the role that ecological integrity has played, and must play, in governance for environmental sustainability in order to ensure the future survival of life on earth.

Ecological integrity encompasses not only the necessity of respect for nature, but also the human right to a sound and healthy environment. The author shows that on this basis, acceptance of its primacy in law and governance is key to a sustainable and equitable future for all. The book presents a uniquely informed treatise on the term, examining its origins, evolution and position in current debates, and exploring the conflicts which have so far prevented its acceptance.

Written by a leading scholar on the subject, this book provides the most in-depth exposition of ecological integrity available to increase understanding of this crucial concept and encourage its adoption in governance and international law.

Laura Westra is professor emerita (philosophy), University of Windsor, Canada and a sessional instructor at the Faculty of Law, University of Milano (Bicocca), Italy.

Routledge Research in International Environmental Law

A full list of titles in this series is available at: https://www.routledge.com/series/INTENVLAW

Recently published titles

International Environmental Law and the Conservation of Coral Reefs
Edward J. Goodwin

Common Pools of Genetic Resources
Equity and Innovation in International Biodiversity Law
Evanson Chege Kamau & Gerd Winter

The Precautionary Principle in Marine Environmental Law
With Special Reference to High Risk Vessels
Bénédicte Sage-Fuller

International Environmental Law and Distributive Justice
The Equitable Distribution of CDM Projects under the Kyoto Protocol
Tomilola Akanle Eni-Ibukun

International Climate Change Law and Policy
Cultural Legitimacy in Adaption and Mitigation
Thoko Kaime

International Liability Regime for Biodiversity Damage
The Nagoya-Kuala Lumpur Supplementary Protocol
Akiho Shibata

Climate Change, Forests and REDD
Lessons for Institutional Design
Joyeeta Gupta, Nicolien van der Grijp, Onno Kuik

Environmental Governance in Europe and Asia
A Comparative Study of Institutional and Legislative Frameworks
Jona Razzaque

Climate Change and Forest Governance
Lessons from Indonesia
Simon Butt, Rosemary Lyster & Tim Stephens

Research and Development on Genetic Resources
Public domain approaches to implementing the Nagoya Protocol
Edited by Evanson Chege Kamau, Gerd Winter and Peter-Tobias Stoll

Ecological Integrity and Global Governance

Science, ethics and the law

Laura Westra

Routledge
Taylor & Francis Group
LONDON AND NEW YORK

earthscan
from Routledge

First published 2016
by Routledge
2 Park Square, Milton Park, Abingdon, Oxon OX14 4RN

and by Routledge
711 Third Avenue, New York, NY 10017

First issued in paperback 2018

Routledge is an imprint of the Taylor & Francis Group, an informa business

British Library Cataloguing-in-Publication Data
A catalogue record for this book is available from the British Library

Library of Congress Cataloging in Publication Data
Names: Westra, Laura, author.
Title: Ecological integrity and global governance : science, ethics and the law / Laura Westra.
Description: New York : Routledge, 2016. | Includes bibliographical references and index.
Identifiers: LCCN 2015047180 | ISBN 9781138647220 (hbk) | ISBN 9781315627168 (ebk)
Subjects: LCSH: Environmental law, International. | Ecological integrity. | Environmental ethics. | Sustainability. | International cooperation. | Globalization. | International organization.
Classification: LCC K3585 .W48 2016 | DDC 344.04/6--dc23
LC record available at http://lccn.loc.gov/2015047180

ISBN 13: 978-1-138-61828-2 (pbk)
ISBN 13: 978-1-138-64722-0 (hbk)

Typeset in Times
by Saxon Graphics Ltd, Derby

For Peter

"The sustainability of the human enterprise hangs on entangled threads of ecological integrity and social justice swinging precariously in the void yet to be occupied by effective global governance. Laura Westra's latest book weaves the safety net of science, ethics and international law the world community needs to save itself from itself."

– William Rees, University of British Columbia, Canada

"Global Environmental Governance has many flaws as is commonly known, but this book uncovers their root cause. Summarizing much of her impressive lifework, Laura Westra makes a strong case for ecological integrity as a fundamental principle to guide law and governance. Governments and decision-makers ignore this book's vital message at their peril."

– Klaus Bosselmann, University of Auckland, New Zealand

"With this new book, Laura Westra has added to her prodigious output of scholarly work on the topic of ecological integrity. She continues to give meaning to the vital concept, this time with an emphasis on its importance to law and global governance. Most of Westra's past work on ecological integrity, including on environmental ethics, policy and law, human rights and global justice is interwoven throughout this masterful analysis."

– Kathleen Mahoney, University of Calgary, Canada

"Laura Westra offers an impressive multidisciplinary discussion of the concept of "ecological integrity" aimed at developing it as a working legal category in the making of a cosmopolitan and yet practical ecology of law. This is the best kind of contribution that a philosopher can offer to the challenges of Anthropocene. A must-read."

– Ugo Mattei, co-author of Plunder: When The Rule of Law is Illegal *and of* The Ecology of Law

"Westra has followed the scientific, ethical, philosophical, legal, social, local, and global dimensions of ecosystem integrity across three decades. She is on the front lines in her clarion call that ecosystem integrity is foundational for respecting life on this wonderland Earth."

– Holmes Rolston III, Colorado State University, USA

"The lack of consideration for "ecological integrity" is the key to explain how states and corporations disregard human rights, public health, as well as problems posed by forced migrations, food and water deprivation and climate change. This book is not radical, but radically logical and even balanced in its proposals."

– Tullio Scovazzi, University of Milano-Bicocca, Milan, Italy

Contents

Introduction

In 1972, for the first time, the concept of biological integrity entered the realm of law, in the US Clean Water Act. In 1978, the concept reappeared in the US/ Canada Great Lakes Water Quality Agreement, and it entered into the discourse of ecologists, biologists, economists, toxicologists, regional planners, philosophers and legal scholars. Aldo Leopold had spoken of the foundational value of integrity a long time before these novel uses of integrity (see Chapter 1).

But it was after 1992 that the Global Ecological Integrity Project began to give shape, content and eventually an exhaustive definition to that elusive concept. The original group of scholars began with local or nearby Great Lakes policy meetings; eventually the group expanded to become the Global Ecological Integrity Group, and meet every year, moving beyond the problematic conditions of the Great Lakes, and the clear results of the loss of integrity in the area. Jack Manno, our group's historian, said:

> overfishing, toxic chemical pollution and invasion of alien species decimated native populations of salmon and trout, the top predators of the Great Lakes food web. The smaller bait fish on which salmon and trout once fed multiplied without check.[1]

And this aspect of disintegrity only represented the "top-down crisis". In addition, the "bottom-up" aspect of the disaster was the "overfertilization of the Lakes, from the runoff of nutrients from agriculture, and house hold and industrial use of phosphorus containing detergents".[2] At the time, after having worked at many Canadian and US universities on a contractual basis, teaching primarily environmental and other applied ethics, I was finally awarded a permanent post in 1990 at the University of Windsor, where I remained until retirement in 1999. From a regular, tenure-track position, I was able to apply to and secure grants from Canadian Government sources in 1992 (SSHRC), and that enabled me to bring together those who wanted to understand and flesh out the language of the Great Lakes Water Quality Agreement (GLWQA) between Canada and the US, and the goal "to restore and maintain the chemical, physical and biological integrity of the Great Lakes basin ecosystem".[3]

That goal led to actions that fostered eventually the recovery of Lake Erie, and to some limited control over the pollution affecting the other Great Lakes, based upon the work of the great "systems ecologists" of the time, such as E. P. Odum and Thomas Jorling.[4] But the scholars researching integrity were following not only the insights of Aldo Leopold, but also those of Rachel Carson and Thea Colborn, both of whom used their groundbreaking research to explain the connection between ecosystem integrity and human and non-human health.

The group's scholars also included William Rees who, together with Mathias Wackernagel, was the originator of the ecological footprint analysis, so that he added a "human ecology" and social component to our work, thus far primarily done by natural scientists and environmental ethicists. However, "biological integrity" first emerged in law, as we saw, so that, after reaching our joint definition in 2000 (see Chapter 1), our next meeting was a joint one, including the representatives of the Earth Charter, in Urbino, Italy: at that meeting for the first time, we were joined by several legal scholars.

The Earth Charter was the first, and remains the only, "soft law" charter that has ecological integrity as one of its principles.[5] Among the legal scholars who joined the group, outstanding was Prue Taylor, a staunch supporter of environmental human rights.[6]

The group had also been collaborating with a number of doctors and epidemiologists, from Dr Roberto Bertollini (WHO), who hosted our group's meeting in Rome, Italy, in 1998, to Colin Soskolne, an epidemiologist who arranged for our meeting in WHO offices in Budapest the following year, with the help of economist Philippe Crabbé.

This expansion of collaborating disciplines was foundational for the expanding reach of our research, although the focus was increasingly centred on law and governance, particularly including the most vulnerable, Indigenous peoples, the poor and, lately, asylum seekers and refugees.

And this is the main reason for researching and writing this work. How can the newly "enriched" understanding of integrity, now incorporating a deeper appreciation of its multiple facets, perhaps suggest a different approach to legal regimes? The present environmental instruments are clearly not up to the task. Thus we need to show how integrity is inescapably linked to basic human rights, then seek out whether there might be a novel, more appropriate way of establishing ecological governance that gives primacy to biological/ecological integrity.

The first two chapters of this book review the scientific and practical information that will explain how the recovery of integrity and its protection is of basic importance to the survival of humanity and of the Earth that supports that survival. Equally important are the strong links that emerged between integrity and public health. All these strands must be brought together to ensure that the new forms of governance that are being advocated do not stop simply by advocating "sustainable development", or "environmental concern", or even other forms of "green" governance.

What is required is to insert integrity as the primary goal, the foundational principle of legislation affecting/controlling all areas that relate to human rights.

A deepened understanding of integrity helps to direct all diverse areas which, as we will show, affect all aspects of human needs and endeavours, from the need for food and water, to a safe environment not inquinated by the products of industrial corporate interests, to a climate that can support life.

Once we start from that basic premise, I believe, this work unfolds in a way that appears radical, but is simply radically logical. Chapter 1 explains in detail the meaning of integrity, as that forms the basis of the argument that follows. Chapters 2–4 show all the "conflicts" that exist against the support and promotion of integrity. Chapter 2 shows the attacks of capitalism and globalization, as all human rights are increasingly at risk as disintegrity advances.

The first human right that is not respected under those circumstances is the human right to health, which is based on the biological integrity of the human organism. The right to health is proclaimed in international law, but the jurisprudence that deals with cases where human health is under attack from human industrial activities, demonstrates the total disregard of health not only of individuals, but of whole communities. Chapter 3 argues that when integrity is clearly under attack as it happens in the case of the numerous ongoing conflicts the world over, the disregard for the human rights of those affected shows the component that permits, and in fact encourages, such disregard: racism. Discrimination is viewed as a grave threat to human rights; it is forbidden and is an *erga omnes* obligation in international law. However, that fundamental aspect of the disregard for integrity (and with it human health and right to life) has been consistently ignored, despite the many ill effects that follow.

Those effects include the use of the worst instruments of war, such as bombs using depleted uranium, land mines and the continuous threat of the use of nuclear weapons, primarily by the two "rogue" states as defined by Noam Chomsky: the US and Israel. Chapter 4 further examines the presence of attacks on human rights through disintegrity, to yet another basic need: the need for food. The right to food includes that to water and to a climate favourable to maintaining a habitat capable of supporting and feeding humanity in a just and equitable manner.

In Chapter 5 we pass from the review of the direct and indirect consequences arising from disintegrity, to a consideration of the legal instruments needed to correct the ongoing situation. In Chapter 2 we spoke of the need to return to cosmopolitanism, to the respect for human rights everywhere, globally. In this chapter we attempt to review what might exist in law capable to effect the return to the primacy of integrity we advocate. As the present environmental legal regimes are incapable of protecting integrity, and with it, the related basic right, we are forced to consider some novel approaches that might be more successful.

We are not suggesting that the proposal to seek out unusual legal instruments as applicable to the goal we are pursuing represents *lex lata* at this time: we are clearly in the realm of *de lege ferenda*, supported by argument and appeal to principles, rather than to jurisprudence or *opinio juris*. In contrast, Chapter 6 reviews the many other recent proposals, suggested by various scholars in recent times, in order to achieve the necessary ecological governance. There has been a proliferation of recent volumes on the topic of ecological governance, and in this chapter we review them in sequence. Their proposed strategies range from the acknowledgment of the importance of resilience to the urgency to radically alter current capitalist practices, and further to the resurgence of the commons and "commoning", leading away from globalization to regionalism, and the emphasis on the fiduciary relation between people and their governments, or even people and the sources of global governance.

All these proposals and strategies have much to recommend them, and Chapter 7 starts with the analysis provided by a religious leader and head of state, Pope Francis. His June 2015 encyclical, *Laudato Si'*, has been treated as a major step forward by environmentalists everywhere, for the incisive analysis it provides of the world's ecological conditions, and for the intimate relation between globalization and the ecological conditions that threaten us all starting with the poor and those in the third world.

Hence we start by following the similarities between the encyclical and the work of the Global Ecological Integrity Group for the past 24 years. After acknowledging this closeness, we also review both the favourable aspects of the theories discussed in Chapter 6, and the drawbacks that emerge from the possible pursuit. Finally we acknowledge that all the proposals we have seen depend on some other radical change, which is not acknowledged as such, but assumed in each of the proposals.

Thus, rather than choosing one or another of those strategies as the goal to achieve environmental governance, I simply propose that, while those ideals are being realized, there may be some legal strategies that might be pursued *right now*. These strategies may or may not prove to be the ideal or the best possible solution for ecological governance. The solution proposed meets some of the criteria needed for a new, improved form of governance that respects and defends the Earth, together with all its most vulnerable inhabitants, human and non-human alike.

Notes

1 Jack Manno, 2013, "Why the Global Ecological Integrity Group?", in L. Westra, P. Taylor and A. Michelot (eds), *Confronting Ecological and Economic Collapse*, Routledge, London, pp. 9–20, here p. 10.
2 Ibid.
3 Cited in ibid., p. 11.
4 Ibid., p. 14.
5 Principle 5 states: "Protect and restore the Integrity of the Earth's ecological systems, with special concern for the biological diversity and the natural processes that sustain life" (see www.earthcharterinaction.org/content/pages/Read-the-Charter-html).
6 Prue Taylor, 2008, "Ecological Integrity and Human Rights", in L. Westra, K. Bosselmann and R. Westra (eds), *Reconciling Human Existence and Ecological Integrity*, Earthscan, London, pp. 89–108.

1 Ecological integrity

Between ethics and law

Ecological or biological integrity originated as an ethical concept in the wake of Aldo Leopold (1949) and has been present in the law, both domestic and international, and part of public policy since its appearance in the 1972 US Clean Water Act (CWA). Ecological integrity has also filtered into the language of a great number of mission and vision statements internationally, as well as being clearly present in the Great Lakes Water Quality Agreement between the United States and Canada, which was ratified in 1988.

The generic concept of integrity connotes a valuable whole, the state of being whole or undiminished, unimpaired, or in perfect condition. Integrity in common usage is thus an umbrella concept that encompasses a variety of other notions. Although integrity may be developed in other contexts, wild nature provides paradigmatic examples for applied reflection and research.

In my work, I consistently based my argument on the scientific understanding of ecological integrity, because to accept it, as some have done, as a socially definable notion, means to lose it as a firm point of reference. In that case, it could not be understood as a firm starting point, if it were open to a variety of opinions. I proposed the principle of integrity, as a solid principle of a new ethics,[1] reaching beyond a simple environmental ethic, to a moral principle that acknowledges the primacy of a consideration for human rights and the human good, even the right to life, all must start with the protection for the habitat of mankind which also – at the same time – ensures respect for the biological integrity of all human beings.

That understanding, based on science, was eventually fleshed out in its full meaning and connotations, by the members of the Global Ecological Integrity Group (GEIG), initially funded by SSHRC (1992–1999). Since then it has been meeting every year, starting with the 2000 meeting funded by NATO for 50 per cent Eastern Europe participation, which took place in Budapest. The final collectively agreed upon definition was published combining the work of ethicists, conservation biologists, ecologists and other scholars.[2]

Essentially, the Global Ecological Integrity Project (as it was known at the start) has been guided by two complementary policy imperatives: conserve integrity and live sustainably.[3] I have defined sustainability as a system's capacity to retain its specific functions, that is, its critical life-support processes as well as its parts or components.[4] The emphasis on the scientific meaning of integrity was never lost by the Group, but, after 2000, when the final definition was reached, basing ourselves primarily on the work of James Karr, and the development of his Index of Biotic Integrity,[5] fidelity to the scientific consensus reached remained constant.

This starting point was established against the arguments of philosophers of science,[6] but also against the practical resistance of globalized corporate interests, strongest at Great Lakes Meetings and other venues. Their mantra of "development" at all costs contradicts the very basis of strong sustainability my Group and I have supported,[7] which renders ecological integrity both hard to implement and unpopular.

As well, aside from the hostile responses to the primacy of integrity on the part of others, from various standpoints, there is also the somewhat "despairing" position of one of our founding members, William Rees:

> Ecological footprint analysis, developed by William Rees and his students, is another important tool for diagnosing unsustainability in relation to off-site impacts. It is not enough that one's immediate habitat or environment is stabilized … We need to ensure that the distant terrestrial and aquatic ecosystems we "appropriate" through trade and by exploitation of the global commons … also remain in a productively healthy state.[8]

But Rees also identifies a further grave difficulty, for which we cannot blame only external factors and economic interests: our own propensity to accept "social myths", while totally ignoring the "ecological reality that surrounds us", which makes us prey to "a collection of shared illusions".[9] Thus one of the foremost names in Canadian ecological economics and regional planning, William Rees, is co-author of the introductory chapter of a law textbook currently used to teach environmental law, which is specific to Canada, something that would not likely be found in the US, for instance.

Another unique Canadian trait, as we shall see, is the frequent reference one finds in law to Canadian First Nations, particularly in legal scholarly work regarding the environment. At any rate, in 1998 I proposed eight "secondary order principles" (SOPs) to supplement the principle of integrity and to expand on it, attempting a response to the question: how can we conserve integrity and live sustainably, with concern for environmental justice and the rights of those living in the third world? The necessary step from theory to public policy suggested these principles for practical guidance:

SOP 1 In order to protect and defend ecological integrity, we must start by designing policies that embrace complexity.

SOP 2 We should not engage in activities that are potentially harmful to natural systems and to life in general. Judgments about potential harms should be based on the approach of "post-normal" science.

SOP 3 Human activities ought to be limited by the requirements of the precautionary principle.

SOP 4 We must accept an "ecological worldview" and thus reject our present "expansionist worldview" and reduce our ecological footprint.

SOP 5 It is imperative to eliminate many of our present practices and choices as well as the current emphasis on "technical maximality" and on environmentally hazardous or wasteful individual rights.

SOP 6 It is necessary for humanity to learn to live as in a "buffer." Zoning restraints are necessary to impose limits both on the quality of our activities, but also on their quantity. Two corollary principles follow: (a) we must respect and protect "core"/wild areas; (b) we must view all our activities as taking place within a "buffer" zone. This is the essential meaning of the ethics of integrity.

SOP 7 We must respect the individual integrity of single organisms (or micro-integrity), in order to be consistent in our respect for integrity and also to respect and protect individual functions and their contribution to the systemic whole.

SOP 8 Given the uncertainties embedded in SOPs 1, 2 and 3, the "Risk Thesis" must be accepted, for uncertainties referring to the near future. We must also accept the "Potency Thesis" for the protection of individuals and whole in the long term.[10]

No doubt, philosophers may still be cringing at my use of an "is" to generate an "ought". But, *pace* Hume, Kant's support of the infinite value of life, is closer to the approach I have been taking. Onora O'Neill discusses the difference between globalization and cosmopolitanism. While the former is primarily *procedural* in its structures, and primarily influenced by powerful, market-oriented powers, the latter is based primarily on *substantive* moral principles of justice that include but also transcend the economic realm, and rely on Kantian principles. States may or may not be fully just within their own borders but, even at best, they may well injure those outside their borders by exclusionary practices, and these are *direct* injuries.[11] The practices we don't accept provide *indirect* injuries instead. This is a form of indirect injustice as "destroying parts of natural and manmade environments injures those whose lives depend on them". In addition:

> Secondly, the principle of destroying natural and manmade environments, in the sense of destroying their reproductive and regenerative powers, is not universalizable.[12]

Ecological and biological integrity is precisely what O'Neill terms "regenerative and reproductive powers", or true sustainability:

> Environmental justice is therefore a matter of transforming natural and man-made systems only in ways that do not systematically or gratuitously destroy the reproductive and regenerative powers of the natural world, so do not inflict indirect injury.[13]

This is what has been argued from a scientific and a moral point of view in the work of the "Global Ecological Integrity Project",[14] and referenced and summarized here.

In O'Neill's terms, moral principles represent the "blueprint" and the "specifications", which define the "product" to be eventually produced. In a similar sense, strategies based upon principles are not, as such, the strategic tools to use in order to achieve just aims, but they define what forms such tools might take. O'Neill says:

> The move from abstract and inconclusive principles of justice toward just institutions, policies and practices is analogous to moves from design specification towards finished product.[15]

Cosmopolitanism based on Kantianism, can supply the principles and also the guidelines that are largely absent from even the best among the advocates of liberal democracy, as the roots of injustice are seldom sought out by these thinkers:

> The idea that our economic policies and the global economic institutions we impose make us causally and morally responsible for the perpetuation and even aggravation of world hunger, by contrast, is an idea rarely taken seriously by established intellectuals and politicians in the developed world.[16]

O'Neill's focus is on the role of conservation and respect for natural systems, as she acknowledges the interface between these and human rights. Following along these lines, we can add the insights Alan Gewirth proposes.

The foundational arguments proposed by Alan Gewirth help to shed light on that basic connection between humans and their habitats. Gewirth argues that human rights are not based primarily on human dignity,[17] but that this Kantian principle is only partially right. He prefers to base "human rights on the necessary conditions of human action",[18] as morality is intended to give rise to moral action. Gewirth adds that "human rights are the equivalent to 'natural' rights, in that they pertain to all humans by virtue of their nature as actual or prospective agents".[19] He cites five reasons in support of his claim:

1 "the supreme importance, of the conditions of human actions" (and we will return to this point below);
2 action is "the common subject matter of all moralities";
3 "action" is more specific and less vague than "dignity" or "flourishing";
4 thus "action" ultimately secures "fundamental moral status" for persons; and
5 "action's necessary conditions provide justification for human rights – as every agent must hold that he has a right to freedom and well-being as the necessary conditions of his actions".[20]

Beyleveld and Brownsword argue that the "basic" or "generic needs" that represent the preconditions of all action including moral action are "freedom or voluntariness" and "well-being or purposiveness", where the former are procedural and the latter "substantive",[21] and they view freedom as instrumental to well-being. I want to propose inverting this order. Life, health and the mental ability to comprehend and choose precede the exercise of voluntariness, and are not only necessary for it, but sufficient, when all these conditions are in fact present.

In essence, this has been the argument of the previous section: "basic rights"[22] represent the minimum all humans are entitled to, and they are prior to all other rights, both conceptually and temporally. For Gewirth as well, life and the capacities named above can be "threatened or interfered with".[23] Thus to say we have rights is to say equally that the preconditions of these rights represent something we are entitled to have not only in morality but also in the law. In other words any legal instrument that supports the existence of human rights, *ipso facto* ought to proclaim the requirement that their preconditions be equally supported and respected.

Some argue that the dignity of human beings is only partially the ground of human rights and that dignity itself is based on agency, still the argument allows the introduction of at least a further point in favour of extending human rights to life and health. The introduction of "preconditions" means the introduction of conditions that are not only conceptually but temporally prior to agency, hence the protection of these pre-conditions entails the acceptance of potential consequences in the protection of agency. Thus, not only does the scientific approach and the ensuing definition of integrity foster and support the interface between ecological integrity and human rights, but that connection may also be found in the thought of moral philosophers, although the explicit reference to ecological integrity, a recent scientific concept, is clearly missing.

However, the most significant aspect of ecological integrity relating to Canada, can be found in the multiple areas where biological or ecological integrity figure prominently in the law. It is present in the Great Lakes Water Quality Agreement (1978, rat. 1988). It is sad to acknowledge that its mandates, however, are only paper tigers, as they are largely ignored in a series of annual or biennial meetings, where a minor advancement is described as a great success, while, except for the notable clean-up of Lake Erie, for the rest, it is mostly business as usual.

In contrast, there are two other areas of law where ecological integrity or its equivalent takes centre stage, at least on paper: first, the environmental legal regimes regulating Canadian Parks, and second, the extensive jurisprudence past and present regarding the rights of First Nations. The role of ecological integrity in Canadian law is explained by Shaun Fluker:

> human activity necessarily impairs ecological integrity and thus paradigm ecological integrity is found ecosystems protected from human disturbance … It thus comes as little surprise that the norm of ecological integrity figures prominently in the management of Canada's national parks.[24]

After a study mandated by the Minister of Canadian Heritage,[25] the appointed scientists confirmed what Canadians know well, especially our environmentalists, that is, that ecological integrity was not central to park management, despite the stated goal of maintaining ecological integrity as its preservation was listed as the primary purpose of our parks. But such "first priority" has often been lost to other interest, proposing the primacy of human activities in the parks, thus the "overriding primacy" of ecological integrity instead.[26] Hence, two sections were added to Canadian legislation in 2001:

> Section 2(1) – Definitions
> "ecological integrity" means, with respect to a park, a condition that is determined to be characteristic of its natural region and likely to persist, including abiotic components and the composition and abundance of native species and biological communities, rates of change and supporting processes.
>
> Section 8(2) – Ecological Integrity
> Maintenance or restoration of ecological integrity, through the protection of natural resources and natural processes, shall be the first priority of the Minister when considering all aspects of the management of parks.

However strong the language of these mandates for Canadian Parks, the facts on the ground contradict the high-sounding environmental concern here expressed. Nowhere is this contradiction clearer than in the cases where tenure is a conflict between a First Nations interest, and that of a natural park which is adjacent to their lands. A prime example is the case regarding Wood Buffalo National Park.[27] This park straddles the province of Alberta and the Northwest Territories. In 1998 the municipality of Fort Smith submitted an application to Parks Canada, "seeking approval to construct and operate a road crossing the park from east to west along the Peace River".[28]

The Park had been originally set aside in 1922 to protect the Wood buffalo, and the proposed road was not found to serve any park purpose, but it would advance economic interests of others outside the Park instead.

Parks Canada approved the road's construction in 2001, with no reference to ecological integrity; and Justice Gibson ruled, in a requested judicial review, that Parks Canada's lack of consideration for ecological integrity, did not invalidate the decision.

In contrast, there was at the same time another lawsuit pending, based on the legal rights of the Mikisew First Nation instead, which was eventually heard by the Supreme Court of Canada. In that case[29], Madam Justice Hansen stated that although ecological integrity was perhaps not the first priority in reaching a decision, reaching a balance with the interests of those living near the Park was paramount. Hence the importance of the rights of First Nations to aboriginal hunting and their traditional lifestyle would prevail.[30]

Thus despite the explicit wording added to Canadian Parks legislation, the rights of First Nations to their unspoiled habitat, thus maintaining wildlife, take precedence. In that case, the connection between the natural environment wherein they reside, and its ecological integrity, is inescapably tied to their cultural integrity, their rights to their religious practices and, in general, their traditional lifestyle.[31]

In conclusion, whether explicitly cited or not, ecological integrity is more than a foundational necessity for sound moral principles in defence of human rights; it also acquires a specific Canadian flavour, not only because of the amount of research funded by Canadian sources (Social Sciences and Research Council of Canada, and Health Canada), but also because of the legal rights to the "commons",[32] which is expressed in Canadian regulatory regimes, whether directly, as in Parks Canada's explicit language, or indirectly, as a substantive aspect of the rights of Canadian First Nations.

Notes

1 Laura Westra, 1994, *The Principle of Integrity*, Rowman Littlefield, Lanham, MD.
2 Laura Westra, David Pimentel and Reed Noss (eds), *Ecological Integrity: Integrating Environment, Conservation and Health*, Island Press, Washington, DC; the definition of integrity is in chapter 2 of that book: Laura Westra, Peter Miller, J. R. Karr, William E. Rees and R. Ulanowicz, "Ecological Integrity and the Aims of the Global Integrity Project", pp. 19–41.
3 Westra et al., *Ecological Integrity*, p. 3.
4 See Laura Westra, 1998, *Living in Integrity*, Rowman Littlefield, Lanham, MD, ch. 8.
5 See J. R. Karr, 1981, "Assessment of Biotic Integrity Using Fish Communities", *Fisheries* 6(6), pp. 21–27; J. R. Karr, 1996, "Ecological Integrity and Ecological Health are not the Same", in P. Schulze (ed.), *Engineering within Ecological Constraints*, National Academy Press, Washington, DC, pp. 97–109.
6 See K. Shrader-Frechette and E. D. McCoy, *Method in Ecology*, Cambridge University Press, New York.
7 Klaus Bosselmann, 2008, *The Principle of Sustainability*, Ashgate, Aldershot, UK.
8 Westra et al., *Ecological Integrity*, p. 32; see also Mathias Wackernagel and William Rees, 1996, *Our Ecological Footprint*, New Society Publishers, Gabriola, BC.
9 William Rees and Karin Mickelson, 2003, "The Environment: Ecological and Ethical Dimensions", in E. Hughes, A.-R. Lucas and W. A. Tilleman (eds), *Environmental Law and Policy*, 3rd edn, Emond Montgomery Publications, Toronto, pp. 1–40.
10 Westra, *Living in Integrity*; see also Westra et al., "Ecological Integrity and the Aims of the Global Integrity Project", pp. 33–34.
11 Onora O'Neill, 1996, *Towards Justice and Virtue*, Cambridge University Press, Cambridge, p. 175.
12 Ibid., p. 176.
13 Ibid., p. 177.
14 See for example David Pimentel, Laura Westra and Reed Noss, 2000, *Ecological Integrity: Integrating Environment, Conservation and Health*, Island Press, Washington, DC; R. F. Noss and A. Y. Cooperrider, 1994, *Saving Nature's Legacy*, Island Press, Washington, DC; Westra, *Living in Integrity*.
15 O'Neill, *Towards Justice and Virtue*, p. 181.
16 Thomas Pogge, 2002, *World Poverty and Hunger*, Cambridge University Press, Cambridge, p. 15.
17 Alan Gewirth, 1982, *Human Rights: Essays on Justification and Applications*, University of Chicago Press, Chicago, IL.
18 Ibid., p. 5.
19 Ibid., p. 7.
20 Ibid., p. 5.

21 Deryck Beyleveld and Roger Brownsword, 2001, *Human Dignity in Bioethics and Biolaw*, Oxford University Press, Oxford, p. 71.
22 Henry Shue, 1996, *Basic Rights: Subsistence, Affluence, and American Public Policy*, Princeton University Press, Princeton, NJ.
23 Beyleveld and Brownsword, *Human Dignity in Bioethics and Biolaw*, p. 70; Gewirth, *Human Rights*, p. 54.
24 Shaun Fluker, 2013, "Environmental Norms in the Courtroom (The Case of Ecological Integrity in Canada's National Parks)", in Laura Westra, Prue Taylor and Agnes Michelot (eds), *Confronting Ecological and Economic Collapse*, Routledge/Earthscan, London, pp. 21–31, here p. 23.
25 Parks Canada, Canadian National Parks Act, SC 2000, c.32.
26 Fluker, "Environmental Norms in the Courtroom", p. 23.
27 *Canadian Parks and Wilderness Society v. Canada* (Minister of Canadian Heritage) 2001 FCT 1123.
28 Fluker, "Environmental Norms in the Courtroom", p. 25.
29 *Mikisew Cree First Nation v. Canada* (Minister of Canadian Heritage) 2001 FCT 1426.
30 Canada's Constitution Act, 1982, c.11, s.35(1), states; "The existing aboriginal and Treaty rights of the aboriginal peoples of Acanda are here recognized and defended."
31 Laura Westra, 2007, *Environmental Justice and the Rights of Indigenous Peoples*, Earthscan, London, especially ch. 1–2.
32 Laura Westra, 2011, *Human Rights: The Commons and the Collective*, University Press of British Columbia, Vancouver, BC.

2 Integrity in conflict

Introduction

As described in Chapter 1, ecological integrity is an entirely positive concept basic to the life of both humans and non-humans, present and future. Hence, if integrity is not openly accepted everywhere, if it is not incorporated openly in environmentally oriented and human rights legal instruments, as well as in national constitutions, then there must be some deep-seated conflict blocking that possibility. The question is how the protection of ecointegrity could be viewed as conflicting with other major human interests when – in contrast – it is basic to the protection and enjoyment of all human rights. Judge Christopher Weeramantry affirmed that that was the case for "environmental rights in general",[1] and the protection of integrity is fundamental to environmental rights.

The previous chapter indicated the irreplaceable life-support role that integrity has in the continuation of all planetary life. The biological integrity of individuals (human, non-human animals, plants) represents their health and fitness to exist and to persist through time, each according to their specific nature. The presence of all these "fit" individuals within an ecosystem secures its maximum ability to persist while, at the same time, it remains capable of performing its support role for all individuals within it. The eventual development trajectory of each individual, when each is terminated, continues through the role it plays when it is no longer a living whole.

However, any alteration of these life trajectories, to the interjection of man-made substances into the system, that is, the production and use of substances that do not have a naturally evolving role to play within the system, represents a threat, at least *prima facie*, and this threat may be more or less grave to the continuity and the evolution of life. Everything that is either added or removed from an original ecosystem, at least in principle, is a threat to its continued existence, in its natural, optimal form.

Yet, satisfying multiple human needs and wants, part of the very lifestyle of modern developed/industrial countries, depends entirely on using all manner of materials removed from natural systems near and far. That is what constitutes our ecological footprint,[2] which includes what we use, and the waste we return to the environment. All international environmental law consists in the attempts to regulate both additions and subtractions to ecosystems in a way that does not (or should not) cause the diminution, or even the elimination, of the elements upon which we depend absolutely, or result in various "natural disasters".[3]

However, none of the instruments designed for that purpose are actually binding, or enforceable, and their range and limits are ultimately prescribed by politicians and economists, not ecologists. Therefore our present situation that includes multiple disasters, mounting extinctions of species and – in general – the creation of conditions inimical to the continuation of life from the Arctic to Africa, demonstrates beyond a doubt not only the presence of ecological emergencies present in any part of the globe, but also the effects on humankind of this lack of legal limits and restraints, typical of the modern institutional approach to the violence perpetrated in and through the environment with impunity.

This reality characterizes the modern age since the emergence of the Universal Declaration of Human Rights of 1948, that is, after Westphalia and the interstate system which, at this time, is also characterized by the legal take-over by corporate interests primarily but not exclusively in North America.[4] This take-over includes the disregard of the relation between science and policymaking. In both environmental and health matters, state-of-the-art scientific research ought to inform public policy. In addition, the precautionary principle ought to be basic to decisions.[5]

Yet the ultimate arbiter , the final word in all environmental issues, is and remains the WTO, and Article XX (the *Chapeau*), which sets out the tests for the *manner* in which a trade measure is applied. Three standards are stated in the *Chapeau*:

- arbitrary discrimination;
- unjustifiable discrimination; and
- a disguised restriction on international trade.[6]

Clearly the only concern is trade as substantive environmental matters are not even considered as part of the decisions reached by that body. In fact, from the standpoint of the disregard of biological integrity, the scientific Principle of Innovation is the main culprit so far. That principle is in direct opposition to the precautionary principle as, most often, the benefits of Innovation "may be overstated due to the underestimation of the cost of failure to anticipate potential harms", particularly for risks involved in the production and use of chemicals.[7]

The innovation principle appears to push the limits of safety regarding the introduction of chemicals into the environment. It presumes to judge the effects of untried new substances, while the great majority of such chemicals, thus far only "judged safe" by the manufacturers themselves, have proven to be highly toxic to the environment and hazardous to public health.[8]

What is needed is a radical revision of the regulation of pesticides and other toxic substances, to replace the presently existing "tolerance levels" based on the 1993 National Academy of Sciences (NAS),[9] because the "tolerance levels" were problematic at several levels:

> A first problem was that they were not health-based. Instead the tolerance-setting process weighed the protection of human health against the costs of regulation to agricultural producers and tried to strike a balance between the two, often to the detriment of public health. A second, even more serious shortcoming was that the older pesticide tolerances paid no attention to the unique exposures or special susceptibilities of infants and children. They assumed that the population was comprised solely of adults and that a single tolerance level would protect people of all ages against pesticides in agricultural products.[10]

In contrast, ensuring safety for children also *ipso facto* will protect older children and adults from toxicants. Even if the innovation principle is not explicitly advocated by all corporate activities, the fact that their goal is to ensure that their next project should proceed as expeditiously as possible, without "red tape" or with only minimal or non-existent external restraints, implies that that principle is implicitly present. The result? In Carl Cranor's words:

> Some industrial chemicals, pesticides, pharmaceuticals, and pollutants have already caused harm from in utero exposure. Others pose live risks, especially during development. Some may trigger transgenerational effects and others have become known to act in concert with other contaminants to pose unexpected risks.[11]

Cranor adds: "Currently the law permits toxic contamination and live risks to our children. The law is the culprit; it also holds the solution."[12]

Existing laws do not help to prevent harm, whether the toxicants affect the human being directly, through effluents in the air or in the water, or indirectly, as pesticides or other additives in the food system. But the basis for all harms is that the main right belongs to corporate persons, to "innovate" until the substance is "proven guilty" through causing obvious multiple diseases or deaths. These persons maintain the right to harm humans and their habitat, as the testing is and remains in the hands of those who profit from these substances' production.

So far, we have discussed a number of issues, arising from present policies and approaches, unquestioned and in fact fostered and supported by present legal systems. But it is necessary to start by examining more closely just how the disregard for integrity originates, and its clear conflict with present practices and accepted goals and lifestyles. However, we also considered in turn where and how the prevailing economic trends based on capitalism and globalization impact on the support for integrity. After this brief, cursory review, it will be necessary to return in some detail to the results of ignoring the effects the neglect of integrity has on public health in general, and on human rights, specifically.

Starting with the next section in this chapter, subsequent chapters will range further afield, to consider the effects of the ongoing legal and illegal conflicts on both biological and ecological integrity not only during the conflict, but also after it, as refugees attempt to flee the unliveable situations in which they find themselves. But, as we consider the different negative aspects of the interface between integrity and the current world order, we will also need to review whether there are any existing instruments that advocate or legislate integrity in various jurisdictions. Apparently, existing regulations are insufficient to support the most necessary life-support systems, thus we will need to reach outside the expected legal purviews in order to propose alternative venues for the defence of integrity.

Capitalism and globalization in conflict with the integrity of life-support systems

> In his book *Uneven Development* the geographer Neil Smith brilliantly formulates how capitalism historically has produced a particular kind of nature and space, an unevenly developed landscape that integrates poverty with wealth, industrial urbanization with agricultural diminishment. The culmination of this process is imperialism, which dominates, classifies, and universally commodifies all space under the aegis of the metropolitan centre.[13]

The examination of the interface between culture and imperialism is beyond the scope of this work. But the relation between Western imperialism and others who were either colonized in earlier times or controlled and treated as inferior by the dominant cultures, is highly relevant to our topic. As Said describes it, the "massive colonial system whose economy, functioning and history had acquired the status of a virtual fact of nature", depends upon considering other peoples and other races as "inferior, dependent, subject".[14] The capitalist enterprise, ultimately expanded into globalization, entails domination, not only of workers, as Marx had it, but beyond them.

"The idea of Western salvation and redemption through its civilizing mission"[15] always entails fostering and promoting the idea that somehow violence, directed to both the environment and to humans, is somehow justified, part of the political goals of Western affluent countries, but also totally ingrained as part of the culture of those Western nations.[16] The only possible way that colonization could be justified, is by originating from a deep-seated belief in the inferiority of the colonized, coupled with the equally unshakeable belief in the "mission" to bring about "the steady improvement in the condition, character and custom of primitives as a result of their contact with European civilization".[17]

Whatever their language, traditions, beliefs, these "colonized" individuals were victims. But the end of colonization did not mean either the end of national greed, or that of the belief in the inferiority of those who could be exploited and dominated, even as "free people" under such fictional categories as, for instance, "sustainable development". Europe's imperialism is based on the aspect of cultural "improvement" derived primarily from Eurocentrism.[18] In contrast, the whole foundation of American imperialism was and is based on the "commercial cause of empire",[19] and the claimed superiority which includes still the possession of a moral higher ground, while pursuing an unrestrained policy of plunder.[20] The true goal of plunder is the exploitation of land and peoples, and for many decades it has been supported by the armed violence of American exceptionalism.[21]

Since colonization is now obsolete according to international law, whatever happens now must be judged from the perspective of the customary rule of internal self-determination:

> Internal self-determination means the right to an authentic self-government, that is, the right of a people really and freely to choose its own political and economic regime – which is much more than choosing among what is an offer perhaps from one political or economic position only. It is an ongoing right.[22]

This rule, as Cassese points out, entails that "any use or exploitation of natural resources of a territory under colonial domination ... without a foreign acting in the exclusive interest of the people at issue, amounts to a gross infringement of the rights of people to self-determination".[23]

Hence this rule, derived from the indisputable authority of the former one, can be seen most clearly as the illegal ongoing occupation by the Zionist Israeli government of the Palestinian territories.[24] Leaving aside for the moment the exploitation of the Palestinian peoples and territories, and the multiple human rights breaches committed by the illegal occupation and the presence of the apartheid wall, we can simply review the legal ongoing plunder and exploitation practiced by Western nations, determined to continue to avail themselves of former "colonies" and lands for their exclusive interests.

The internal self-determination of peoples and the protection of integrity

> [T]he legal basis for the transformation of self-determination into *jus cogens* cannot of course be found in views – however authoritative – put forward by persons acting in their individual capacity.[25]

The main point is that internal self-determination may not be explicitly cited as a *jus cogens* norm, but it is based on customary rules although the law does not provide procedures for allowing self-determination,[26] while several states have gone on record as supporting the status of *jus cogens* for self-determination.[27]

At any rate, economic self-determination presents a challenge for states to be free to dispose of their national resources, as a true indication of real independence.[28] In fact, scholars have understood this challenge in two separate ways:

> Thus courts and scholars came up with two different forms of self-determination: internal and external. The former, potentially applies to all peoples, and signifies that all peoples should have a set of respected rights within the central states. Minority groups should have cultural, social, political rights and those rights should be respected by the mother state.[29]

The main case in point is the Canadian case on the Secession of Quebec[30] which distinguishes clearly between these two forms of self-determination as it would apply to the Quebecois.[31]

Of course, in our context, the main issue is not the relation between a people and the "mother state" only, but the interface between people and the powerful corporate persons intent on depriving them of their resources for profit, even if that includes the means for their survival. However, the latter has not "crystallized into a rule of international customary law, applicable to and binding on all states".[32]

One can understand the reason for the legal neglect of this alternative: for the most part the complicity between what Sterio terms "the Great Powers"[33] and the largest and most powerful among the multinational corporations (MNCs) is not explicit in law. As well, corporations are not legally bound by any international instrument, or directly accountable for human rights violations.[34]

The aspect of self-determination that supports the defence of integrity is neither explicitly recognized nor even implicitly acknowledged in any international or domestic legal instrument. This basic lacuna in fact remains the most important reason for the lack of support for the ecological integrity of systems, and the biological integrity of individual organisms, including humans.

What is at stake is the "internal self-determination" of peoples, that is, their *de facto* ability to "determine" their own forms of governance, including the use or disposal of their own resources. But this right, although acknowledged, is not without limits. Just as people have the *right* to their own resources, they also share "transborder obligations",[35] in the case of their natural ecology, to transcend their own specific interests, in the interest of the survival of global society, as in today's world, no nation or country is "a closed system isolated from other societies" as Rawls had it instead.[36]

Hence, it appears that the very presence of global ecological integrity is necessary to counter the existence of global ecological problems. These indisputably attack the very notion of "closed societies" as survival is and remains the common concern of humanity. In contrast, although international legal instruments defend at best the rights of individuals, ecologically speaking, those rights cannot be protected without protecting the rights of the collective.[37]

Thus the weakened state,[38] with its porous borders, is not such that the transboundary citizen remains bound and committed to her "nationality" as in older days, while the citizen now tends to be committed to obligations beyond state borders. The quest for global obligations is based on cosmopolitan theory; in fact, ecological integrity is the one moral ideal/goal that is essentially meaningless unless its application is based upon cosmopolitanism.

Biological/ecological integrity and cosmopolitan theory

> Legally or institutionally strong cosmopolitanism translates easily into notions of world or global government, an ancient idea that remains attractive to some. It is also evident in much contemporary discussion amongst lawyers

> who are preoccupied with the "goal", though not yet perhaps convinced of the need for global government.[39]

In our case, the argument proceeds from the foundational role that the scientific understanding of biological/ecological integrity has in regard to the survival of all life, including human life. The second step is the acknowledgment that local regulatory regimes – even if binding and resulting in serious consequences, at least in principle – can be hopelessly inadequate to protect life, unless they are as global in reach as the harms imposed by globalization are. One could argue that even local restraints on industrial pollutants and other toxic substances, even if they could be enforced, could be added to other such local ordinances, thus contribute to eventual global controls.

However, the possibility of coordinating legal instruments, presupposes coordinated state policies. Such coordination is reasonably present and even effective on many issues in the states of the European Union, but nowhere else, and the greatest polluting states are in turn largely controlled by corporate powers. Corporations today are capable of controlling directly the policies of one state at a time, at least if we exclude the powerful associations such as the World Trade Organization (WTO), for instance; that is, an organization whose apparent aim is that of supporting and protecting the common interests of corporations, and the promotion of international trade in general. The very composition of GATT, the WTO and the related dispute settlement bodies precludes the serious consideration of ecological and public health issues:

> There is no provision in the Understanding on Rules and Procedures governing the Settlement of Disputes (DSU) for panels adjudicating environmental cases to have specific environmental expertise, in contrast with, for example, the requirement that panels adjudicating "prudential issues and other financial matters" under GATT have the necessary financial services expertise.[40]

In addition, the possibility of addressing conflicts between GATT and multilateral environmental agreements, which are far from being ecologically demanding or binding on state or non-state actors, remains remote. The cases/disputes that appear to seek an environmentally protective role, so far, tend to protect wildlife, and are few and far between, and they involve no major global issue, such as the protection of climate or the Arctic, which are the most grave.[41]

The WTO is perhaps the most powerful tribunal in the world. At the same time, it is the least transparent, and the most secretive one, as it allows no open doors and no appeals for its final decisions. That power needs to be countered by an equally powerful tribunal, one staffed primarily by biologists, ecologists toxicologists and other scientists, as well as legal scholars. An example might be the environmental tribunal proposed by Amedeo Postiglione and the ICEF,[42] as well as several other emerging proposals. But, most of all, it is necessary that the connection between justice and ecological integrity be made explicit in law, and protected. Thus ecointegrity should be viewed as foundational to basic human rights, and its role should be acknowledged as a primary value in international law. Yet international law has only two existing principles on which it could rely for such protection, despite its connection to the survival of life on the planet: *jus cogens* norms and the existence of *erga omnes* obligations, neither of which is often used in the courts or even explicitly connected to life support in any way.

According to the International Court of Justice (ICJ), the principles and rules concerning basic rights of the human person are "[b]y their very nature" the concern of all states, and thus impose obligations *erga omnes* upon them. The reference to nature, as opposed to conventional obligations as the starting point, reaffirms that the rationale for the possibility of obligations *erga omnes* is not to be found in extrinsic principles, such as the presumed or effective predominance of the will of the majority of states or the more powerful states over a dissenting minority, but in the universal validity of the moral values that these obligations were meant to protect.[43]

No matter how convincing might be the arguments of the previous sections, we are still firmly based in *de lege ferenda* – in what should be done, rather than what can be done right now in the courts. In addition, even if courts might be persuaded to consider such arguments in their decisions, the main problem remains: the flawed and incomplete legal instruments that do not forbid or at least work to mitigate the activities that result in harms, thus eventually may result in court cases.

The main issue is the lack of connection between ecology and human rights in law; as well, human rights are mostly viewed as *individual* entitlements and the question of collective rights has not been seriously addressed in international law at this time.[44] In this sense, both racial discrimination and especially genocide are – almost by definition – examples of collective harms, as a person may be the target of discrimination for her race only if the race itself is considered less worthy than one's own.

Similarly genocide, or the extermination of a "genus", cannot be limited to one person, whatever the degree of intent or at least knowledge regarding the harmful activities is accepted. Hence the present focus on *jus cogens*, or universally applicable norms, and the appropriateness of *erga omnes* obligations, both of which were used in earlier cases. One such case is the Corfu Channel Case[45] where the court referred to "general principles" and "well recognized principles", and to the "elementary considerations of humanity".[46]

But the problem is that neither the "general principles" nor any "considerations of humanity" are included in binding agreements or other instruments, as they are – at best – limited to the preambular portions of these documents, so that the harms continue to be imposed as the harmful activities are not explicitly forbidden. Particularly apt is the Reservations to the Genocide Convention, where the IJC's Advisory Opinion makes clear which principles provide guidance (and we will discuss some aspects of both the case and the Opinion in the next section):

> the principles underlying the Convention are principles which are recognized by civilized nations as binding on States even without any conventional obligation (1951) ...[47]

> the rights and obligations enshrined by the Convention are rights and obligations *erga omnes* (1996).[48]

Further, there is the Advisory Opinion in the *Nuclear Weapons Case*; and even more significant for the argument of this work, a similar approach is present in the Advisory Opinion of the Legal Consequences of the Construction of a Wall in the Occupied Palestinian Territory, as Salomon points out that "rules of international humanitarian law incorporate obligations which are essentially of an *erga omnes* character".[49]

More examples can be adduced but, as Cassese notes, for a state to invoke *jus cogens*, such state must be a party to the treaty "it intends to have declared contrary to *jus cogens*", as well as being a party to the Vienna Convention.[50] In general only exceptional circumstances will permit invoking *jus cogens*, which therefore indicates that such rules today remain in a state of "potentiality" only.[51]

Further, given the legal difficulties involved, any state invoking *jus cogens* must be prepared to "submit to arbitral or judicial determination",[52] thus rendering the final arbitration or judicial decision possibly still dependent on the same world order we are asking to alter. Yet peremptory norms are not only binding on states, but also the UNSC which should ensure that current examples of grave human rights breaches should be pursued by the international law instruments that are appropriate, but also by the UN through all its organs. Because this is not what happens today, it is vital to seek radical changes to the international legal order.

International law versus cosmopolitanism: the need for global governance

> Conceptually cosmopolitan law should receive its own legitimacy from a worldwide legislative assembly. However, politics does not follow a logical path and it is difficult to imagine the ICC being set up in any other way; no institutions exist for the citizens of the world, and even if they did they would not have sufficient powers to oblige the states to collaborate.[53]

International law should not conflict with cosmopolitanism, as it now deals with individual human rights as well as with the relationship between states, nevertheless, it does not function as it should, as Archibugi notes above. In contrast, states are "united" primarily in pursuing their own interests, but, as we noted, the organizations that rule their interaction are oriented exclusively to trade and the quest for economic advancement. Thus, citing either environmental multilateral instruments, or such imprecise human rights as that to a safe environment or even to health, remains totally insufficient. The major principles discussed are not able to substitute the present international legal instruments, presently lacking in both force and consequences for non-compliance.

At any rate, the general principles and *jus cogens* norms are not part of binding agreements, and their explicit presence in declarations, *Obiter Dicta*, and Preambular Sections of Treaties, indicates the main reason why radical changes are now required.

Both individual governments and multiple alliances, as well as specific MNCs, pursue their own interests, barely keeping within the law in most cases, and flaunting international law altogether when their only "punishment" will be the lack of approval from a powerless international community; as an example consider the legal aspects of the so-called "war on terror", including the murder of Hamas member Mahmoud al-Mabhouh, and the "extent to which basic principles of international law have been torn up under the war on terror".[54]

As far as the US government and its allies are concerned, extra-judicial executions and so-called targeted killings, now constitute a legitimate State activity and do not warrant comment, let alone condemnation.[55]

In contrast, Chaloka Beyani argues for the need to strengthen States, because "the protection of human rights is primarily a function of states".[56]

But, as we argued, "democratic" states give primacy to their economic interest, and to the interests of industry, as long as the latter supports them and their aims. Hence, the paragraph cited at the start of this section is problematic: cosmopolitanism does *not* require legitimacy from a world assembly or any form of "counting of heads". Whether arising from the Stoics, the specific version of the Roman philosopher/statesman Cicero or Immanuel Kant, cosmopolitanism depends on principles, not votes. Hence, desirable as a democratic state might be, the will of states is for the most part in direct conflict with cosmopolitanism and with the rule of law based on fundamental principles and moral values, and we shall return to this difficult topic in the final chapter of this work.

At any rate it will not be easy to move away from a positivist approach to international law, let alone world governance, given the current weakness of the UN and the most often one-sided approach of the Security Council. The ICJ should have "powers of judicial review" over the Security Council, but scholarly opinion is divided on this issue, and on the "nature" of the relation between the ICJ and the Security Council: if what is meant is an automatic constitutional process of review with compulsory effect, both the UN Charter and the International Court are silent in that respect.[57]

This difficulty will be one of the topics of Chapter 6. Thus far, the obvious conclusion is that even the existence of democratic states and of eloquent and well-drafted constitutions is insufficient to achieve a just system of governance internationally. The power within the UN is too uneven and the political power is heavily weighted in favour of the West.

But the problem is not, as some have argued, the lack of democratic states (as currently understood), or the universality of human rights promoted by the West,[58] which promote unfairness and racist practices, but the lack of implementation and enforcement of these rights within the present globalized world governance.

Patrick Glenn says it well; the desperate need exists for a form of governance that is based on cosmopolitanism, given the failures of existing forms of governance:

> National industrialization has created trans-border pollution and global ozone depletion. Liberal political economists created transborder flow of capital. Technology nationally promoted has opened transnational space to abuse,

> in the air and at the bottom of the seas ... We are subject to an indefinite accretion of interdependent elements and there is no one in control, or even possibly in control.[59]

However, the very idea of a centralized, worldwide control, or power, works against the acceptance of cosmopolitanism: the ideal of democratic states governed by freely voting citizens sounds far more acceptable, despite the increasingly obvious failure of that system. Those who cannot accept the thought of world governance – even when "world law" would be based on highly desirable principles, based on the UN Charter itself – do not acknowledge that a centralized power and "control" already exists.[60] That existing and functioning central power originates from financially oriented organizations, supported by wealthy MNCs, discussed briefly above.[61] These associations and organizations attack ecological integrity and the biological integrity of humans (and other life-forms), on one hand, and existing human rights, on the other.

Biodiversity and biological integrity: the connection between ecology and public health

> Biodiversity, ecosystems and the essential services they deliver are central pillars for all life on the planet including human life. They are sources of food and essential nutrients, medicines and medicinal compounds, fuel, energy, livelihood and cultural and spiritual enrichment ... Each of these functions has direct and indirect consequences for our health and well-being, and each is an important component of the epidemiological puzzle that confronts our efforts to stem the tide of infections and non-communicable diseases.[62]

When we speak of cosmopolitanism, we speak of universal rights, hence we need to start with the most basic ones, those which apply to all human beings in the world. The right to one's biological integrity is primary among these. Yet even the 2015 document quoted above represents only a review of the state of knowledge, not an instrument stating policies binding on all states, let alone on other legal or natural persons. In fact, despite the emphasis on biodiversity and ecosystem services, three major problems remain:

1 Despite the repeated mention of "biotic and abiotic component",[63] that is, the acknowledgment of the need to move beyond biodiversity itself, in the whole document there is only one mention of the concept that should be foundational for the argument advanced (i.e. integrity): "In response to these challenges, the Rockefeller Foundation and the Lancet have formed a Commission to review the scientific basis for linking human health to the *underlying integrity of the Earth's natural systems* (The Commission on Planetary Health) and set out recommendations for action to the health community and policymakers working in sectors that influence healthy development and the biosphere."[64]

2 We need more than "to influence policy" for such an urgent endeavour; but the basic, foundational necessity is not even mentioned, that is, the need for laws, both domestic and international, that would codify and implement the findings of the Commission named above, given the present difficulties regarding the interface between environment and health in law.[65]

3 The ongoing insertion of "development" as a component of the needed radical changes, despite the current instantiations of "development" as an unsustainable neoliberal quest for profit, with no consideration whatever, for either public health or the ecological realities of our existence.[66]

In this chapter we will briefly address no. 2 and no. 3 in turn as they form the basic platform from which to address the major issues considered in the following chapters.

The first problem, that is the lack of an explicit connection between the topic of the WHO document discussed above and biological integrity, can be expected, given the controversial status of that concept. But it is precisely this status that precludes the acceptance of that basic notion in the development of legal instruments. Yet it is the force of the law, not simply the presence of desirable sentiments in exhortations or in declaratory, non-binding instruments, that is absolutely necessary to ensure any progress. In fact it is primarily legal persons and groups (with the complicity of state bureaucracies) that are responsible for the greatest damage to both health and environment, leading to the gravest breaches of human rights.

Human rights and corporate accountability in international law

> Human Rights Watch establishes a special unit on corporations and human rights; in 1999 it issued two lengthy reports, one accusing the Texas based Enron corporation of "corporate complicity" in human rights violations "by the Indian government", and another one accusing Shell, Mobil and other international oil companies operating in Nigeria of cooperating with the government in supporting political opposition.[67]

Steven Ratner argues that international law should "provide for human rights obligations directly on corporations", and that corporate duties should also extend to the elimination of their complicity with states that may be viewed "as the prime source of human rights abuses".[68]

The background to the present situation originated when European states left their colonies, and the process of decolonization started. It was to be based on the sovereignty and equality of all states, and any relation with the former colonial power had to be based on a "clear choice by the people of the territory".[69] The most important document for that period was the *Charter of Economic Rights and Duties of States*, emphasizing the obligations of the North to the South.[70]

But human rights law is not limited to state interaction, and the presence of both the ICCPR and the ICESCR as well as treaties on women's and children's rights, as well as covenants against racial discrimination and torture, all contributed to diminish the inviolability of state sovereignty, as the legality of intervention replaced the former duty of non-interference in the internal affairs of individual states.[71]

Although states had tried to limit the power of MNCs in the 1980s and early 1990s, the increasing spread of globalization in the 1990s gave rise to a counter-reaction with a strong emphasis on corporate rights.[72] The reality is that MNCs are becoming "more embedded in the economy of the host states than ever before"[73] but, while governments have obligations to their citizens under human rights law, the question of the corporations duties under international law has not been fully clarified,[74] especially in developing countries, where Indigenous peoples are often based. These impoverished states are far more interested in foreign investment and trade than in protecting their citizens and ensuring compliance with domestic or international law; and the corporate position was that "The citizenry's human rights were the government's responsibility, not theirs. In short, the race to the bottom was on."[75]

When we consider the interface between powerful corporate actors and indigenous communities under the category of international law, the problem of *mens rea* recedes in importance. The states have been retreating from their duties, to foster their own economic interest so that the corporations have taken on a direct role vis-à-vis the communities, not as one or another individual with clearly spelled human rights. Yet, ultimately, it is indeed individuals who are harmed both singly and as part of groups.

Because of the laxity of states in enforcing existing laws, whole territories are in fact given controls over vast tracts of indigenous, traditional lands.[76]

> The Inadequacy of state responsibility stems fundamentally from trends in modern international affairs, confirming that corporations may have as much or more power over individuals as governments.[77]

It is commonplace almost to affirm that many corporations have a budget hence economic power, in excess of that of many developing countries.[78] Even without turning to developing nations and indigenous groups, one sees the subtle and widespread power MNCs wield, even in a developed country like Canada. Mosanto corporation, for instance, offered funds to the university of Toronto for a "research institute", and the result was that they effectively muzzled any scientific dissenting voice that might have arisen against their policies and practices, based on complete disregard for human rights and scientific truth, as exemplified in the Percy Schmeiser case in Saskatchewan.

In conclusion of this part, it is worth noting that at best these cases address these crimes as "torts", whereas the direct impacts on human health and life itself ought to place each of these events squarely among breaches of humanitarian law, if a conflict is involved, or human rights law, and that they should be treated as crimes against humanity.

No discussion of such examples would be complete without at least a mention of the few existing European cases: *Guerra v. Italy*, *Lopez-Ostra v. Spain*,

Oneryildiz v. Turkey and *Fedeyeva v. Russia.*[79] These cases demonstrate the presence of grievous harm to the life and health of human beings through environmental means and conditions. But all are discussed under the aegis of article 8(1), and only refer to the loss of "family life".

I am well aware of the convoluted reasons why in these cases the law cannot speak simply and openly of the "right to life". But this circumlocution unfortunately obscures the very real harm and danger posed by such environmental violence. The implications are equally worthy of note: does it mean that unless one is part of a "family", one's life is not worthy of protection? What about single individuals? Students in schools and colleges? Religious or monastic orders? In the interest of strengthening the tenuous link between environment and human rights, perhaps the time has come to call a spade a spade and note the danger to health and life, whatever the possible implications and conflicts with feminist contingents.

The final lacuna is in the listing of *erga omnes* obligations in the Barcelona Traction case.[80] Although some of the scholarship in the abundant discussions of that issue propose that serious environmental harms would be appropriate as a further addition to the limited list presented in that decision,[81] thus far no one has attempted to extend our common obligations in that direction, as should be indicated by our common responsibility, confirmed by recent scientific research on environmental/health connections.[82]

Employing public health for global justice and the hazards of development

> In confronting the insalubrious ramifications of globalization, human rights scholars and activists have argued for greater national and international responsibility pursuant to the human rights to health … However, in pressing for the highest attainable standard for each individual, the right to health has been ineffective to address burgeoning inequalities in underlying determinants of health focusing on individual medical treatments at the expense of public health.[83]

It is easy to see the major difference between the proposal discussed in the last section and this approach: the major underlying problem is evident, as the dominance of neoliberalism and globalization. The latter's emphasis on individuals, particularly individuals in affluent Western states at the expense of the "underlying determinants of health", necessary for the protection of collective public health, is the main issue that needs to be addressed.

Although Meier does not cite the environment directly, coupling "neoliberal economic policies" on one side with health hazards, and contrasting them with the collective right to public health[84] entails the implicit acknowledgement of how the former adversely affect the latter. The two major symptoms of globalization are:

- the weakening of the state powers, and
- the spread of "development".

Both affect disproportionately the poor and people of colour everywhere,[85] hence re-affirming the conclusions drawn so far about the doctrine of social justice as the necessary foundation from which to seek novel institutions.

The weakening of state powers, now secondary to the mandates of such economic organizations as GATT, NAFTA or the WTO, implies that the gains made in developed countries regarding public health,[86] cannot always be sustained in the face of the increasing powers of the trade related organizations. These organizations deny states their legitimacy as protectors of the health of their citizens, if any possibility of trade "protectionism" might be alleged.[87]

"Development" as the neoliberal engine of globalization has served to exacerbate the disparities in health between rich and poor.[88] Global trade itself promotes the spread of infectious diseases beyond national borders,[89] as do accelerated and widespread travel patterns.

In addition, measures such as quarantines, originally designed to protect some populations from exposure, are no longer sufficient to restrain the spread of disease and to ensure protection.[90] Further, current so-called "agricultural" practices such as industrial factory farms, with the multiplication of hog farms, beef and chicken operations, with their overuse of antibiotics to counter the unnatural overcrowding and hazardous living conditions of those animals, directly increases antibiotic resistance in those who eat meat grown under those conditions, which are also undesirable from many other perspectives:

> The dominant economic and development perspectives that inform the present market-based model of agrifood governance tend to champion agro-industrial techniques and the development of technological methods of intervention in agriculture. Such methods focus on increasing production and are reliant on biotechnology, fossil fuels and genetic modification.[91]

Hence there are issues that render current agro-industrial practices contrary to social justice, beyond the overuse of antibiotics that eventually increase the dangers faced by meat consumers whose infectious diseases spread by globalization no longer respond to such medications. For instance, even aside from other North/South injustices connected to the systems of production upon which agro-industry is based, the spread of non-infectious diseases in developing countries is also depending (at least in part) on the increases of obesity, cancers and cardio-vascular diseases that start with the overuse of fatty meat products laced with chemicals.

In addition, there are other direct environmental harms that eventually rebound on individuals and countries through climate change:

> Agriculture and food production account for 10–12% of greenhouse gas emissions. Livestock farming is responsible for four-fifths of these emissions, which include methane (a greenhouse gas more potent than CO_2) emitted by ruminant animals, land-use changes, including deforestation for livestock production, and substantial further emissions. Increasing affluence boosts

> meat consumption, and forecasts predict that livestock production will increase dramatically in the future to meet consumer demand.[92]

The spread of meat consumption even in "low- and middle-income" countries, already produces increases in "heart disease, diabetes, some cancers and other diseases connected with over nutrition, high fat diets and reduced exercise".[93]

The increase in non-infectious diseases in developing countries beyond the affluent West, indicates yet more culpable activities causing harm on the part of legal commercial persons, through globalization. It is

> the "double disease burden" of both infectious and non-communicable diseases [that] has risen to unprecedented levels, creating a heightened need for expanded national health responses. Paradoxically, however, just as the burden of disease is reaching its apex, additional public health systems are being downsized to meet the requirements of international financial intuitions.[94]

In fact, it is the subjection of public health and environmental concern to "international financial institutions" that has prompted the research of this work regarding a revamped world law. Essentially, what renders the public health approach superior to pursuing other avenues is the fact that, for any organization based on public health, there is no need to argue/prove the connection between environmental conditions and human rights to life/health: the causality is direct, rather than indirect, as it would be if the central mandate remained the protection of the environment. Thus even starting from an ecocentric position, from the standpoint of principles and morality, requires a legal approach based on human collective rights to health for the implementation of those principles.

Concluding thoughts and plans for the next steps

The first two chapters have dealt briefly with science, including ecology and biology, and with principles both moral and legal, with the goal of showing the failures of the present system of governance and its regulatory regimes. The main problem is not even that the most important issues and values are not recognized or accepted. The problem is that the scientific realities are not acknowledged as relevant and basic to several facets of human rights. These include such acknowledged values as the right to health, to life, to a community's natural resources, to a safe environment.

In the next chapters we will move from theory and principles to present realities that force us to reconsider existing forms of governance, as they move us to attempt a new way to redress the current grave problems by applying a cosmopolitan approach. It is clear that despite the assurances found in the preambles of international legal instruments and declarations, present legal regimes are not drafted to deal with human rights according to the established principles for which we have argued. Thus after having acknowledged this flaw, which also represents a marked dissonance between the main principles of the UN

Charter and other major covenants and the results of their implementation, we should review some of the issues we must confront, and propose solutions that would bring us closer to the UN Charter and other major documents.

The present, largely uncontrolled state system has fostered first the growth of capitalism, then the completion of the neoliberal agenda through globalization, and finally the widespread attack on life coupled with state impunity with which we are increasingly faced today. These are the clearest indications that the current system of governance is untenable. Some of its most obvious failures are reflected in many of the present situations that are impossible to handle within the current regulatory regimes.

These include climate change, uncontrollable mass migrations, and global water and food scarcity in the largest portion of the world, coupled with the gross overuse of both for profit in the rest of the world. But, even if the argument of this chapter is convincing, given the scientific understanding of integrity offered in the first chapter, we need to examine some of these "failures", that is issues that result in problems so grave, so intractable and widespread that present regimes cannot begin to cope. The reasons for this inability are easy to understand: the issues are global, and the only global controls, the only organizations potentially capable of dealing with them in support of life in general and human rights in particular, are oriented to the primacy of trade and to support of the interests of the so-called "Great Powers".[95]

Both of these situations are foundational to the conflict with integrity, hence it is clear that we cannot rely on their efforts to redress the problems they themselves have created. Therefore, in the following chapters we will use some of these situations as "case studies" of sorts, in order to show how the present form of governance and the legal infrastructure that supports it, in each case contribute to the general situations. We will not be able to show through parallel case studies how the adoption of cosmopolitan principles will lead to better approaches and solutions, but showing that the present opposite approach is untenable should support our conclusions.

Notes

1 See *Gabčíkovo-Nagymaros Project (Hungary/Slovakia)*, Judge C. Weeramantry Separate Opinion, at www.icj-cij.org/docket/index.php?p1=3&p2=3&case=92.

2 Mathias Wackernagel and William Rees, 1996, *Our Ecological Footprint*, New Society Publishers, Gabriola Island, BC.

3 Patricia Birnie, Alan Boyle and Catherine Redgwell, 2009, *International Law and the Environment*, Oxford University Press, Oxford.

4 Laura Westra, 2013, *The Supranational Corporation*, Brill, Leyden, The Netherlands.

5 Caroline Raffensparger and Joel Tickner, 1999, *Protecting Public Health and the Environment*, Island Press, Washington, DC.

6 Birnie et al., *International Law and the Environment*, pp. 774–775.

7 See http://healthandenvironmentonline.com/2014/10/29/scientificadvice-innovation-and-the-precautionary-principle.

8 Philippe Grandjean, 2013, *Only One Chance: How Environmental Pollution Impairs Brain Development – and How to Protect the Brains of the Next Generation*, Oxford

University Press, Oxford; Philip Landrigan and Ruth Etzel, 2013, *Children's Environmental Health*, Oxford University Press, Oxford.

9 National Academy of Sciences, 1993, *Pesticides and the Diets of Infants and Children*, National Academic Press, Washington, DC.

10 Landrigan and Etzel, *Children's Environmental Health*, p. 20.

11 Carl Cranor, 2013, *Legally Poisoned*, Harvard University Press, Cambridge, MA, p. 132.

12 Ibid.

13 Edward W. Said, 1994, *Culture and Imperialism*, Vintage Books, New York, p. 2251. See also Neil Smith, 1984, *Uneven Development: Nature, Capital and the Production of Space*, Blackwell, Oxford, p. 102.

14 Said, *Culture and Imperialism*, p. 134.

15 Ibid., p. 131.

16 Ibid., pp. 162–163.

17 Ibid., p. 168.

18 Ibid., pp. 221–222.

19 Ibid., p. 221.

20 Ugo Mattei and Laura Nader, 2008, *Plunder*, Blackwell, Oxford.

21 Laura Westra, 2014, *Revolt Against Authority*, Brill, Leyden, The Netherlands, pp. 118–120; see also Donald E. Pease, 2009, *The New American Exceptionalism*, University of Minnesota Press, Minneapolis, MN.

22 Antonio Cassese, 1995, *Self-Determination of Peoples*, Cambridge University Press, Cambridge, p. 101.

23 Ibid., p. 100.

24 H. Awartani, 1992, "Israel's Economic Policies in the Occupied Territories: A Case for International Supervision", in E. Playfair (ed.), *International Law and the Administration of Occupied Territories*, Oxford University Press, Oxford, pp. 399–417; Peter Sand, 2009, *United States and Britain in Diego Garcia*, Palgrave Macmillan, New York.

25 Cassese, *Self-Determination of Peoples*, p. 135; with reference to Judge Ammoun's sep. op. in the Barcelona Traction Case, ICJ Reports, 1970, 304, 312.

26 Cassese, *Self-Determination of Peoples*, p. 131.

27 Ibid., p. 137.

28 Ibid., p. 99.

29 Milena Sterio, 2010, "On the Right of External Self-Determination: 'Selfistans', Secession and the Great Powers Rule", *Minnesota Journal of International Law* 19, pp. 137–176.

30 Secession of Quebec [1998] 2 SCR 217.

31 See also Michael P. Scharf, 2003, "Earned Sovereignty: Judicial underpinnings", *Denver Journal of International Law and Policy* 31, pp. 273–379, where Scharf discusses the different forms of self-determination available to people, which include autonomy, self-government, free association, and ultimately secession.

32 Ibid., p. 378.

33 Sterio, "On the Right of External Self-Determination", p. 140.

34 John Gerald Ruggie, 2007, *Business and Human Rights: The Evolving International Agenda*, June, Working Paper 38, John F. Kennedy School of Government, Harvard University, Cambridge, MA.

35 H. Patrick Glenn, 2013, *The Cosmopolitan State*, Oxford Press, Oxford, p. 172.

36 John Rawls, 1971, *A Theory of Justice*, Harvard University Press, Cambridge, MA, p. 8; as cited in Glenn, *The Cosmopolitan State*, p. 173, where Rawls's doctrine is faulted for its basic premise, but also for the lack of an egalitarian component.

37 Laura Westra, 2011, *Human Rights: The Commons and the Collective*, University Press of British Columbia, Vancouver, BC.

38 Saskia Sassen, 2006, *Territory, Authority, Rights: From Medieval to Global Assemblages*, Princeton University Press, Princeton, NJ.
39 Glenn, *The Cosmopolitan State*, p. 174.
40 Birnie et al., *International Law and the Environment*, p. 765.
41 For instance, see US-Import Prohibition of Certain Shrimp and Shrimp Products, WT/DS58/R (1998); US-Restrictions on Imports of Tuna, Report of the Panel, 30 ILM (1991).
42 Amedeo Postiglione, 2010, *Global Environmental Governance: The Need for an International Environmental Agency and an International Court for the Environment*, Bruylant, Brussels, Belgium.
43 Margot Salomon, 2007, *Global Responsibility for Human Rights*, Oxford University Press, Oxford, p. 171; Maurizio Ragazzi, 1998, *The Concept of International Obligation Erga Omnes*, Oxford University Press, Oxford, p. 466.
44 Dwight G. Newman, 2004, "Collective Interests and Collective Rights", *American Journal of Jurisprudence* 49, pp. 127-163.
45 *Corfu Channel* case (Merits) *United Kingdom v. Albania* 1949.
46 Ibid., para. 22.
47 Reservations to the Convention on the Prevention and Punishment of the Crime of Genocide, 1951.
48 Case Concerning Application of the Convention on the Prevention and Punishment of Genocide, *Bosnia Herzegovina v. Yugoslavia*, 1996.
49 Salomon, *Global Responsibility for Human Rights*, p. 167; Legal Consequences of the Construction of a Walk in the Occupied Palestinian Territory, Adv. Op. 2004.
50 Antonio Cassese, 2004, *International Law*, 2nd edn, Oxford University Press, Oxford, p. 204.
51 Ibid.
52 Ibid., p. 205.
53 Daniele Archibugi, 2008, *The Global Commonwealth of Citizens*, Princeton University Press, Princeton, NJ, p. 171.
54 See "The Dubai Assassination and the 'War on Terror'", World Socialist Web Site, 2 March 2010, at www.wsws.org/en/articles/2010/03/pers-m02.html.
55 Ibid.
56 Chaloka Beyani, 1999, "The Legal Premises for the International Protection of Human Rights", in Guy S. Goodwin-Gill and Stefan Talmon (eds), *The Reality of International Law: Essays in Honour of Ian Brownlie*, Clarendon Press, Oxford, pp. 21–36, here p. 22.
57 Susan Lamb, 1999, "Legal Limits to United Nations Security Council Powers", in Goodwin-Gill and Talmon, *The Reality of International Law*, pp. 361–388.
58 Upendra Baxi, 1999, "Voices of Suffering and the Future of Human Rights", *Transnational Law and Contemporary Problems* 8, pp. 125–169; Rosalyn Higgins, 1963, *The Development of International Law through the Political Organs of the United Nations*, Clarendon Press, Oxford.
59 Glenn, *The Cosmopolitan State*, p. 169.
60 Laura Westra, 2011, *Globalization, Violence and World Governance*, Brill, Leyden, The Netherlands, ch. 1.
61 Westra, *The Supranational Corporation.*
62 Braulio Ferreira de Souza Dias, 2015, "Foreword by the Executive Secretary of the convention for Biological Diversity", in World Health Organization and Secretariat of the Convention on Biological Diversity (hereafter WHO & CBD), *Connecting Global Priorities: Biodiversity and Human Health – A State of Knowledge Review*, World Health Organization, Geneva, Switzerland (available at www.cbd.int/health/SOK-biodiversity-en.pdf), p. ix.
63 Executive Summary, in WHO & CBD, *Connecting Global Priorities*, p. 6.

64 Sir Andy Haines, "Preface to the Chair of the Rockefeller Lancet Commission on Planetary Health", in WHO & CBD, *Connecting Global Priorities*, p. 5; italics added.

65 Laura Westra, 2012, "Life, Health and Environment: The Denied Connection", in Laura Westra, Colin Soskolne and Donald Spady (eds), *Human Health and Ecological Integrity*, Earthscan, London, pp. 7–19.

66 Mattei and Nader, *Plunder*; Wackernagel and Rees, *Our Ecological Footprint*; Westra, *The Supranational Corporation.*

67 Steven R. Ratner, 2001, "Corporations and Human Rights: A Theory of Legal Responsibility", *Yale Law Journal* 111, pp. 443–447. See also Human Rights Watch, 1999, "The Enron Corporation Complicity in Human Rights Violations", at www.hrw.org/report/1999/enron; Human Rights Watch, 1999, "The Price of Oil: Corporate Responsibility and Human Rights Violations in Nigeria's Oil Producing Communities", at www.hrw.org/reports/1999/nigeria.

68 Ratner, "Corporations and Human Rights", p. 449.

69 Ibid., p. 454; GA Res. 2625, Declaration on Principles of International Law Concerning Friendly Relations and Co-operation Among States in Accordance with the Charter of the United Nations, UN GAOR, 25th Sess., Supp. No.28, at 121, 124, UN Doc. A/8028 (1970); *Western Sahara*, 1975 ICJ 12, 39 (1 October), noting the legal status of nineteenth-century territories.

70 Charter of Economic Rights and Duties of States, GA Res. 3281, UN GAOR, 29th Sess., Supp. No. 31, at 50, UN Doc. A/9631 (1974).

71 Ratner, "Corporations and Human Rights", pp. 455–456.

72 Ibid., p. 458; Development and International Economic Co-operation: Transnational Corporation, UN ESCOR, 2d See., UN Doc. E/1990/94 (1990); Draft United Nations Code of Conduct on Transnational Corporations, UN ESCOR, Spe. Sess. Supp. No. 7, Annex II, UN Doc. E/1983/17/Rev.1 (1983).

73 Ratner, "Corporations and Human Rights", p. 459.

74 Ibid., p. 460.

75 Ibid. See also Eyal Benvenisti, 1999, "Exist and Voice in the Age of Globalization", *Michigan Law Review* 98, p. 167; Jeffrey L. Denoff and Joel P. Trachtman, 1999, "Economic Analysis of International Law", *Yale Journal of International Law* 24(1), pp. 54–55; both view the problem solely in economic terms.

76 Ratner, "Corporations and Human Rights", p. 462; see also Michael C. Howard, 1994, "Mining, Development and Indigenous Peoples in Southeast Asia", *Journal of Business Administration* 22, p. 93.

77 Ratner, "Corporations and Human Rights", p. 461.

78 Susan Strange, 1996, *The Retreat of the State: The Diffusion of Power in the World Economy*, Cambridge University Press, Cambridge, MA, p. 47.

79 *Guerra v. Italy* (1998) 26 EHRR 357; *Lopez-Ostra v. Spain* (1994) 20 EHRR 27; *Oneryildiz v. Turkey* (2004) 41 ECHR 325, 48939/99; *Fadeyeva v. Russia* (2005) ECHR 55723/00.

80 *Barcelona Traction, Light and Power Co. Ltd*, second phase, Judgment ICJ Reports, 1970, p. 3.

81 Ragazzi, *The Concept of International Obligation Erga Omnes*.

82 Hans Jonas, 1984, *The Imperative of Responsibility*, University of Chicago Press, Chicago, IL.

83 Benjamin Mason Meier, 2006, "Employing Health Rights for Global Justice: The Promise of Public Health in Response to Insalubrious Ramification of Globalization", *Cornell International Law Journal* 39(3), pp. 711–752, here pp. 711–712.

84 Ibid.

85 Laura Westra and Bill Lawson, 2001, *Faces of Environmental Racism*, Rowman & Littlefield, Lanham, MD.

86 Ibid.; A. J. McMichael and R. Beaglehole, 2000, "The Changing Global Context of Public Health", *The Lancet* 356, pp. 495–499.

87 See NAFTA ch. 11.
88 Meier, "Employing Health Rights for Global Justice", p. 715; Jim Yong Kim, Joyce V. Millen, Alex Irwin and John Gershamn, 2000, *Dying for Growth*, Common Courage Press, Monrow, ME.
89 David P. Fidler, 2001, *International Law and Public Health*, Transnational Publisher, Ardsley, NY; Allyn L. Taylor, 1997, "Controlling the Global Spread of Infectious Diseases: Towards a Reinforced Role for International Health Regulations", *Houston Law Review* 33(5), pp. 1327–1362; J. A. Patz, D. Campbell-Lendrum, T. Holloway and J. A. Foley, 2005, "Impact of Regional Climate Change on Human Health", *Nature* 438, pp. 310–317.
90 Meier, "Employing Health Rights for Global Justice", p. 717; Ruth L. Berkelman et al., 1994, "Infectious Disease Surveillance: A Crumbling Foundation", *Science* 264, pp. 368–370.
91 Dario Bevilacqua and Jessica Duncan, 2010, "Towards a New Cosmopolitanism: Global Reflexive Interactive Democracy as a New Mechanism for Civil Society Participation in Agri-food Governance," *Global Jurist* 10(1) (Advances), article 2, at www.bepress.com/gj/vol10/iss1/art2.
92 Sharon Friel, Alan D. Dangour, Tara Garnett, Karen Lock, Zaid Chalabi, Ian Roberts, Ainslie Butler, Colin D. Butler, Jeff Waage, Anthony J. McMichael and Andy Haines, 2009, "Public Health Benefits of Strategies to Reduce Greenhouse-Gas Emissions: Food and Agriculture", *The Lancet* 374(9706), 12 December, pp. 2016–2025.
93 Ibid.
94 Meier, "Employing Health Rights for Global Justice", p. 718; Derek Yach, Corinna Hawkes, C. Linn Gould and Karen J. Hofman, 2004, "The Global Burden of Chronic Diseases: Overcoming Impediments to Prevention and Control", *Journal of the American Medical Association* 2914, pp. 2616–2622.
95 Sterio, "On the Right of External Self-Determination", p. 140.

3 Integrity against racism in conflict situations and migrations

Introduction

> [W]e have stressed … the extent to which neo-liberal ideology of "the market" constitutes a façade behind which the planning principle of the state as "big government" with its "big bank" and commanding heights "big MNCs" operate as an expropriation machine preying on real economic activities wherever these remain.[1]

The previous chapter has argued for the importance of achieving a radical re-organization of the present system of governance, based upon cosmopolitan principles, involving the restoration of ecological integrity as basic, and the respect for the life and dignity of all human beings. That desirable goal would be reached only by following a series of steps, starting with the elimination of the present position of states as the only locus of authority and institutional support of all citizens.

In other words, the first step is to do away with the "big bank" and the "big MNC" (including both Big Pharma and Big Ag), which now constitute "big government". The problem, however, is to replace the organizations and institutions upon which we depend for vital support and services beyond those available from co-operatives or other socially-based service systems. The latter may well be restored when some centralized state services are replaced.

The problem is that basic social services are, and have been for centuries, part of the obligations of states to be provided to citizens. The perversion and substitutions of these necessary services which are now mostly subject to privatization, is endemic to globalization. This seems to be the major "elephant" in the room, the topic ignored even by those who openly advocate the demise and even the reversal of capitalism and the elimination of the multiple ills of globalization. This is a position openly advocated by such diverse scholars as UN Special Rapporteur Olivier de Schutter, ecological economist/scholar William Rees[2] and Marxist political economy scholar Richard Westra.[3] The difficult question is what happens after that, if social, local communitarian groups are successful in eliminating the lethal combination of "Big Government" and "Big Bank".[4]

At that happy juncture, we may ask the obvious question: is what we are proposing any more likely to give a feasible answer, or at least a reasonable answer, to the question the status quo cannot give? As we proceed through the examples we have proposed, starting with this chapter, we need to keep in mind whether there is a possible relation between our suggestions and the policy implementations that are vital to restoring the conditions necessary for life, or at least reversing the present ongoing attacks upon it.

There is one aspect of the cosmopolitanism we propose that is superior to most other proposed policies: it is based upon the principles of the UN Charter, a global constitution, which would support a great number of positive policies as such. Our unfortunate position regarding human rights protection today is due to the deliberate alteration of that constitution for political and economic advantage, primarily by the US and its allies.

This reference to an acknowledged constitution is necessary in order to ensure a basic starting point from which to combat the "ecological imperialism" that was and is the main reason for disintegrity. The only way that state and non-state actors may feel confident in their own immunity sufficiently to continue along their destructive path, is that they will continue to act on their belief in racial, ethnic, or class difference among the affected human beings; differences grave enough that they may justify radically different treatment between the actors and the "other".

Thus an initial appeal to the basic tenets, not only of cosmopolitanism, out of the UN Charter itself, appears to provide the best starting point for our quest for radical change. This chapter will support that contention as we shall see that the ongoing conflicts on almost all continents, together with the resulting conditions, which force mass migrations, are all initially based upon the us/they relations, and founded upon the acceptance of a discriminatory intent toward the victims of the activities designed to produce profits and other advantages for the actors.

As Patrick Glenn remarked (see Chapter 2), there is no one in charge, or even potentially in charge, charged with addressing the multiple disasters that face us, both ecological disasters and the breaches of human rights that follow upon them. What is lacking is precisely the presence of a global assistance, capable of responding to numerous urgent situations, but without the political baggage of NATO and other R2P enterprises. An example in the realm of public health is Médecins Sans Frontières, an international NGO that enjoys global respect and support, given its impeccable reputation.

In contrast, there is no such organization present and available for ecological human rights emergencies, and the primary reason for this lack is that the connection between ecological disasters or even uncontrolled ecological conditions arising from globalized industrial activities and human rights, is neither acknowledged nor accepted, as we saw in the previous chapter.[5] At any rate, because biological integrity is foundational to all organisms, and it is equally so for the life of human beings, perhaps the first attack on it, that is, on both individual organisms and natural systems, is the presence of ongoing conflicts, both legal and semi-legal, that involve numerous areas in the world. In most cases, the original cause of most of these conflicts is the same as the original cause of climate change:

> Throughout this period of rapid change, the climate and trade negotiations closely paralleled one another each involving landmark agreements within a couple of years of each other … in 1992 governments met for the first United Nations Earth Summit in Rio, where they signed the UN Framework Convention on Climate Change … in 1994 negotiations establishing the World Trade Organization concluded, going into effect two years later. What is most remarkable about these parallel processes – trade on one hand – climate change on the other – is the extent to which they functioned as two solitudes.[6]

These "two solitudes" pretending not to be aware of the intimate relations they share, as well as the additional interface between the commitment to economic gain at all costs that is the origin of both, and at the same time it represents the start of the multi-faceted attacks on integrity. We will show these connections as we consider the various symptoms of the same malady in the sections that follow in this chapter and the next ones. We will start with the most obvious attacks on both individuals and systems; that is, the conflicts that flow from the imperialistic drive primarily of the US and other major powers.

Disintegrity in conflicts

> Given the history of environmental destruction in international conflict and the improbability of persecution of environmental war crimes as stand-alone violations, the international community should focus on prosecuting environmental destruction when conducted to achieve another atrocity, such as genocide or crimes against humanity.[7]

There are treaties and customary laws intended to address the prevention of environmental destruction, starting with the revised Report of the United Nations Conference on the Human Environment, held at Stockholm,[8] which established the "fundamental right to … an environment of a quality that permits a life of dignity and well-being", followed by the Rio Declaration on Environment and Development, which recognized that "warfare is inherently destructive of sustainable development", as well as "states shall therefore respect international law providing protection for the environment in times of armed conflict and cooperate in its further development as necessary".[9] More recently (after the Vietnam war), the Convention on the Prohibition of Environmental Development Techniques,[10] as well as the Geneva Convention, Protocol I,[11] forbids using "methods or means of warfare which are intended, or may be expected, to cause widespread, long-term and severe damage to the natural environment",[12] which states:

> Care shall be taken in warfare to protect the natural environment against widespread, long-term and severe damage. This protection includes a prohibition of the use of methods and means of warfare which are intended or may be expected to cause such damage to the natural environment and thereby to prejudice the health or survival of the population.[13]

The existence of specific documents, even coupled with international humanitarian law (IHL), particularly as it applies to *jus in bello*, however, has not resulted in the abundant jurisprudence one may expect, given the multiple conflicts harmful to both land and civilians in recent times, and ongoing today. Paolo Benvenuti explains the function of IHL:

> On the one hand it limits the choice of means and methods of conducting military operations (this branch is traditionally referred to as the Law of The Hague); on the other hand, it obliges the belligerents to spare persons who do not or no longer participate in hostilities (this branch, concerning the victims, traditionally is referred to as the Law of Geneva *stricto sensu*).[14]

The UN Charter (art. 2, para. 4) also states:

> All Members shall refrain in their international relations from the threat or use of force against the territorial integrity or political independence of any state, or in any other manner inconsistent with the Purposes of the United Nations.

However, the "territorial integrity" referred to in this paragraph is only intended in the quantitative, *not* in the qualitative sense of the expression. This is a common flaw in both international and domestic law, the latter particularly as it applies to Indigenous Peoples, such as the First Nations of Canada.[15] This is a basic flaw, unacknowledged and uncorrected in any environmental law or human rights regime, despite the grave problems inflicted on both ecological integrity and the biological integrity of individuals by climate change and other hazards of human origin.

In part, the reason for the missing case law is the fact that, rather than wars governed by the law of war, today almost everywhere we are afflicted by illegal conflicts, that is internal conflicts taking place within nations, rather than between nations, most of which are not legally declared wars. The conflicts tend to have their origin in the economic or power interests of the "Great Nations" who presently support one or another warring faction, often with the support of the UN and its institutions, such as NATO.[16] Then there are the unrecognized wars of liberation, primarily in Palestine, where the citizens are desperately trying by various means to shake off the illegal Israeli occupation, persisting against all UN Resolutions, declarations and related legal instruments, for over half a century.[17]

Thus, even beyond the deliberate avoidance of the interface between human rights to health and environmental hazards,[18] ongoing conflicts demonstrate the effects of the same powerful interests that support the approach to climate change denials. Another powerful illegal form of "war" is the so-called war on terrorism, or counter-terrorism, a "war" that does not recognise IHL or the rules of war, and one that respects neither active participants (not acknowledged as enemy combatants), nor civilians who somehow no longer deserve due process or even a proven crime, before being condemned to death by drone or other means.[19]

It is noteworthy that, whether legal or illegal the reasons for the outbreak of conflicts, IHL is "ready to step in, notwithstanding the prohibition on the use of force, whenever a war breaks out, whether or not there is any justification for that war".[20] In fact, IHL also applies to cases of internal conflicts, although not with equal strength.[21] Nevertheless, despite the many instances when war has been devastating to the environment, and the latter used deliberately to inflict harm on whole populations, from the "scorched-earth policies" against the Persians of 512 BC to the use of Agent Orange in the Vietnam war in the 1970s, no prosecutions in international law have followed.[22]

All these practices imply a previous judgement that the harm that will befall others is justified by their lesser status, in comparison to that of the authors of these practices. The same discriminatory approach is basic to all conflicts: group or community X does not possess the same rights to life and to its members' biological integrity that the attackers possess, must be the starting point. In fact most atrocities committed within either war or an internal conflict are humanitarian in nature, and they include "rape, murder, genocide and other crimes against humanity".[23]

It is easy to see why environmental crimes, or the destruction of the environment needed by these "inferior beings" for their survival, are far less likely to be prosecuted or even acknowledged. Tara Weinstein proposes that the commission of the direct humanitarian crime that accompanies the environmental destruction would be brought to a tribunal together with it, as a way of ensuring the criminalization of environmental attacks, at least as part of another grave crime.

However, even if this approach were to succeed, it would still ignore the basic discrimination that fosters both crimes which, instead, remains the cause of both kinds of crime and – most important – is already singled out as a grave breach of human rights in international law, and which imposes a non-derogable obligation on all states. The racism and discriminatory intent that permits practices that ignore human rights were acknowledged clearly in the Principles of Nuremberg,[24] beyond (a) crimes against peace and (b) war crimes:

> Article 6(c). Crimes against Humanity: namely murder, extermination, enslavement, deportation, and other inhumane acts, committed against any civilian population, before or during the war or persecutions on political, racial or religious grounds, in execution of or in connection with any crime within the jurisdiction of the tribunal, whether or not in violation of the domestic law of the country where perpetrated.

It is significant that the full listing of all possible inhumane acts is not present in this article, and also that the *means* of accomplishing the "extermination" and "deportation" of the targeted population or community is not specified. Further, the document refers to "leaders", "organizers", and "instigators and accomplices participating in the formulation or execution of a common plan or conspiracy" (art. 6(c)) as being all equally responsible for the execution of the criminal acts, and that the position of such individuals (participating in the common plan), whether they are heads of state or other responsible government officials, would not free them from either responsibility or punishment.

Finally, the presence of "superior orders" would also not eliminate accountability for the actions committed (art. 8), and – in fact – whenever these individuals are tried, the Tribunal, at its discretion, "may declare ... that the group or organization of which the individual was a member was a criminal organization" (art. 9).

This inclusive list of the aspects of individual accountability would appear to be sufficient to indict whoever is responsible for the collateral effects of conflicts, whether they are due to ecological disasters, as consequences of global warming, or to the deprivations and plunder of the means of sustenance of populations, or the deprivation of their water, or the health effects of disintegrity. It is not clear whether this approach can be used to advance the defence of eco-integrity in law and policy.

At least it proposes an approach based on principles that are already entrenched in law through international legal instruments, such as the principles of Nuremberg Tribunal, or even the International Convention on the Elimination of All Forms of Racial Discrimination.[25]

Discrimination and the use of force in conflict situations

> Article 2(4). All Members shall refrain in their international relations from the threat or use of force against the territorial integrity or political independence of any state, or in any other manner inconsistent with the Purposes of the United Nations.[26]

Charter rules followed the Second World War, so that both article 2(4) and article 51 on self-defence were exclusively directed to conflicts between states. But, since 1945, there have been any number of illegal or semi-legal conflicts, civil wars, struggles of national liberation, even the recent "war on terror". All of these foster various aspects of the "use of force" that are clearly completely different from interstate conflicts, understood as traditional wars were at the time the Charter was established. In addition, the differences of opinion between developed and developing states, and between East and West appear to have changed completely the context of the use of force as it exists today:

> The prohibition of the use of force led to fundamental divisions as to whether the prohibition of the "Use of force" included economic coercion, the scope of the right to self-defence, the right to use force to further self-determination and to intervene in civil wars.[27]

The "use of force" needs to be understood as the violent, unconsented actions that deprive people of their resources, as we shall see in the next chapter, but also the more general deprivation of liveable conditions entailed by the imposition of disintegrity. All the multiple actions that produce that result represent a form of violence that should – minimally – be characterized as "the use of force". They include "economic coercion" and ultimately result in threats/hazards to life itself, as the environmental conditions required for the continuation of life are increasingly eliminated.

If a population *or* community is dealing with unwarranted force, surely that form of attack should justify the use of self-defence in order to further self-determination. The latter ought to be understood as the right to repeal ecologically -based attacks on one's life, indirect as they may be, and especially the right to control one's living situation. Hence, this sort of the "use of force" is the basis of numerous conflicts, as Western powers, no longer able to hold their colonies, attempted to maintain their profits and their powers through imperialistic policies, using semi-legal, or otherwise unacceptable policies, although most of the other states in the international community were not prepared to acquiesce and tolerate:

> certain newly independent and socialist states began more clearly to claim legal rights not only to self-determination but also for national liberation movements to use force under international law and for third state to use force to help them. The colonial powers and western states resisted such claims.[28]

These "great powers" did not truly accept the legitimacy of international law; for instance General Assembly Resolution 2105(1965) "recognizes the legitimacy of the struggles by the peoples under colonial rule to exercise their right to self-determination and independence", without, however, clarifying the meaning of "struggle"; that is, whether "armed struggle" would be equally acceptable as a peaceful version.[29] Christine Gray cites the early use of another unclear term, "legitimacy" (rather than "legality" itself), to characterize the rights of peoples in their struggle, "by all means at their disposal".[30]

In 1981 the "Declaration on the Inadmissibility of Intervention"[31] affirmed "the right and duty of states to support self-determination included the right of these people to wage both political and armed struggle".[32]

The issue of the right to use force in the quest for self-determination, has lost its poignancy today, as most countries have accepted decolonization, and South Africa, for instance, "has given up on apartheid",[33] a condition which, however, persists in the Zionist state of Israel. In fact, the issue is at the heart of the present-day international law and politics:

> The issue is still important in the context of the Palestinian struggle for self-determination in the territories of the West Bank and Gaza, occupied by Israel since 1967. The states that support the Palestinian intifada generally prefer to make their case in terms of violations by Israel of the law of belligerent occupation; they are reluctant to argue for a legal right to use force for self-determination.[34]

This reluctance persists, despite the legal reaffirmation of the right of the Palestinians to self-determination.[35] The Israel–Palestine situation remains an ongoing glaring example of the many "international failures" listed in the 2014–15 Amnesty International Report:

> The July assault on Gaza by Israeli forces caused the loss of 2000 Palestinian lives. Yet again, the great majority of those – at least 1500 – were civilians. The policy was as Amnesty International argued in a detailed analysis, marked by callous indifference and involved war crimes. Hamas also committed war crimes by firing indiscriminate rockets into Israel by causing 6 deaths.[36]

Nor is this approach contrary to the letter of the law. Antonio Cassese views self-determination "as a continuing right" and as "freedom from outside interference". He says:

> Given that the people of every sovereign State have a permanent right to choose by whom they are governed, it is only logical that they should have the right to demand that the chosen central authorities exploit the territory's natural resources so as to benefit the people. Herein orders article1(2), which provides the right to control and benefit from a territory's natural resources lies with the inhabitants of that territory.[37]

The right to one's resources surely also applies to the ecological conditions that foster the presence of such resources. The elimination or pollution of such resources, whether because of corporate economic interests or because of conflicts in the area, should be equally proscribed. As Cassese argues, "The Problem lies not in understanding the nature of the right, but in ensuring state compliance".[38] That, of course, is the main problem, one that is all pervasive as it applies primarily to wealthy "democratic" countries. Richard Falk explains it well: the main problem is the prevalence of "lawfare".

Human rights and lawfare

> Issues of law and "lawfare" are recurring features of foreign policy debates in the United States. On the side are efforts by peace activists and others to condition the behaviour of all states, and especially the United States, by reference to authoritative limits on national discretion, as encoded in the UN Charter, a binding treaty. In opposition to a law-oriented foreign policy for the United States are a variety of arguments that rely directly or indirectly on a version of American exceptionalism.[39]

"Lawfare" represents the "instrumental use of law to achieve valued ends, positive or negative".[40] What characterizes these "valued ends" is their lack of universality: they are, one and all, specific to the state or organization that is pursuing them.

Thus Falk also defines "lawfare" as "soft power geopolitics", best suited to those who are short of hard power. "Lawfare" can be viewed as neutral, but in today's world, the "weak", that is the states and organizations that have been victimized by the Powers that control the Security Council remain the losers, thus directing much of what the United Nations can do – or rather what the UN is coerced *not* to do.

After 9/11, the US has proclaimed the "war on terror", and neoconservatives under George W. Bush decided that dependence on or respect for international law was a weapon best left to the weak. Again, Israel's policy against the Palestinians is a case in point: the latter have been the recipients of numerous favourable GA Resolutions, and have enjoyed the support of world renowned legal scholars such as John Dugard, Richard Goldstone and, most recently, William Schabas, all favourable to their position, on grounds both legal and accepted by the global community.[41]

Yet their situation has not changed for decades, because of the twisted machinations of the Zionist authorities in Israel, and the US. Many people are convinced by the US, and the spin they put on the illegal actions of both Israel and the US itself; those who are not convinced can be coerced in various ways, ranging from the US's endless efforts to spin acts of resistance and attempts to achieve self-determination, in various illogical ways, such as Bush's own explanation at the time of 9/11: "they hate our freedom".

Another example is the use of "false flag" episodes, such as the likeliest explanation of the 2015 killings in Paris, following the earlier Charlie Hebdo offensive cartoons depicting Islam. The Israeli Prime Minister, Netanyahu, was not invited, yet he marched in solidarity with European heads of state, after thoughtfully (and very quickly) providing Mossad's help to kill the "terrorists". That episode was the culmination of Western countries (mostly the US and Canada) viewing and treating attacks against Muslim beliefs and practices as instances of almost sacred "free speech", while any critique of Israel, no matter how well founded in law, was and is treated as "anti-semitism", hence impermissible. That recent episode, splashed across the media both print and television globally, represents one of the clearest examples of the negative uses of lawfare. Falk says:

> I find it clarifying to distinguish between positive and negative uses of lawfare. I identify positive uses to be efforts to insist that international law be upheld to the extent that it serves values of peace, justice and human dignity, and that its guidelines and conceptions of right and wrong be generally treated as authoritative in diplomatic arenas concerned with the peaceful resolution of conflicts ...[42]

These positive uses of lawfare entail the pursuit of justice and they aim to hold the perpetrators of the actions that lawfare condemns accountable in law. In contrast, in its negative aspect, lawfare demonstrates disdain for international law, and it views its constraints as inappropriate, because they pose possible limits to the pursuit of US policy. In addition, Falk remarks on the very issue that cosmopolitan scholars such as Glenn find most problematic today, that is, the lack of any central authority capable of adjudicating the principles guiding state decisions. Falk adds:

> given the absence of any central governing authority or legislative institution on a global level to pronounce upon disputes about interpretation or to agree upon changes in governing rules. As a result, many "violations" of international law serve as precedents for the establishment of new norms: power generates law and its interpretation, whether or not it serves the causes of justice.[43]

One of the most egregious examples of such "precedent" is the origin of the so-called "war on terror" since 9/11. Antonio Cassese says:

> I shall not dwell on the use of the term "war" by the American president and the whole US administration. It is obvious in this case "war" is a misnomer. War is armed conflict between two or more states. Here we are confronted with an extremely serious terrorist attack by a non-state organization against a state.[44]

Further, "terrorism" itself is not definitely defined in international law. Cassese addresses this question as well:

> For more than thirty years States have debated in the UN the question of punishing terrorism. However, they have been unable to agree upon a definition of this crime. Third World countries staunchly clung to their view that the notion could not cover acts of violence perpetrated by so-called freedom fighters, that is individuals and groups struggling for the realization of self-determination.[45]

I have discussed this difficult issue and the use of these terms ("war", "terrorism") in detail elsewhere.[46] It is undeniable that the global community is driven to condemn and punish those with even the smallest connection to a "crime" that is undefined, without any effort to seek out and redress the reasons for these occurrences, let alone to actually prove the guilt of "suspected" individuals in a court of law.

The various Acts produced especially in North America, in the US since 2001,[47] and, unfortunately, also being followed by Canada with an Act to be presented to Parliament as Bill C-51 in February 2015, despite the vehement opposition of law professors and scholars from coast to coast.[48]

The main issue is the uncritical desire on the part of former prime minister Harper (enjoying at best a third of Canadian votes), to follow the US in depriving citizens of their rights, from privacy, to protest, all based on nebulous concepts, which the current government extends to all protests. Included are the protests against "tar sands" and the Big Oil interests that support them, in direct conflict with the rights of Canadian First Nations in the area.

Hence the possible extension of criminal law to the protests of those who would defend environmental right and safety together with Indigenous rights, equally concerned about the environment, are close to the interests of those who would protect ecological integrity, needs a radical review. It is sad that the countries who support these forms of governance against people's rights are the very countries that claim for themselves strongly the mantle of democracy.

Disintegrity and the racist roots of the fight against terrorism

> I identify here three types classified by agent, or actor: non-state terrorism, state terrorism, and what I call "amphibolous" state-cum-non-state terrorism, each of which has subcategories according to objective or method.[49]

Rama Mani also distinguished between "self-determination terrorism" and "hate terrorism" and two different aspects of non-state terrorism. We discussed the former in the previous section, using the Palestinian situation as the main example, although we could also have cited the acts of terrorism by the Irish Republican Army (IRA), or that of the Chechen Rebels in Moscow in 2002.[50] Hate terrorism in contrast included the actions of white supremacists or neo-Nazis, and other similar groups in Europe and others in the US, as well as other revolutionary "fronts" in Sierra Leone, Uganda and other similar areas, although some will not acknowledge these as acts of terrorism.[51]

Less convincing is the description of mixed terrorism, described as combining state and non-state terrorism, and the primary example Mani related is that of al-Qaeda, which he defines as "a collusion between non-state and state actors with strong business, financial and criminal connections".[52]

However, this is a description, not an explanation, and I am not convinced that this represents a better definition of their motive then the one we cited earlier, offered by Osama bin Laden himself. For Al-Qaeda as for many other terrorist attacks, the "root cause" may be less obvious. Mani adds, "Terrorism is not a philosophy or a movement. It is a method. To state the obvious, the search for root causes is futile if the definition of terrorism itself is consistently shifting."[53]

In contrast, Thomas Homer-Dixon argues, correctly I believe, that "analyzing root causes was not a pretext for justifying terrorism, but rather was done to prevent its recurrence".[54] That represents the most important focus of this research: root causes are absolutely necessary in order to comply with the mandates of the UN regarding the *prevention* of terrorism and the importance on non-aggression. Although the exact motivation of each single attack may not be immediately clear, claims of randomness and the lack of a serious cause, amount to the dismissal of the issues many consider grave enough to merit putting their own life on the line.

In this sense, the superficial denial of a serious reason for the attack is clearly a major part of the problem: such denial will continue to elicit attacks – and that with some justice – as the issues that are most important to some, are simply dismissed as non-existent, by others. In fact, some believe that "understanding" leads directly to "legitimizing" terrorism. Those who take that position believe that it is unacceptable to try and listen, in order to understand what motivates terrorism. Both Ted Honderich[55] and Chomsky[56] plead for understanding. Meisels criticizes this position as she presents Derrida's: "to condemn unconditionally certain acts of terrorism … without having to ignore the situation that might have brought them about or even legitimated them".[57] Meisels adds that Natanyahu finds the quest for "root causes", to be "perplexing" as too close to legalization.[58]

However, we must acknowledge that unless we come to these attacks prepared to listen and understand, our real goal, that is, the prevention of terrorism, will never be reached, as it has not been reached by the violent practices that have prevailed in recent times. We should recall with David Sturm, that "Human rights … are more than means of individual advance they are attributes of concern for each other".[59]

Unless we are prepared to honour our common humanity and respect our differences rather than hide behind walls of separation and discrimination between "us" and "them", it will not be possible to work for the prevention of terrorism and the diffusion of peace. Thus, *pace* Mani, Meisels, Netanyahu and others, even if one essential single general cause of terrorism cannot be found, we can affirm that the root cause hinges on the lack of respect for the human rights, basic, but also cultural and religious of all individuals and peoples. Both are firmly entrenched in international law, and basic to the letter and the spirit of the UN Charter and other foundational documents.

Hence we need to discover what other causes motivate terrorist attacks, beyond the quest for self-determination and/or territorial integrity. No doubt, not all motives once discovered, will justify the "legitimization" of terrorism, but each position may represent a varying shade of grey, rather than an uncompromising black or white, and each should be judged on its own merits.

We will return to this point in the conclusion of this chapter. At this point we should return to the question of motives beyond self-determination, understood as external self-determination. In contrast, internal self-determination is different, but it remains a motive that may spur communities embedded within states to revolt, or to act forcefully to defend themselves from state terrorism, the topic of the next section. For now it is important to keep in mind the following:

> In 1982, the UN Human Rights Commission and the Economic and Social Council approved the establishment of a working group on Indigenous Populations under the Subcommission of Prevention of Discrimination and the Protection of Minorities.[60]

The protection from discrimination of minorities and others includes the right of Indigenous Peoples to (internal) self-determination, but the focal point of minority protection is the issue of discrimination, already entrenched in international law, according to article 27 of the ICCPR:

> In those States in which ethnic, religious or linguistic minorities exist, persons belonging to such minorities shall not be denied the right in community with

> other members of their group to enjoy their own culture, to profess and practice their own religion, or to use their own language.[61]

Howard J. Vogel discusses this point as he adds that it was understood that the language of article 27 included "the use of affirmative action" or what international law terms "special measures", to ensure the right enumerated.[62]

However, neither the ICCPR nor the sub-commission on prevention of Discrimination specify what "measures" – if any – are legitimate in the affirmation of these rights, failing the appropriate legal procedures. In other words, aside from the presence of the system of the international courts, what are the rights of the citizens who are the victims of discrimination and apartheid, to name two basic and ongoing issues? There is no legal "permission" to employ terrorist tactics, to be sure, but the question is what else can be done, when the UN system is and remains practically unresponsive or insufficient, as we can see for instance from the number of resolutions against Israel, from the UN, all blocked by *one* veto: that of the US.[63]

In the previous sections we identified the quest for self-determination as the major causal source of terrorism as currently understood. We also showed the support in international law for both self-determination rights and for the struggles that accompany that goal. Denying the right to colonize weaker nations to major Western powers was basic to that approach. But both colonization and the denial of rights to self-determination are based on racist/discriminatory beliefs, or at least cannot exist without that belief. Similarly the "war on terror" is a combination of illegal practices based on the strong belief in the difference between "us" and "them", the latter being for the most part non-whites, mostly non-Christian, and comprising various ethnic and racial groups.

All these forms of racism confirm the presence of a strong legal basis upon which to rest the condemnation of all practices that attack the health and integrity of environments and human beings; The International Convention Against All Forms of Discrimination.[64] This prohibition represents a *jus cogens* norm, thus a non-derogable obligation not only for the discrimination country, but also for the entire international community.

Thus, as we explore the multiple forms of conflict that deliberately or otherwise also represent attacks on the integrity of life, new developments emerge, aside from the historical episodes that since antiquity have represented at least a collateral damage arising from warfare. Today's globalization economic activities, whether they support climate change or the deprivation of resources, increase the ongoing conflict with integrity, the gravest danger that confronts humanity today. One of the results driven by globalization, is the increasing number of mass migrations.

Ecological refugees and others escaping from conflicts and racial discrimination

Although "overt racism [is] going out of fashion", and "civil rights movements at home and anti-colonial movements abroad undercut the legitimacy of racial exclusion and discrimination",[65] "global apartheid" is now imposed, separating "the global North from the global South".[66] This separation is especially important as it affects refugees at all points in their saga: in the exposure to the conditions that render them asylum seekers; in the situation they find, when they are lucky enough to be able to flee; and even in the conditions of life they find when they reach their goal, life in another country.

Juss puts it well:

> When one considers the root causes of flight in many developing nations, however, it is clear that a focus on narrow political interpretation of persecution excludes the bulk of the world's refugees today, thereby making such a definition wholly inappropriate for a global application. Thus the definition can exclude those suffering economic and social persecution. It can exclude those suffering from the effects of war. It can exclude the victims of natural disasters in countries where the state offers no protection. It can accordingly all too easily exclude the migration of people attributed to climate change. In short it excludes most of the world's humanitarian refugees.[67]

It seems clear that the effort to render refugee law more relevant, thus ensuring a better fit between its regulations and the situation of those it is intended to protect, should be to switch the focus of relevant regimes to human rights. As well, the attempt to separate the conditions and the needs of asylum seekers from those of migrants, is not conducive to either an understanding of the causes and conditions leading to the forced exodus of whole groups, or even to better knowledge of the situation of refugees who succeed in their flight, after their arrival in their chosen country.

For many reasons connected to the presence of "global apartheid", the main issue regarding today's asylum seekers is the existence of multiple human rights breaches; we need to respect their dignity and their rights from the start. Their rights must be respected at their original location, at the start, as mass flights are better reduced by eliminating the causes, than by attempting to redress the problems, after they have occurred. In addition, their rights must be respected at the border, after they flee, if the harmful conditions that face them persist. Finally, their rights must be respected after their arrival.

> Conscious of their duty to achieve the total liberation of Africa, the peoples of which are still struggling for their dignity and genuine independence, and undertaking to eliminate colonialism, neo-colonialism apartheid, Zionism, and to dismantle aggressive foreign military bases and all forms of discrimination, particularly those based on race, ethnic group, colour, sex, language, religion or political opinions ...[68]

This paragraph could apply to any of the third world countries from which come the overwhelming majority of refugees: they are, in various measure, "struggling for their dignity", as well as for their life, against different forms of aggression, all based upon the effects of ongoing discriminatory practices. In fact, all the circumstances that have been discussed in Part I as being causally determinant of the forced displacement of whole populations, start precisely with the discriminatory practice that underlies the harmful activities that force displacement.

Hence, there is a specific reason for choosing the African Charter to start this section's discussion. If we consider the origins of the disparate activities that result in (a) climate change, (b) famine and the illegal deprivation of peoples' natural resources, and (c) the ongoing illegal conflicts, we note one common theme all these human rights breaches share: the total depreciation of the rights, hence the human dignity and value of those who are eventually affected by the consequences of the activities themselves.

I have argued that the commonality of all the phenomena leading to migrations, is manifested in the crippling poverty all refugees share.[69] The additional common denominator that unites the activities that eventually make the flight inevitable, is the discriminatory intent of those whose operations first create, then impose those conditions:

> Economists have focused on how best to provide incentives so that individuals and firms take into account their externalities: steel producers should be forced to pay for their pollution, and those who cause accidents should pay for the consequences. We embody these ideas for instance, in the "polluter pays principle", which says that polluters should pay for the full consequences of their actions.[70]

Stiglitz adds that non-compliance is equivalent to rewarding the corporations involved by offering them a subsidy for their operations. For instance, "nuclear power plants and offshore oil rigs are shielded from bearing the full costs should they explode".[71] As we saw, at the time of Chernobyl (Ukraine), and we still see today after the Fukushima disaster in Japan, the question of possible malfunctions is only a small part of the ways in which these entities can impose harm. The gravest threat posed by nuclear power plants, is the unsolved (and unsolvable) problem of radioactive waste, right from the start of their operations, that is, with the uranium mining that is also evidence of discriminatory intent, in the way those operations are located and staffed.

Another example of industrial harms can be found for example in uranium mining.[72] The history of uranium mining in the four-corner area (Utah, Colorado, Arizona and New Mexico, and the Navajo Reservation between the Grand Canyon and the Petrified Forest National Park), appears to have been written in blood.

The evidence of the narrative is unequivocal. It is consistently one group and one group alone that is targeted. I have termed this approach "institutionalized ecological violence", and the author is correct in pointing out that this form of violence does more than destroy the unfortunate miners, working in hazardous unventilated "dog holes", accumulating in one week multiple doses of the yearly maximum "safe" radiation exposure in their bodies, and eventually succumbing to untreatable cancer and other diseases.

Some mill workers also had up to 60 micrograms of uranium in their urine samples. The yellowcake dust they inhaled and swallowed was making them radioactive from the inside out. This intolerable violence also destroys families who attempt to survive on the pitiful sums allotted to them, or with no compensation at all for surviving wives and children. Finally, this same violence, discriminating against Native Americans, also attacks their survival as people, hence the appeal to genocide in this case. Although we all depend on a healthy, non-toxic environment, Native people have a particular right and claim to the lands they inhabit and from which they assert their identity as a Nation.

Nor is the United States the only country with that problem. A 2006 report from Australia relates a similar story:

> Cancer rates among Aborigines near Australia's biggest uranium mine, according to a study by the Federal Government's leading indigenous research body, appear to be almost double the normal rate. The study also found there had been no monitoring in the past 20 years of the Ranger mine's impact on the health of local indigenous peoples. Yet since 1981 there have been more than 120 spillages and leaks of contaminated water at the mine located in the World Heritage listed Kakadu National Park.[73]

Energy Resources of Australia (majority owned by Rio Tinto), which operates the mine, denied that the aboriginal peoples in the area were exposed to radiation, and in fact announced that the mine would continue to operate until 2020, despite the fact that a study "compared Aborigines diagnosed with cancer in the Kakadu region with the cancer rate among all Aboriginal peoples in the Northern Territory from 1994 to 2003". It found the diagnosis rate "was 90 percent higher than expected in the Kakadu region".[74]

In this case as well, neither the corporation(s) responsible for the extractive activities nor the Australian government that allowed and in fact defended this operation, accepted responsibility for the harms they had perpetrated, or attempted to close the mine and redress the injustice for which they shared responsibility.

Examples can be multiplied, thus, it is neither the facts nor the science that are lacking, but the functionalist approach of industry and institutions that needs to accept the scientific reality and enact the required corrections.

Of course it is not only the internal stakeholder that is at risk from the nuclear industry. The whole world is under threat. Consider the 2011 earthquake and explosion that damaged the nuclear plant at Fukushima in Japan:

> The Fukushima disaster in Japan has brought to the forefront the dangers of a worldwide nuclear radiation. The crisis in Japan has been described as "a nuclear war without a war". Nuclear radiation, which threatens life on planet earth, is not front page news.[75]

This reality speaks to the role and aim of the corporation, intended to serve the public good. As well, nuclear power workers at all levels contribute to the manufacture, stockpiling and use of nuclear weapons, with horrifying results for public health for decades following their use.

The most recent abuse of public health and human rights can be observed in the effects of so-called "spent uranium" by the US in Iran, and Israel in Palestine.[76] As there are no US official findings regarding these children's horrible fate, so too, there are no research data regarding the workers who assembled the ammunitions that used spent uranium.

Disintegrity and a major threat to humanity

> The International Court of Justice has issued an advisory opinion of great weight on the legality of nuclear weaponry. It is the first time ever that an international tribunal has directly addressed this gravest universal threat to the future of humanity.[77]

Before considering the International Court's Opinion on this question, it is best to consider the context against which these weapons are developed, and the International Pleadings of Australia and New Zealand as part of that context. Nuclear power, in all its applications, represents one of the most hazardous products and process on earth.[78] As such it is one of the clearest cases demanding immediate concern and legal action on several fronts: it is hazardous in the mining of its required materials, or throughout the "fuel cycle";[79] it is hazardous in all its uses, not only as a weapon; and it is especially hazardous in it disposal phase. Nuclear power is indeed "risky business" from cradle to grave,[80] and the results of its impact exhibit all the characteristic harms this work confronts: immediate harm to human health, delayed threats to health, life and normal function, and long-term harm to the "diversity of life"[81] and to its very survival, through direct and indirect (genetic) impacts.[82] Finally it is extremely and unpredictably hazardous through its disposal.[83]

It is not hard to find extensive and clear philosophical support not only for the immorality of the use of nuclear weapons, but also for threats intended as nuclear deterrence.[84] In law one finds direct reference only to two aspects of nuclear power use:

- testing; and
- the threat and use of nuclear armaments.

This is somewhat surprising: the occurrence of a terrible accident such as Chernobyl, as well as the routine production of low-level ionizing radiation through the normal, peace time operation of nuclear power stations, has not been officially pursued in international law, to the best of my knowledge, although both have been discussed in the literature.[85] For instance, despite the presence of an old, often malfunctioning power station like Fermi, right over the Canadian border, and Windsor, although it is located between Michigan and Ohio, no legal cases have arisen from these hazardous circumstances.

On the question of the legality of atmospheric nuclear testing, Australia and New Zealand instituted separate proceedings against France before the International Court.[86] Atmospheric Nuclear Tests clearly spread unwarranted radioactive material indiscriminately to any and all countries adjacent to the tests. Even France, who wanted to test, did not attempt to conduct such tests over its own soil. France must have recognized that the atmospheric tests were neither desirable nor risk-free, as they defended their strategy: France claimed it needed to perform these "last tests" in order to end atmospheric testing altogether. This declaration ensured that "the International Court did not pronounce either jurisdiction or the merits of the cases, relying on the obligation undertaken explicitly by the French government".[87]

But the importance of the case does not lie with the majority view expressed above. Rather, the four judges who wrote a forceful dissent (Judges Onyeama, Dillard, Jiménez de Arechago, Sir Humphrey Waldock) asserted that the "object of the applicant States was to obtain a declaratory judgment" instead.[88] The pleadings in these cases show that the intentions of the states were not simply to stop France on this single occasion, but to make a universal point of principle. France, according to these pleadings, had violated important rights: the protection of New Zealand's sovereign rights to be free of radioactive nuclear fallout and contamination. This was described as a right that belonged to "all members of the international community".[89]

Hence, especially for New Zealand, the obligation was *erga omnes*, and all states possessed correlative rights of protection. The fact that France (with China) had not been a signatory to the Treaty Banning Nuclear Weapons Tests in the Atmosphere, in Outer Space and Under Water[90] was not relevant. Nevertheless, the additional fact that 104 states did become parties to the Moscow Treaty over the next 10 years, enabled Australia and New Zealand to argue that "customary rule had gradually emerged" in the international community, and to assert, at the same time, the *erga omnes* character of France's obligation.[91] Ragazzi "infers" that the obligation is indeed *erga omnes,* from the following arguments found in the pleadings:

> the obligation (a) is stated in "absolute" terms (the dictum refers to "absolute" and "unqualified" obligations);
>
> (b) reflects a "community interest" (the dictum refers to the "concern of all States");
>
> (c) protects fundamental goods, namely "the security, life and health of all peoples" and the "global environment" (security, life and health are also some of the basic goods protected by the four examples of obligations *erga omnes* given in the dictum);
>
> (d) has a prohibitory content (like the four examples given in the dictum);

(e) is not owed to particular States, but to the "international community" (the dictum refers to the "international community as a whole"); and

(f) its correlative rights of protection "are held in common" (the dictum provides that "all States can be held to have a legal interest" in the protection of obligations *erga omnes*).[92]

The "dictum" here referred to is the one found in the *Barcelona Traction* case. This argument is of foundational importance, because it introduces the principled approach sought later by the WHO. Although originally the UN turned down the request of the WHO, eventually, the World Court Advisory Opinion on the "Legality of the Threat or Use of Nuclear Weapons"[93], shows the transition from state treaties as sole arbiters of the status of nuclear armaments, to an Opinion whose history and background served to bring a normative issue to the forefront of public opinion.[94]

Falk traces the history of the movement that culminated in that request, from several groups in civil society, as "the push to achieve elimination [of nuclear weapons] often merges with the view that weapons of mass destruction cannot be reconciled with international humanitarian law".[95] Falk shows how world opinion as well as the work of many committed non-governmental organizations prepared the ground for the very possibility of asking for an Opinion, from the time of the 1985 London Nuclear Warfare Tribunal, where those weapons were defined as "unconditionally illegal", hence, that even a threat of their use would amount to a "crime against humanity".[96]

The main point that emerges is that neither politics nor economic factors, nor even the advantage of groups of nuclear states, could be allowed to decide on the use of these weapons. Hence, at first the UN General Assembly and the WHO posed a difficult question to the World Court, and although the question could be evaded as "health", narrowly construed, was the WHO concern, later, an Opinion was given. Implicit in both the original request and the eventual opinion is the fact that "Nuclear Weaponry, with its global implications, raises questions of legality that affect not just the citizenry of the nuclear weapons states, but the entire world".[97] This position supports, once again, the *erga omnes* status of the question. Falk does not use this language in regard to either the question or the Opinion itself, but he adds:

> Although not so formulated the radical element in this request was to transfer the question of nuclear weapons policy from the domain of geopolitics, where it had remained since the first attacks on Hiroshima and Nagasaki, to the domain of international law.[98]

And if it has not transferred the question to treaty law, clearly both incomplete and insufficient to deal with this global threat, then Ragazzi's argument for placing its normative aspect among the few *jus cogens* norms generating an *erga omnes* obligation appears to be correct.

Geoffrey Danton cites the late Burns Weston in his recent work:

> in this burgeoning human rights era especially respecting an issue that involves potentially the fate of human civilization itself, is not only appropriate, but mandated that the legal expectations of all members of human society official and non-official be duly taken into account.[99]

The fate of humanity is indeed at stake, as a brief comparison between the bombing of Hiroshima and Nagasaki and a possible similar bombing today demonstrates. Survival seemed possible after that nuclear attack, but the bombs used in 1945 were only 15 kilotons of explosive power; they represented the end of a war; there was no nuclear retaliation on the part of the country attacked; both struck cities were not the main centres of Japan. Also – highly significantly – the "small bombs" used in Hiroshima and Nagasaki could not produce the nuclear winter which would be the result of the use of the much more powerful weapons available today.[100]

That is why employing the doctrine of "military necessity" in defence of the use of nuclear weaponry as many do today, forces us to relinquish any respect for legality or morality:

> Where is the military necessity in incinerating entire urban populations, defiling the territory of neighbouring and distant neutral countries, and ravaging the natural environment for generations to come? If so, then we are witness to the demise of Nuremberg, the triumph of Kriegsraison, the virtual repudiation of the humanitarian rules of armed conflict … the very meaning of "proportionality" becomes lost, and we come dangerously close to condoning the crime of genocide, that is, a military campaign directed more towards the extinction of the enemy, than towards winning a battle of conflict.[101]

Nuclear power's effect 55 years later

> Ahmed el-Hadj Hamadi was huddled into a building with the rest of his community by French soldiers early in the morning. They were instructed to lie down, close their eyes and cover their ears. He then remembers a sound like "the world coming to an end" and the windows turning white. A cord above their prone bodies swung erratically until the light bulb it held shattered.[102]

When we consider the effects of nuclear power alone, even before it is used in warfare, we see clearly the connection between the discriminatory basis of colonialism, and the ongoing examples seen in the locations of tests and, as we already saw, in the very roots of the industry upon which all forms of nuclear power is based. Uranium operations take place in areas inhabited by Indigenous peoples, not anywhere near the offices or residences of those who derive economic or other benefits form nuclear operations, whether peaceful or not. The same is true of the chosen locations for nuclear tests. In addition, the latter's dire effects are not communicated to the local populations, nor has informed prior consent been sought.

In the Algerian case, the French soldiers made sure that the local people were "huddled into a building"; and after the sound like "the apocalypse", the people were sent out to pick up the garbage. "The ground was all burned, white liquid". The estimates of the affected Algerians "range from 27,000 to 60,000". Yet only 17 victims have been compensated to date, despite the fact that France, after relocating its testing location, "experimented with more than 90 nuclear bombs from 1966–1996".[103]

A litany of uncompensated (and often uncompensable) medical issues followed upon the tests:

> Babies born with atrophied limbs; cancers of the liver, stomach and skin; cases of temporary blindness among those who saw the brutal flash of light as it ripped through the Maghreb about 6:30 a.m.[104]

Ammar Mansouri called the events "the most despicable crimes perpetrated by colonial France in Algeria".[105] Yet France was a retroactive signatory with the International Atomic Energy Association in 1997, on the Treaty on radioactive waste management. Eventually France ratified a plan known as the Morin Law, which estimated that "at least 150,000 people" have been exposed in areas where France executed its tests.[106]

Applications for compensation may take over a year to be processed and so far the average amount of compensation has been about $80,000. The US Congress also took about "50 years to ratify a program recognizing those who suffer from illnesses related to nuclear testing or uranium mining", eventually "awarding almost $2 billion to 42,000 citizens – about 70 percent of applicants". The UK tested two nuclear bombs in the Monte Bello Islands in Australia, and in 1993 "granted nearly 30 million to the Australian government to cover plaintiffs" for death and illness resulting from radiation.[107]

These terrible stories combine grave harms to both ecology and humanity, through threats that are (and were) well-known to the governments of all three countries, France, the United States and the UK. It is also worth knowing that the threats were deliberately placed in areas far from those inhabited by the white citizens of each of the countries involved. The victims in all cases were those who did not share equal rights with other citizens: native populations, Indigenous citizens of other countries, and the inhabitants of previously held colonies, thus confirming the inherently racist and discriminatory aspects of these governments' activities.

The Advisory Opinion on nuclear weapons and the protection of the environment

> The environment is not an abstraction but represents the living space, the quality of life, and the very health of human beings including generations unborn.[108]

With these words the ICJ places nuclear weapons control closer to human rights law than to humanitarian law and the rules of war.[109] This connection is cemented further by the Human Rights Committee, General Comment No. 14:

> It is evident that the designing, testing, manufacture, possession and development of nuclear weapons are among the great threats to the right to life which confront mankind today. This threat is compounded by the danger that the actual use of such weapons may be brought about not only in the event of war but even through human or mechanical error or failure …
>
> The production, testing, possession, deployment and use of nuclear weapons should be prohibited and recognized as crimes against humanity.[110]

Hence the question of nuclear weaponry is not debated for its possible use in war situations alone, but starts from the most basic human right of all, the right to life:

> The right to life, which the committee discusses in this General Comment, is indeed the central human right without which all others are rendered meaningless. It is a non-derogable human right rising to the level of a *jus cogens* norm, meaning that it will override inconsistent treaty or customary norms.[111]

Hence it is important to separate these weapons, largely acknowledged for their "very ghastliness",[112] from considerations of the *lex specialis* and for discussions regarding the use of force in armed conflict. In fact, although some preferred to discuss nuclear weapons simply in connection with general issues regarding armaments in international humanitarian law,[113] the main point regarding these weapons is that they are different *in kind* from regular weapons that permit to focus on a specific target, rather than providing a general attack on the environment and on humans without any possibility of distinguishing legal from illegal targets.

A strong case for the *sui generis* status of nuclear weapons has been made by Judge Christopher Weeramantry.[114] Weeramantry argues strongly for the right to life, a universal right that cannot be supported by any country that would even consider the use of weapons that "ha[ve] the potential to kill between one million and one billion people".[115] This statement is particularly relevant for its applicability to the present work, because the diffuse killing arising from nuclear weapons is, in fact, killing in a manner that arises from environmental sources, further, from environmental sources as increasingly identified through scientific research, as Weeramantry also suggested in his other landmark Separate Opinion in 1997.[116]

The horrific effects of exposure to the effects not only of nuclear weapons but also of "their possession, manufacture, and stock piling in peacetime",[117] are effects that persist long after their use, or any possible justification for their use even in a "just war". Thus there are two major aspects that are seldom mentioned in any assessment of the permissibility of manufacturing or stockpiling nuclear weapons for possible future use in the exceptional case of a nation being dependent on their use for its survival. The first *sui generis* characteristic is the terrible effects they produce long before and after their use, hence the staggering number of innocent, civilian victims, none of whom have even a remote connection with "enemy combatants". The second is the comparably terrible harms to the environment itself, thus compounding the totally unjustified attacks directly to humanity. Hence, if we consider *jus in bello* as our starting point, we immediately note that we must refer to nuclear weapons as *sui generis*, not just one among many more or less "acceptable", or at least tolerable weapons.

These special characteristics apply equally to so-called "spent uranium" munitions.[118] They are, one and all, such that:

- they cannot be considered to be limited to one or even several identifiable acts;
- they cannot be considered as limited to one or even several identifiable, specific times or time-frames; and
- their results cannot be understood to be limited to one or even several legitimate targets.

Thus the UN Sub-Commission on Prevention of Discrimination and Protection of Minorities, links the very existence of these weapons to the right to life:

> The use of or threat of use of weapons of mass destruction and, in certain circumstances, the production and sale of such weapons are incompatible with international human rights and/or humanitarian law.[119]

Yet the *Bulletin of the Atomic Scientists*, Sept./Oct. 2014, estimates that:

> There are approximately 16,300 nuclear weapons located at some 97 sites in 14 countries. Roughly 10,000 of these weapons are in military arsenals; the remaining weapons are retired and awaiting dismantlement. Approximately 4,000 are operationally available and some 1,800 are on high alert and ready for use on short notice.[120]

They are, one and all, the gravest, most blatant threat/attack to the biological integrity of our ecology or to the essential life-support of the planet. Further, at least in North America, those who would protest against the threats to the ecology that sustain us and the corporate/industrial interests that promote and foster the proliferation of all such threats, are viewed as "terrorists", that is as similar to those who violently attack the public in the pursuit of political change, as a tentative definition, but are left undefined in both the US Patriot Act of 2006, and in 2015, in the proposed Bill C-51 following the same path if approved to become law in Canada, by the conservative Canadian government of Steven Harper.[121]

We are therefore moving far beyond the "Nuremberg Legacy",[122] because of two separate but interwoven causal roots. On one hand, there are vast advancements in the scientific research linking environmental exposures to harms to the normal functioning of the ecological systems, such as the causal links between GHG emissions and climate change.[123]

On the other hand, there are the giant steps in scientific research, connecting grave human harms to industrial exposures of all kinds, not only among those who work in such enterprises, or deal direct with the materials and products involved, but with all possible users, all humans starting from the embryonic stage of development.[124]

The vast and largely unchecked proliferation of industrial chemicals, coupled with the proliferation of nuclear armaments, indicates where the basis for the worst threats facing humanity lie, now, but such that they have been increasing since the start of the Anthropocene period.[125] It is worth noting that both these clusters of threats are entirely man-made, hence they were, in principle, entirely preventable and are still such that they could be reduced through a sustained goodwill effort on the part of the richest and most powerful nations.

Landmines: a somewhat similar threat against biological integrity

> Landmines should be outlawed, it was argued because they are victim-activated; because 80 to 90 percent are civilian; because injuries inflicted by landmines are of a horrific nature; and because landmines continue to cause death and injury for decades after being sown. They are the weapon of mass murder in slow motion.[126]

The Convention on Landmines deals with much that is similar to the effects of nuclear weapons: they share the lack of temporal limits to some of the harms caused; they also share their indiscriminate nature and the gravest effects affecting civilians. They also fit the definition here offered, equally appropriate for ecological damages to soils and climate; they are weapons "of mass murder in slow motion", long after their initial murderous (and planned) effect.

In addition, nuclear weapons are instruments of murder, injustice, and death long before they are deployed. Ecological harms, such as those that follow the use of industrial chemicals and pesticides, fit that model as well. It is insufficient to view them, as they have been viewed, as requiring the controls of "measures that make up the laws of international conflict".[127] In contrast, the awareness of their effects suggests that they too should be considered to be contrary to human rights laws.

The Ottawa Convention[128] was intended to be binding on states, but it seems that the main power of the Convention may lie in the "process of stigmatization and anathematization"[129] of the guilty state. Aside from the difficulty of isolating a truly "just war" today, that is, a war that was initiated for a just cause, and following the appropriate steps before initiating hostilities (*jus ad bellum*), neither the nuclear weapons nor landmines fit the permissible conduct within the conflict (*jus in bello*).

> For either set of weapons, states may attempt to exempt themselves from customary legal prohibitions by pointing to a sustained pattern of objections,

> [but] this will not protect them from violations of a "peremptory norm" of general international law (*jus cogens*).[130]

Jus cogens norms include prohibitions on the use of force, the right of self-determination, prohibitions against genocide,[131] and other grave breaches of human rights. It seems obvious that the prohibition of antipersonnel mines (APL) should be included among these worst crimes. Both humanitarian groups and NGOs have long been asking to have these cheap weapons ("as little as US$3 each") banned.

Objections, as expected, came from industry and defence departments, who wanted to keep these weapons in use without any consideration of the multiple harms to innocent civilians and to the land and the environments where they have been placed, nor even of the high cost of clearance (between US$100 and US$1000 each).

Therefore this Convention was yet another example of US exceptionalism, but the modifications of the document demanded by the US would have represented too extreme a modification of the document, as affirmed by the Oslo Conference.[132] Together with the US's secretive supportive position on Israel's stockpile of nuclear weapons, and its position on climate change until recent times, when denial would have become unconscionable, these political stances, unfortunately, confirm where lies the origin of the gravest threats to humanity and to the Earth.

However, some perceive the US abstention as a signatory to both the Ottawa Convention and the Rome Statute[133] as a sign of resistance to "international legal imperialism".[134] Yet the author, Kenneth Anderson, does not consider the most important point of all: the fact that what he terms "international legal imperialism", that is, the presence of truly international legal instruments, such as the Ottawa Convention and the Rome Statute, both of which were created primarily to erect a solid protection on the side of human rights, were also, at the same time, systems capable of resisting the partisan exceptionalism that drives the US imperialism.

That imperialism has no real interest in human rights or humanitarian principles, in fact, no interest in international law in general, despite its affirmations to the contrary. Anderson wrote in 2008, perhaps before the worst abuses that followed 9/11, the brutal so-called "war on terror" with its recently uncovered torture regimes, and the ongoing US support of Israel's illegal dispossession on Palestinians, occupation of their lands, and the multiple illegal attacks of that rogue state against Gaza. The intent of that illegitimate power is acknowledged by Anderson himself as he critiques the very hope of international legal resistance to US imperialism:

> expressed brutally, what profound change can these treaties purport to signal if the largest, most powerful state, the world's only superpower, the only military power capable of projecting force across the globe, stands aside from them?[135]

Given that this "superpower" can no longer claim any ties to morality, let alone UN principles of legality, it is clear that "international legalism" is the only possible response to a blatantly rogue state, with no apparent respect for the letter or the spirit of the law. The same disregard has manifested itself in regard to all sorts of environmental issues, from climate change, to the control of pesticides or GMOs, as we shall argue in the next chapter.

Essentially, US unilateralism acts in too many ways that are contrary to the most deeply held beliefs and principles; hence its actions are not simply "a matter of power, guns and butter",[136] but are based on clearly illegitimate, but nonetheless real, "moral and political claims to legitimacy, normalcy not merely within its borders, but upon the world's stage".[137] At any rate:

> There is, to be sure, US imperialism: it is a fact of international life. But international law is the non-imperial alternative to US imperialism and hegemony, and it ought to be celebrated as such.[138]

This reality, and this assessment of the US position, attitude and goals, indicates both the necessity, and at the same time the almost impossibility of affirming and establishing the primacy of ecological and biological (individual) integrity on the world stage. The presence of a superpower determined, against law, traditional state power, and the moral principles of civilized nations, to impose the primacy of its own economic interests over all else, demonstrates the reason why ecointegrity is deliberately marginalized together with most aspects of human rights.

The semi-legal presence of both landmines and nuclear power, together with multiple ongoing human rights breaches, both serve to confirm the gravity of the situation and the immense difficulty of the path the world must pursue.

The effects of unliveable environments: forced migrations, displaced persons and desperate asylum seekers

> The Chagossians – the rightful inhabitants of the islands – have sustained a very different sort of torture. They were not beaten or raped, they were not waterboarded or forcibly deprived of sleep, but they were threatened, they were ripped from their homelands (ancestors, communities, schools, homes), they were forced onto the hull of a ship, and they were dropped off on foreign islands and forgotten. And this didn't happen in long ago history, it happened only 40 years ago – a slow and pronounced torture that continues today.[139]

The outrageous case of the dispossession of the "ecological refugees" or the displaced inhabitants of Chagos have been thoroughly studied by many, especially Peter Sand,[140] who termed Diego Garcia a "legal black hole" from the standpoint of human rights, but also from the standpoint of environmental laws, such as the Convention on Biological Diversity. A brief review of that situation may be useful, as the case involves several notable elements:

- the deliberate elimination of a people's resources;
- the pollution of a pristine environment where wonderful, well-known coral colonies were thriving;
- the planned deprivation of a people's traditional means of survival; and
- the deprivation of that community's cultural integrity.

Forced relocation, deprivation of human rights and genocide

> The plaintiffs in this case are persons indigenous to Chagos their survivors or direct descendants ... they bring this action against the United States and various current and former officials of State and the department of Defence ("the individual defendants"), for forced relocation, torture, racial discrimination, cruel, inhuman and degrading treatment, genocide, intentional infliction of emotional distress, negligence and trespass.

Although the Chagos Archipelago of 52 islands was administered by the UK Government, but leased to the US, the US was now responsible under the British Indian Ocean Territory Agreement ("BIOT Agreement"). In the late 1960s and early 1970s, the whole Chagos population was moved to Mauritius and Seychelles, to allow a US military facility to settle in their space. The original inhabitants were not allowed to return,[141] and were offered no compensation to help ease their transition into a new environment and the loss of their homes.

Those who had not left had to suffer from being forced on "overcrowded ships for Peros Banhos and Salonen, from whence they eventually were taken to Mauritius and Seychelles".[142] The US Congress went ahead with the construction of a military base on Diego Garcia island, despite hearings where multiple human rights violations were detailed, from the lack of relocation assistance, to harsh removal conditions that caused injuries to the survivors, including miscarriages, and eventual living conditions that include still poverty, unemployment and other deprivations.[143]

Before the judgement proper could be decided, the "individual defendants" all claimed that they had been obeying superior order, based on "the statutory immunity granted to the Federal Officers under the Federal Employee Liability Reform and Tort Compensation Act".[144]

Yet the gravity of the effects of the forced removal brings to mind the language of the Nuremberg principles, hence the international law's denial of such claims of immunity. Even if the individual defendants are eliminated from the action (justly or unjustly), that leaves the United States as the sole defendant. However, all those who perpetrated knowingly the actions involving the Chagos indigenous population, violated the tenets of international law:

> Pursuant to the Alien Tort Claims Act, 28 USC & 1350 ("ATCA"), "the district courts shall have original jurisdiction of any civil action by an alien for a tort only committed in violation of the Law of Nations or Treaty of the United States".[145]

Other issues used to rebut the plaintiff's claims were the fact that they had "failed to exhaust their administrative remedies", despite the fact that they were not allowed to return to their home base, now a US military base (in Chagos), nor in the other islands, where the United Kingdom itself was not likely to offer an impartial forum after entering into an agreement with the US, that led to the very actions in question.

Another issue was "the judicial expertise" of the court, as it was required to pass judgement on US policy:

> Neither our federal law nor customary international law provide standards by which the court can measure and balance the foreign policy considerations at play in this case such as the containment of the Soviet Union in the Indian Ocean thirty years ago, and today the support of military operation in the Middle East. The court concludes that it is ill-equipped to review the conduct of the military operation challenged in this case, because they implicate foreign policy and national security concerns.[146]

Essentially, if the US Government political branches made a decision thirty years earlier, the court was not prepared to second guess that decision today.[147] Of course, even if the court was not prepared to question either the decision of the US Government at the time those decisions were made, or the reasons for those decisions, the *way* those decisions were carried out appears to remain untouched by this argument. Even if a country's political or other decision cannot be judged under ATCA, "Article 2(3) of the Torture Convention explicitly states that 'An order from a superior official or public authority may not be invoked as a justification for torture.'"[148] Torture is forbidden by *jus cogens* norms, and so is genocide, so that appealing to this Article appears to be appropriate, and we will address this question below.

This point is also made clearly in the *Filartiga v. Pena Irala* case.[149] In that case, the US Supreme Court recognized that the law of nations "may be ascertained by consulting the work of jurists writing professedly on public law; or by the general usage and practice of nations, or by the judicial decisions recognizing and enforcing the law".[150]

Nevertheless, one thing must be acknowledged:

> Unlike the criminal remedy, there is no treaty that clearly obliges or even authorizes courts to take jurisdiction over civil actions respecting torture committed abroad with the exception of the US, there is no domestic legislation in any other country that expressly grants a court jurisdiction with respect to these matters.[151]

Because ATCA permits individual citizens to sue for torture and other such injuries, without the far more complicated requirements of initiating a criminal action for an International Court of Justice or International Criminal Court, this avenue appears to remain the preferred one by claimants in various venues:

> While it is premised on the principle that victims of torture must be compensated, its true role in many cases is admittedly symbolic: the third country tort remedy provides recognition for, and emotional vindication of, the victims of torture and places moral and political pressure on rights abusing governments.[152]

The end of the story: R (on the application of Bancoult) v. Secretary of State for Foreign and Commonwealth Affairs

> On 3 November, 2000 the Divisional Court (Laws LJ and Gibbs J) gave judgment in favour of Mr. Bancoult.[153] They decided that a power to legislate for the "peace, order and good government" of the territory did not include a power to expel all the inhabitants.

Beyond the ATCA trials, Bancoult and other Chagossians also attempted to find justice from the other superpower involved in their case: the UK Government. Lord Hoffman describes the original lifestyle of the inhabitants of Chagos, working for the "Company" (Chagos Agalegal Company Ltd.), tending coconut trees and producing copra, working their gardens and keeping chickens and pigs to add to the provisions the Company provided for its workers. Yet, despite their lack of education and their simple lifestyles, they had "a rich community life, the Roman Catholic religion and their own dialect, derived from the French".[154]

For this case, their main points of contention were based on the history of their interaction with the UK Government:

- The British Indian Ocean Territories Order (BIOT)[155] had made the Chagos Archipelago a separate colony. The Order also appointed a Commissioner of BIOT, with the power to "make laws for the peace, order and good government of the territory"; hence the inhabitants retained British citizenship.[156]
- In 1966, Her Majesty's Government corresponded with the government of the US: the result was to grant a lease of at least 50 years to the latter, to establish a base on Diego Garcia, and to occupy other islands as required. In 1967 the UK Government bought out the Company which was only allowed to run the coconut plantations until July 1971 when the US required vacant possession. This prompted the commissioner to make the Immigration Ordinance 1971 (section 4(1)) providing that only a special permit would allow the former inhabitants to re-enter the territory.
- From 1968 to 1971 the UK Government removed the whole population, primarily to Mauritius and the Seychelles, without the use of force, but stating that the company was ceasing its operations, and no more supplies would be available to them.[157]
- The whole operation established a "callous disregard for their interests", and the members of the community were left to fend for themselves in the slums of "Port Louis". The ordinance denying them the right to return had been prompted by US concerns about "non-aligned countries" objecting to the

construction of a military base in the Indian Ocean.[158] In more recent times other objections could be raised about the alleged renditions flying into that base, or taking place, with concomitant torture episodes, in ships anchored just beyond Chagos. The miserable conditions of the Chagossians in Mauritius, and their poverty and unemployment, prompted negotiations between Mauritius and the UK, eventually culminating until 1977 ("depleted by inflation") to 595 Chagossian families. The Chagossians sought legal advice, and with the support of Michael Vencatessen, issued a writ in the High Court in London, on behalf of all Chagossians, and eventually a trust fund of £4 million was set up in Mauritius in exchange for abandoning all claims, and this was signed by most Chagossians.

- After the judgement (Divisional Court, Laws LJ and Gibbs J) in favour of Mr. Bancoult on 3 November 2000 effectively quashed Section 4(1) of the Immigration Ordinance as *ultra vires*, Mr. Robin Cook (Foreign Secretary) announced a feasibility study to attempt to resettle the Chagossians in their former territory. He concluded his press release saying:

> This government has not defended what was done or said thirty years ago. As Lord Justice Laws recognized, we made no attempt to conceal the gravity of what happened. I am pleased that he has commended the wholly admirable conduct in disclosing material to the court, and praised the openness of today's foreign office (para. 17).

The points that remained in contention were the Chagossians' right to return and the very legality of the official Constitution Order and the Immigration Order, as well as their "irrationality", as "The Orders were not made in the interest of the Chagossians, but in the interest of the United Kingdom and the United States" (para. 28).

Further, the authority to remove persons of British citizenship from their chosen residence – without any compensation at any time – was also questioned. Lord Hoffman and the other Lords recognized the impact of the law made for a colony, citing Blackstone: "But no power on earth except the authority of Parliament can send any subject of England out of the land against his will; no, not even a criminal."[159]

The Crown, therefore, and its appointed Commissioner, has no authority to transport anyone, against their will (para. 44), by what constituted, essentially, threats of starvation to them and their families. But even the acknowledged wrong that had been done at the time, did not result in a favourable judgement at this time: the main problem was the costs and logistics of total resettlement, although the Chagossains were now permitted to return for a time, to visit family graves and the like.

Were the Chagossians ecological refugees? Perhaps not, or only in the sense that their migration was indeed forced (like many others) by lack of resources and economic pressures from outside, although the main causative factors at the time were clearly political. Their case is worth studying in detail, because of the different treatment they received at the hands of US first, then UK courts. The former appealed to procedural flaws in the case. The UK court instead tackled the factual elements of the case head-on, and admitted its own fault in regard to the series of events outlined above.

In addition, it is important to note the forces of neocolonialism seeking power (rather than natural resources at this time): those who initiated and authorized the Chagossians' displacement manifested the callous disregard for the rights of local and Indigenous communities that is, generally speaking, typical of forced migrations.

Displaced persons and asylum seekers after conflicts: some concluding thoughts

> Responsibility as a *cause*. ... "Responsible for" can, in any number of contexts, be replaced by "caused" or "to have a consequence", or some such expression that indicates a causal connection.[160]

The legal international instruments existing for the protection of refugees and asylum seekers are sadly dated and seemingly unable to cope with the ongoing overwhelming situation, where illegal conflicts and unliveable conditions are present in large portions of the world today.[161] The clearest case combining plunder of resources, grave environmental damage, physical harms and human rights breaches, all in order to support political control on the part of an imperialist state driven by a personal agenda, was that of Chagos, discussed above.

In addition, it should be noted that the only refugees that have some claim to protection in law, are the ones who can be said to be fleeing persecution, whether in conflict or in peace. However, elsewhere I have argued that, in contrast with the stated position of the Convention on the Status of Refugees (CSR), deprivation leading to abject poverty represents the real common denominator of all refugees and asylum seekers.[162]

The final result of those deprivations are obvious as we see wave after wave of desperate asylum seekers, jammed into boats that are barely seaworthy, arriving at ports and borders in Italy and elsewhere in Europe. In North America, the asylum seekers are often children, attempting to come to the United States from South and Central America, only to find cruelty and disinterest after a gruelling trip north, fuelled by hopes never to be fulfilled in the country they hope to reach.[163]

What all migrants share, besides their poverty and the deprivations they are suffering, is the fact that they are victims of the same globalization, driven by the same imperialism that is relentlessly destroying integrity. Despite the many protocols, declarations and conferences designed to address the problem of ongoing mass migrations, the question of the origins of those migrations, the causality from which those movements originate, is never discussed. Thus the responsibility shared by most Western countries for that end result, that is, for mass migrations, remains elusive.

Some mass migrations are indeed the product of conflicts, but the great majority follow today's economic distress of the 99 per cent in contrast with the thriving 1 per cent.[164] Hence we will discuss the situation of those millions fleeing from unbearable circumstances in the next chapter. The reasons for their plight are many and can be listed; however, those who are responsible, both states and other legal actors, have not been held accountable so far.

Notes

1 Richard Westra, 2015, *Exit from Globalization*, Routledge, London, p. 142.
2 Mathias Wackernagel and William Rees, 1996, *Our Ecological Footprint*, New Society Publishers, Gabriola Island, BC.
3 Westra, *Exit from Globalization.*
4 Ibid., p. 142.
5 Laura Westra, 2012, "Life, Health and the Environment: The Denied Connection", in Laura Westra, Colin Soskolne and Donald Spady (eds), *Human Health and Ecological Integrity*, Earthscan, London, pp 7–19.
6 Naomi Klein, 2014, *This Changes Everything*, Allen Lane, London, pp. 75–76.
7 Tara Weinstein, 2004, "Prosecuting Attacks that Destroy the Environment: Environmental Crimes or Humanitarian Atrocities?" *Georgetown International Environmental Law Review* 17, pp. 697–722, here p. 698.
8 UN Conference on the Human Environment, 16 June 1972, Principle I, UN Doc. A/CONF.48/14, revised by UN Doc. A/CONF.48/14/Corr, reprinted in ILM 1416, 1417 (1972).
9 Rio Declaration on Environment and Development, princ. 23–24, UN Doc. A/Conf.151/26/Rev.l (1991).
10 ENMOD, Convention on the Prohibition of Military or Any Other Hostile Use of Environmental Modification Techniques, 18 May 1977, 31 UST 333, TIA s. no. 9614.
11 Protocol Addition to the Geneva Conventions Relating to the Protection of Victims of Armed Conflicts, 8 June 1977, 16 ILM 1391, UN Doc. A/32/144 (1977).
12 Protocol I, art. 35(3).
13 Protocol I, art. 55.
14 Paolo Benvenuti, 2008, "International Humanitarian Law and the Means for Improving Its Effectiveness: A Comprehensive Appraisal", in I. Papanicolopulu and T. Scovazzi (eds), *Quale Diritto nei Conflitti Armati*, Giuffre' Editore, Milan, pp. 3–44, here p. 3.
15 Laura Westra, 2007, *Environmental Justice and the Rights of Indigenous Peoples*, Earthscan, London, ch. 2.
16 Laura Westra, 2013, *The Supranational Corporation*, Brill, Leyden, The Netherlands.
17 Laura Westra, 2012, *Faces of State Terrorism*, Brill, Leyden, The Netherlands.
18 Westra, "Life, Health and the Environment: The Denied Connection".
19 Westra, *Faces of State Terrorism*, ch. 4.
20 Benvenuti, "International Humanitarian Law and the Means for Improving Its Effectiveness", p. 5.
21 Ibid., p. 8.
22 Weinstein, "Prosecuting Attacks that Destroy the Environment", p. 5.
23 Ibid.
24 The Charter of the International Military Tribunal at Nuremberg, 8 August 1945.
25 Adopted and opened for signatures and ratification by General Assembly Resolution 2106 (XX) of 21 December 1965, into force 4 January 1969.
26 The United Nations Charter, 24 October 1945, 1. UNT.S. XVI.
27 Christine Gray, 2008, *International Law and the Use of Force*, 3rd edn, Oxford University Press, Oxford, p. 7.

28 Gray, *International Law and the Use of Force*, p. 60.
29 Ibid., p. 61.
30 UNGA Res. 2708(1970); 2652(1970); 3295(1974).
31 UNGA Res. 36/103 (1981).
32 Gray, *International Law and the Use of Force*, p. 62.
33 Ibid., p. 63.
34 Ibid., p. 64.
35 United Nations, 2004, *United Nations Yearbook*, United Nations, New York, p. 710; see also UNGA Res. 59/502 on the "Right of the Palestinian People to Self-Determination" (179-5-3).
36 Amnesty International, 2014, *Annual Report 2014/15*, available at www.amnesty.org/en/annual-report-201415, p. 5.
37 Antonio Cassese, 1995, *Self-Determination of Peoples*, Cambridge University Press, Cambridge, p. 55.
38 Ibid., p. 56.
39 Richard Falk, 2015, "'Lawfare' and Liberations", 23 February, available at https://richardfalk.wordpress.com/2015/02/23/1821.
40 Ibid.
41 See for instance Ap and Lazar Berman, 2014, "Geneva Conventions invoke Rights of Palestinians: 126 Countries Urge Israel to Halt Construction in West Bank and East Jerusalem; US, Canada, and Australia Stay Away", *The Times of Israel*, 17 December, available at www.timesofisrael.com/geneva-conventions-invoke-rights-of-palestinians.
42 Ibid.
43 Falk, "'Lawfare' and Liberations".
44 Antonio Cassese, 2001, "Terrorism is Also Disrupting Some Crucial Legal Categories of International Law", *European Journal of International Law* 12 (November), pp. 993–1003.
45 Antonio Cassese, 2005, *International Law*, 2nd edn, Oxford University Press, Oxford, p. 449.
46 Westra, *Faces of State Terrorism*, esp. ch. 1.
47 USA Patriot Act of 2001, Pub. No. 107-56, 115 Stat. 272.
48 See "Open Letter to Parliament: Amend C-51. or Kill It", 28 February, available at http://news.nationalpost.com/2015/02/27/open-letter-to-parliament-amend-c-51-or-kill-it, addressed to Steven Harper, Prime Minister, by over 100 of the most prominent legal scholars teaching at major universities across the country, in opposition to this Bill, called the Anti-Terrorism Act 2015.
49 Rama Mani, 2004, "The Root Cause or Terrorism and Conflict Prevention", in Jane Boulden and Thoman C. Wiess (eds), *Terrorism and the UN*, Indiana University Press, Bloomington, IN, pp. 219–242, here p. 220.
50 Ibid., p. 221.
51 Ibid., p. 222.
52 Ibid., p. 223.
53 Ibid., p. 225.
54 Thomas Homer-Dixon, 2001, "Why Root Causes are Important", *Toronto Globe and Mail*, 23 September 2001.
55 Ted Honderich, 2003, *Terrorism for Humanity: Inquiries in Political Philosophy*, Pluto Press, London.
56 Noam Chomsky, 2001, *9-11*, Seven Stories Press, New York.
57 Giovanna Borradroi, 2003, *Philosophy in a Time of Terror: Dialogues with Jugen Habermas and Jacques Derrida*, University of Chicago Press, Chicago, IL; see also discussion in Tamar Meisels, 2008, *The Trouble with Terror*, Cambridge University Press, Cambridge, p. 36.
58 Meisels, *The Trouble with Terror*, p. 38.

59 Douglas Sturm, 2004, "Taking Human Rights Seriously: Relationally and Subjectively", *Process Studies* 33, pp. 235–240.
60 Report of the Sub-Committee on Prevention of Discrimination and Protection of Minorities, UN Doc. E/CN.4/1995/2; E/CN/Sub.2/1994/56, 28 October 1994.
61 ICCPR, UNGA Res. 220 A(XXI), UNGAOR, Supp. no. 16 at 52, UN Doc. A/631 (#966 NTS 171, 23 March 1976).
62 Howard J. Vogel, 2006, "Reframing Rights from the Ground Up: the Contribution of the New UN Law of Self-Determination to Recovering the Principle of Sociability on the Way to a Rational Theory of International Human Rights", *Temple International Comparative Law Journal* 20(2), pp. 443–497, here pp. 456–457.
63 Ted Honderich, 2006, *Humanity, Terrorism, Terrorist War: Palestine, 9/11, Iraq, 7/7*, Continuum, London.
64 ICERD, Committee on the Elimination of Racial Discrimination, Report of the Committee on the Elimination of Racial Discrimination, UN GAOR 1992, 47th sess., Supp. no. 18, UN Doc. A/47/18; Commission on Human Rights, Sub-commission on Prevention of Discrimination and Protection of Minorities, Res. 1994/45, Annex, Draft United Nations Declaration on the Rights of Indigenous Peoples, UN ESCOR, 1994, UN Doc. E/CN.4/1995/2, E/CN.4/Sub.2/1994/56 (1994).
65 Aviva Chomsky, 2014, *Undocumented: How Immigration Became Illegal*, Beacon Press, Boston, MA, p. 2.
66 Ibid.
67 Satvinder Juss, 2008, *International Migration and Global Justice*, Ashgate, Aldershot, p. 171.
68 African Charter on Human and Peoples Rights, Preamble.
69 Laura Westra, Satvinder Juss and Tullio Scovazzi (eds), 2015, *Towards a Refugee Oriented Right of Asylum*, Ashgate, Farnham, see ch. 1, 5.
70 Joseph Stiglitz, 2012, *The Price of Inequality*, Norton, New York, p. 188.
71 Ibid., p. 189.
72 Peter H. Eichstaedt, 1994, *If You Poison Us: Uranium and Native Americans*, Red Crane Books, Santa Fe, NM.
73 Liz Minchin and Lindsay Murdoch, 2006, "Aboriginal Cancer Doubles Near Uranium Mine", 23 November, available at www.theage.com.au/news/national/aboriginal-cancer-doubles-near-uranium-mine/2006/11/22/1163871821 63.html.
74 Ibid.
75 Michel Chossudovsky, 2012, "The Fuel Pools of Fukushima: The Greatest Short-Term Threat to Humanity", 9 April, available at www.globalresearch.ca/index.php?context=va&aid=3207.
76 Robert Fisk, 2012, "The Children of Fallujah: Sayef's Story", 25 April, available at www.counterpunch.org/2012/04/24/the-children-of-fallujah.
77 Richard Falk, 1998, *Law in an Emerging Global Village*, Transnational Publishers, Ardsley, NJ, p. 147.
78 Kristin Shrader-Frechette, 1982, *Nuclear Power and Public Policy*, Kluwer Academic, Dordrecht, The Netherlands.
79 Elaine Draper, 1991, *Risky Business*, Cambridge University Press, Cambridge.
80 Ibid.
81 Edward O. Wilson, 1992, *The Diversity of Life*, Harvard University Press, Cambridge, MA.
82 Theo Colborn, Dianne Dumanoski and John Peterson Myers, 1996, *Our Stolen Future*, Dutton, New York.
83 Kristin Shrader-Frechette, 1993, *Burying Uncertainty*, University of California Press, Berkeley, CA; Robert E. Goodwin, 1980, 'No Moral Nukes", *Ethics* 90(3) (April), pp. 417–449.
84 Richard Wasserstrom, 1985, "War, Nuclear War and Nuclear Deterrence: Some Conceptual and Moral Issues", in R. Hardin, J. Mearsheimer, G. Dworkin and R.

Goodin (eds), *Nuclear Deterrence, Ethics and Strategy*, University of Chicago Press, Chicago, IL, p. 15; Jeff McMahan, 1985, "Deterrence and Deontology", in Hardin et al., *Nuclear Deterrence, Ethics and Strategy*, p. 141; Richard H. Ullman, 1985, "Denuclearizing International Politics", in Hardin et al., *Nuclear Deterrence, Ethics and Strategy*, p. 191; Sissela Bok, 1985, "Distrust, Secrecy, and the Arms Race", *Ethics* 95(3), pp. 712–727.

85 G. Handl, 1997, "Compliance Control Mechanisms and International Environmental Obligations," *Tulane Journal of International and Comparative Law* 5, p. 29.

86 Maurizio Ragazzi, 1998, *The Concept of Obligations Erga Omnes*, Clarendon Press, Oxford, p. 173.

87 *Nuclear Test Cases*; *Australia v. France*; *New Zealand v. France* [1974] ICJ Rep. 253, at 267-70;51

88 ICJ Rep. 1974, 312 and 494; Ragazzi, *The Concept of Obligations Erga Omnes*, p. 175.

89 Ragazzi, *The Concept of Obligations Erga Omnes*, p. 175.

90 "Moscow Treaty", 1963, available at www.un.org/disarmament/WMD/Nuclear/pdf/Partial_Ban_Treaty.pdf.

91 Ragazzi, *The Concept of Obligations Erga Omnes*, p. 177.

92 Ibid., p. 179.

93 Gen. List No. 95, Advisory Opinion of 8 July 1996.

94 Falk, *Law in an Emerging Global Village*, p. 172.

95 Ibid.

96 Ibid., p. 173.

97 Ibid., p. 174.

98 Ibid., p. 175.

99 Burns H. Weston, 1982–1983, "Nuclear Weapons and International Law: Prolegomena to General Illegality", *New York School Journal of International and Comparative Law* 4, p. 252; see also discussion in Geoffrey Darnton, 2015, *Nuclear Weapons and International Law*, Peace Analytics, Bournemouth, pp. 190–191.

100 Darnton, *Nuclear Weapons and International Law*, p. 180.

101 Burns H. Weston, 1983, "Nuclear Weapons Versus International Law: A Contextual Reassessment", *McGill Law Journal* 27, p. 56; see also Darnton, *Nuclear Weapons and International Law*, pp. 229–230.

102 Johnny Magdaleno, 2015, "Algerians Suffering from French Atomic Legacy, 55 Years after Nuke Tests", 1 March, available at http://america.aljazeera.com/articles/2015/3/1/algerians-suffering-from-french-atomic-legacy-55-years-after-nuclear-tests.html.

103 Ibid.

104 Ibid.

105 Ibid.

106 Ibid.

107 Ibid.

108 Advisory Opinion on the Legality of the Threat or Use of Nuclear Weapons, 1996, ICJ Rep. 226, at 241.

109 Karima Bennoune, 2008, "The Intersection of Nuclear Weapons and International Human Rights Law: Implications of the Good Faith Obligation to Negotiate Nuclear Disarmament", paper presented at the Conference on Good Faith, International Law and the Elimination of Nuclear Weapons, 1 May 2008.

110 See Manfred Nowak, UN Covenant on Civil and Political Rights, CCPR Commentary XXIV (1993); UN Human Rights Committee, General Comment No .14 (Article 6), Nuclear Weapons and the Right to Life, 23rd Sess., 1984.

111 Bennoune, "The Intersection of Nuclear Weapons and International Human Rights Law", p. 3.

112 Michael J. Glennon, 2013, *European Journal of International Law* 24(1), pp. 109–127.
113 Written Statement of the Government of the United States of America before the International Court of Justice, Requested by the United Nations General Assembly to an advisory Opinion on the Legality of the Threat of Use of Nuclear Weapons, 42–46, 20 June 1995.
114 Christopher J. Weeramantry, Dissenting Opinion on The Legality of the Threat or Use of Nuclear Weapons, Advisory Opinion, at 506–508.
115 Ibid.
116 *Gabčíkovo-Nagymaros Project (Hungary/Slovakia)* (1997) ICJ Rep., Judge C. Weeramantry Separate Opinion, at www.icj-cij.org/docket/index.php?p1=3&p2=3&case=92.
117 Bennoune, "The Intersection of Nuclear Weapons and International Human Rights Law", p. 5.
118 Samira Alaani, Mozhgan Savabiesfahani, Mohammad Tafash and Paola Manduca, 2011, "Four Polygamous Families with Congenital Birth Defects from Fallujah, Iraq", *International Journal of Research and Public Health* 8(1), pp. 89–96.
119 UN Sub-Commission on Prevention and Protection of Minorities, International Peace and Security as an essential condition for the empowerment of human rights, above all the right to life, Res. 1997/36, Preamble (28 August 1997).
120 Hans M. Kristensen and Robert S. Norris, "Worldwide Deployments of Nuclear Weapons, 2014", *Bulletin of the Atomic Scientists* 70(5), available at http://thebulletin.org/2014/september/worldwide-deployments-nuclear-weapons-20147595.
121 Laura Westra, 2014, *Revolt Against Authority*, Brill, Leyden, The Netherlands, especially ch. 2 and 7.
122 Steven R. Ratner, Jason S. Abrams and James L. Bischoff, 2009, 3rd edn, *Accountability for Human Rights Atrocities*, Oxford University Press, Oxford.
123 Donald Brown, 2012, *Navigating the Perfect Moral Storm Climate Ethics*, Routledge, London.
124 Åke Bergman, Jerrold J. Heindel, Susan Jobling, Karen Kidd and Thomas R. Zoeller (eds), 2013, *State of the Science of Endocrine Disrupting Chemicals 2012*, summary report published as technical document WHO/HSE/PHE/IHE/2013.1, World Health Organization, Geneva, available at www.who.int/iris/handle/10665/78101#sthash.q2ZGAegJ.dpuf; Theo Colborn, D. Dumanoski and J. Peterson, 1996, *Our Stolen Future*, Dutton, New York; Philippe Grandjean, 2013, *Only One Chance: How Environmental Pollution Impairs Brain Development – and How to Protect the Brains of the Next Generation*, Oxford University Press, Oxford; Philip Landrigan and Ruth Etzel, 2013, *Children's Environmental Health*, Oxford University Press, Oxford; Laura Westra, 2014, *Child Law: Children's Rights and Collective Obligations*, Springer, Berlin.
125 Simon L. Lewis and Mark A. Maslin, 2015, "Defining the Anthropocene", *Nature* 519, pp. 171–180.
126 Ramesh Thakur and William Whaley, 1999, "The Ottawa Convention on Landmines: A Landmark Humanitarian Treaty in Arms Control?", *Global Governance* 5, pp. 273–302, here p. 278.
127 Ibid., p. 273.
128 Convention on the Prohibition of the Use, Stockpiling, Production and Transfer of Antipersonnel Mines and on Their Destruction (The Ottawa Convention), 36 ILM (1997) 1507, entered into force 1 March 1999.
129 Thakur and Whaley, "The Ottawa Convention on Landmines", p. 274.
130 Ibid., 277.
131 Ibid.
132 Ibid., p. 280. See also Ramesh Thakur, 1998, "Antipersonnel Landmines", *Pacifica Review* 10, pp. 65–67.

133 Rome Statute of the International Criminal court, 37 ILM (1997) 1507, entered into force 1 March 1999.
134 Kenneth Anderson, 2000, "The Ottawa Convention on Banning Landmines, the Role of International Non-Governmental Organizations and the Idea of International Civil Society", *European Journal of International Law* 11, pp. 91–120, here p. 95.
135 Anderson, "The Ottawa Convention on Banning Landmines …", p. 94.
136 Ibid., p. 96.
137 Ibid., p. 97.
138 Ibid., p. 101.
139 Alyssa Rohricht, 2015, "What the Torture Report Missed", 20 March, available at www.counterpunch.org/2015/03/20/what-the-torture-report-missed.
140 Peter H. Sand, 2009, "Diego Garcia: British American Legal Black Hole in the Indian Ocean", *Journal of Environmental Law* 21(1), pp. 113–137; Peter H. Sand, 2009, *United States and Britain in Diego Garcia*, Palgrave Macmillan, New York.
141 Sand, *United States and Britain in Diego Garcia*, p. 22.
142 Ibid., pp. 22–23.
143 Ibid., pp. 31–33.
144 Federal Employees Liability Reform and Tort Compensation Act of 1988, Fub. L. No. 100–694, 102 Stat. 4563 (1988) (codified at 28 USC 2671–2680).
145 Ibid., para. 24.
146 Ibid., para. 42.
147 Ibid., para. 47.
148 Henry Steiner and Philip Alston, 2000, *International Human Rights in Context*, 2nd edn, Oxford University Press, Oxford, p. 1072.
149 *Filartiga v. Pena-Irala*, US Court of Appeals, 2nd ct, 1980 630 F 2d 876.
150 *United States v. Smith*, 18 US, 153, 160–161, 5 L. Ed. 57 (1920).
151 John Terry, 2001, "Taking Filartiga on the Road: Why Courts Outside the United States Should Accept Jurisdictions over Actions Involving Torture Committed Abroad", in Craig Scott (ed.), *Torture as Tort: Comparative Perspectives on the Development of Transnational Human Rights Litigation*, Hart Publishing, Oxford, pp. 109–129, here p. 110.
152 Ibid., 133.
153 *R (Bancoult) v. Secretary of State for Foreign and Commonwealth Affairs* [2007] QB 1067 (Bancoult 1).
154 Ibid., para. 5
155 British Indian Ocean Territories Order 1865, SI No. 1920.
156 Ibid., para. 6
157 *Chagos Islanders v. Attorney General* (2003) EWCH 2222 (QB), (2003) All ER (D) 166.
158 Ibid., para. 10.
159 W. Blackstone, 1809, *Commentaries on the Laws of England*, 15th edn, vol. 1, Clarendon Press, Oxford, p. 137.
160 Mark Bovens, *The Quest for Responsibility*, 2009, Cambridge University Press, Cambridge, p. 24.
161 CSR 1951; 1967 Protocol.
162 Westra et al., *Towards a Refugee Oriented Right of Asylum*, esp. ch. 3.
163 Westra, *Child Law*.
164 Stiglitz, *The Price of Inequality*.

4 Air, food and water

Ecointegrity for the survival of present and future generations

Introduction

> Resource extraction through mining and fossil fuel development fragments some of the more remote regions, such as Canada's boreal forest. Haddad was surprised by the degree that boreal forest in Canada and Siberia has already been sliced up. Once a forest is segmented, it loses something greater than just the missing square footage.[1]

These results, and even these conditions, are far from surprising: what is surprising is that what is lost is still not called by its name: ecological integrity, with the expected consequences of that loss. The article on which the opening paragraph is based was printed by the American Association for the Advancement of Science, as "Applied Ecology",[2] a thoroughly researched work, incorporating research on areas from Canada and the US, as well as France, England, Brazil, Australia and Borneo.

The article reports on the effects of forest fragmentation on ecosystems: the fragmentation includes demonstrating that "nearly 20% of the world's remaining forest is within 100m. of an edge, in close proximity to agricultural, urban or other modified environments".[3] This almost global, long-term research shows beyond a doubt, how severely (1) "habitat fragmentation affects biodiversity and ecosystem processes";[4] (2) "the ecological consequences of fragmentation";[5] and (3) that "all aspects of fragmentation – reduced fragment area, increased isolation and increased edge – had degrading effects on a disparate set of core ecosystem functions".[6]

The research in this work also shows unquestionably that the harmful changes from fragmentation itself, and the ensuing consequences, are anthropogenic. However, it stops short of showing the effects of the disintegrity of these altered fragmented ecosystems, on the very human communities who brought about the changes. As I have argued in Chapters 1 and 2, loss of biodiversity, productivity and pollination, among other consequences of fragmentation, affect ecosystem services not only to plant and animal species, but to the human species as well: they have been described as "the loss of nature's services".[7]

There is no blame attached to the authors for the scope of an article published as "Applied Ecology", but, as noted above, it is a symptom of the consistent disassociation between ecological conditions and the human rights to a liveable environment that emerge in all areas of study, for a variety of reasons, and is an especially grave symptom of the denial of a connection between ecology and health, present for instance in the growing literature of the principle of "one health".[8]

It is also the gravest symptom of the conflicted situation within which biological (individual) integrity and ecological (general) integrity must assert itself as the basis of life. I have argued for a "denied connection" between integrity and human health.[9] As the global ecological conditions worsen almost daily, and the power and control of those who cause such conditions are also on the ascendant, we can say without exaggeration that the defence of our life, of the right to survival of humanity, dependent as it is on the survival of our habitat, has become desperately important and necessary.

This connection is denied, it is not acknowledged in either domestic or international jurisprudence. In contrast, that interface is recognize by the WHO, in its 2015 report on *Connecting Global Priorities: Biodiversity and Human Health, a State of Knowledge Review*.[10] Biological diversity, ecosystem processes and human health are explicitly linked throughout the document:

> Biological diversity (biodiversity) is "The variability among living organisms from all sources including, inter alia, terrestrial, marine and other aquatic ecosystems, and the ecological complexes of which they are a part; this includes diversity within species, between species and ecosystems." This definition of the Convention on Biological Diversity (Article 2) reflects different levels of biodiversity (including genetic diversity; species and ecosystems) and the complexity of biotic and abiotic interactions. *The attributes and interactions of biotic and abiotic components determine ecosystem processes and their properties*.[11]

Neither the WHO nor the CBD appear to notice that, in the underlined portion of this definition at least, they are no longer simply speaking of "biodiversity" which would clearly contradict the presence of abiotic components, beyond that of biotic ones: that combination, when it refers to well-functioning ecosystems, denotes the ecointegrity of the system, not simply its biodiversity.

The document refers to "integrative approaches" such as the Ecosystem Approach, Ecohealth, and "One Health";[12] and in point 6 it also addresses the connection between the "direct drivers of biodiversity loss" and human health, and these include "landuse change, habitat loss, overexploitation, pollution, invasive species, and climate change". What is undeniably affected is the ecosystems' provision of "essential life-sustaining services", as they "contribute to increased problems for health and well-being".[13]

The disappearance of forests through fragmentation is not mentioned, although "land-use changes", no doubt, contribute to that phenomenon. Thus disintegrity in various forms, from the devastation arising from conflicts, to that arising from industrial expansion and so called "development", continues to ravage the Earth, not as a separate entity, but as the very basis for our survival. We addressed the former in the last chapter, the latter in Chapter 2. For the former Richard Falk puts it well, as he addresses the costs of war:

> This calculus of combat death does not begin to tell the story of the devastation of a foreign society, or the residual dangers that can materialize in death and maiming injuries long after the guns are silent, from lethal unexploded ordinance that litters the countryside for generations, soil contamination by Agent Orange, and warheads containing depleted uranium as well as the legacy of trauma and many daily reminders of war memories in the shape of devastated landscapes and destroyed landmarks of cultural heritage.[14]

This passage shows clearly the link between disintegrity, conflict, US politics and human health in connection with the ecosystem services necessary for survival. When we consider the most basic necessities, air, water and food, we discover that, for the most part, all these are under the control of the law, either domestic or international, but all three are, for the most part, also under the *de facto* control of the power of multinational corporations (MNCs). Thus, in this chapter, we will discuss the specifics of this situation starting from the reverse order of what is needed for immediate survival (air), short-term survival (water), and finally for long-term survival (food).[15]

The right to food and ecological integrity

> In January, U.S. Right to Know released a report titled Seedy Business, on the chemical and food industry's $100 million campaign to keep consumers in the dark about genetically engineered food: how they manipulated the media, public opinion, science and politics.[16]

This passage names only part of Monsanto's interference with human rights to information, as well as to life and health. Another aspect of Monsanto's ongoing attacks on humanity is that scientists employed by the US Department of Agriculture have found their research curtailed and faced censorship investigations and other consequences "arising from research that called into question the safety of certain agricultural chemicals... Research into glyphosate, the key ingredient in Monsanto's Roundup herbicide, and neocotinoid insecticides, which have been linked to honey bee and monarch butterfly endangerment, face particular scrutiny".[17]

Leaving aside for the moment the moral and legal implications of interfering with the work of a government's bureaucracy, whose mandate is to protect the public interest (NOT the economic interests of a corporation), and keeping in mind the focus on the right to life/health, Monsanto is unquestionably the best example of the multifaceted criminality of those who have *de facto* control of food production and distribution, globally. Monsanto is not the biggest, or even the richest MNC in existence; Walmart comes to mind in that regard.[18]

However, Monsanto is the only corporation (to my knowledge) that has actually been identified with a state, in this case, the US, explicitly, and in connection with legal proceedings. Although we are exploring the problems related to integrity and food production, any discussion of Monsanto cannot ignore the precedents of that company, as it collaborated with Dow Chemical to produce Agent Orange used by the US in the Vietnam War. The position of the US Courts in regard to Monsanto and Agent Orange/Dioxin when the International Court of Justice took the US to court for the use of that substance not only as a weapon, but also as a tool of environmental destruction is as follows. After Nuremberg the immunity of states and other actors cannot be claimed for any reason, in the case of war crimes or genocide. The US Courts' positions were clear in this case:

- that Agent Orange/Dioxin was not declared to be a poison at the time it was used;
- that the US government cannot be sued because it has sovereign immunity; and
- that as a "contractor" of the US government, Monsanto shares that immunity.

The first point to note is that after the Second World War, individual responsibility for crimes committed by individuals in such situations was established in the Nuremberg Charter of 1945.[19] Article 6 of that Charter focuses on the individual responsibility of persons:

> The Tribunal established by the Agreement referred to in Article 1 hereof for the trial and punishment of the major war criminals of the European Axis countries shall have the power to try and punish persons who acting in the interests of the European Axis countries, *whether as individuals or as members of organizations*, committed any of the following crimes.[20]

The crimes included "crimes against humanity", including the "participation in a common plan or conspiracy" in war crimes, such as "violations of the laws and customs of war"; also "crimes against peace", and "harming civilian populations", "plunder of public or private property" and the "wanton destruction of cities and towns". Hence the question is, why Monsanto and Dow, whether as individual persons or as organizations, could possibly be "immune from prosecutions as contractors, when even army officers, expected always to obey superior orders, were no longer exempted from responsibility after the Second World War.

Therefore, the question of immunity does not appear to have been judged correctly either in 1984 or later in the appeal or even by the US Supreme Court. Before the Nuremberg Charter of 1945, the London Agreement of 1945 was enacted by the United Kingdom, the United States, France and the USSR.[21] Thus the US was an active participant in the conclusion of an agreement that was basic to the denial of immunity for those complicit in the perpetration of various crimes in war and peace. Many of those crimes were in fact committed during the Vietnam War, with the aid and cooperation of the chemical companies that participated in the manufacturing and providing of the instruments required for those crimes.

In addition, in general criminal cases, US Courts held that "the only intent required to hold a corporation liable is the intent to do the prohibited act".[22] The other problem that remains is that – at most – the guilty corporation could receive only the punishment that was appropriate, that is, a fine, whereas after Nuremberg the individuals responsible could receive a more appropriate punishment for their crimes.

When we combine this "immunity", which recalls US exceptionalism instead of international law, with the 2012 Monsanto Protection act, which created a grave precedent, despite expiring in 2013, it seems that Monsanto is indeed representative of the ultimate corporate power we are seeking to indict, well beyond any regulatory regimes. Yet Monsanto, like other agricultural/pesticide giants, continues to pursue its interests and expand, with no regard for the safety of biological integrity of organisms, or the ecological integrity of natural systems. These are the actions of a criminal organization, and should be treated as such.

The corporation as a criminal

> In its first official confirmation, the National Biodiversity Authority (NBA), India's independent regulator on all matters pertaining to biodiversity protection, conservation and use, has stated that "it is proceeding with lodging a complaint against the alleged violators" of the Biological Diversity Act on grounds of biopiracy in promoting Bt. Brinjal, India's first transgenic GMO food. This information was provided to the Environment Support Group (ESG) in response to a Right to Information query.[23]

This is by no means the only case where the external stakeholders of a corporation are deprived of their basic rights to life and health: starting with the victory of Paul Francois, President of the Phyto-victims network against Monsanto. As well, a recent multi-disciplinary conference emphasized the fact that, in France, "the Senate had recently announced that it would set up a commission on pesticides and health".[24]

The list of the variety of irreversible harms perpetrated by Monsanto, the largest pesticide public health menace, acknowledged that Parkinson's Disease was now to be added to the artificially short list of pesticide-generated disease, including not only the expected cancers, but premature puberty in young girls and the "growing number of micro penis in baby boys".[25]

This important point confirms the ground-breaking research of Theo Colborn,[26] and of Grandjean and Landrigan.[27] It is worthy of note that Colborn published scientific research on endocrine disruptors in a more popular form in the 1996 book cited above, but only after working for many years on the effects of endocrine disruptors on various animals, from gulls to whales, especially in the Great Lakes area and the St. Lawrence Seaway. In 1994, my work on the Principle of Integrity,[28] cited Colborn as part of the argument designed to promote the protection of ecological integrity, and cited the role of endocrine disruptors on Great Lakes Wildlife.

Thus there is surely enough scientific evidence and knowledge, at least from epidemiology, toxicology and medicine, to confirm the effects of exposures on the foetus, so that knowledge, available to the corporation who develop harmful products, produce and distribute them, cannot be denied, and neither can – to say the least – its culpable negligence.

Hence, at this time, it is useful to start with a specific corporation, Monsanto, because of the multiple harms it produces, but also because, in a landmark decision in France, Monsanto's CEO was condemned for its criminal responsibility for the harm inflicted on French farmer Paul Francois.

On 13 February 2012, for the first time, Monsanto Corporation was judged to be responsible for the toxic exposure of the French farmer, Paul Francois, by a tribunal in Lyon, France. This is an unprecedented result, because the manufacturer was found to be guilty, given that Francois's exposure resulted in symptoms which permitted the identification of the specific chemicals involved.[29]

Once the causality has been established, the victims can be compensated, but it is normally the association for the social protection of farmers that pays, that is, society itself. In contrast, in the case of Paul Francois, the farmer has succeeded in establishing the responsibly of the industry that distributes the products which harmed him. No doubt Monsanto will appeal, and it will be hard to sustain the accusation, because it does not involve an "accident, occurring at time *t*", but the case involves effects unfolding over time instead.

At any rate, this case strengthens the ongoing anger in France against Monsanto's other activity: the production of GMOs, which recently prompted national hero José Bové to say, "Culturellement, l'agriculture française ne'existe plus" ("Culturally speaking, French agriculture no longer exists").

On the same day, 13 February 2012, another judgment in Torino, Italy, brought closure to an ongoing case, as the victims of asbestos exposure saw the Swiss billionaire Stephan Schmidheiny, co-owner of Eternit, condemned to sixteen years in prison. This was the biggest and most serious European environmental health case to date.[30]

Thousands died because of the total disregard of worker's health and safety that prevailed. Usually, in such cases, a victim (a worker harmed by asbestos exposure) might sue, and if he could prove the aetiology of his disease, he might have been compensated, in a way similar to the Monsanto case, decided on the same date.

But this case represents a watershed decision: the owner of the corporation was sentenced to sixteen years in jail, a serious sentence reflecting the outrage felt for the thousands of victims his negligence and his disregard for the life of his workers had produced.

The occurrence of two such disparate decisions on the same day, lends some hope that in the future industrial criminals might rethink their cavalier attitude to those they employ and to the general public.

Therefore, although the jurisprudence appears to move forward, as it acknowledges the criminality of those who control certain industrial operations, the legal infrastructure appears to lag behind, as the massive corporate power refuses to accept binding limits, and both single states and the United Nations itself cannot, apparently, force them to accept the limits that are part of all "persons'" duties.

A better situation in Europe?

However, even without reaching the extreme identification we note in Monsanto with the US, even Europe is not immune to agriculture-related lobbies, nor is Monsanto the only corporate criminal:

> Derogations and loopholes are standard business in EU pesticide policy. PAN-Europe already wrote a report on the "120-day derogation" regime, allowing EU Member States to use hundreds of illegal pesticides for almost a full crop season.[31]

As well as the "120 day-derogation", there is also the question of the "essential use" of such chemicals as, for instance, the poisonous gas metam. This gas, used as a soil fumigant, was "officially banned by a 2009 Council decision, but immediately entered again via the backdoor by the same council decision as 'essential use'".[32]

Keep in mind that the European Union is generally far ahead of North America and of most other countries in the control of chemical substances.[33] Yet, when the EU's governing bodies attempt to ban a hazardous substance, such as the "poisonous gas metam", and even extend facilitations such as granting corporations a year to substitute it with a safer product, the industry that produces that substance does not take seriously its responsibility to human life.

Corporate and state responses are far from satisfactory, as they include providing only "vague answers"; not answering at all; relying on industries who try "to relabel metam to sustainable use"; there has even been a case where Dow Chemical was involved, and even funded by the EU.[34] Despite the presence of a directive for the sustainable use of pesticides (128/2009/EC) and the proposed transition to integrated pest management (IPM), ongoing industrial machinations do not allow decisions like the 2009 banning of that dangerous fumigant, or the banning of yet another fumigant, 1,3-dichloropropene.[35]

Both of these fumigants are an essential part of the older-style agriculture, where nature, and all natural elements, were to be eliminated as a pre-requisite for successful agriculture. This system is required for "monocultures and narrow rotations",[36] both of which rely on the effort "to kill biodiversity" and to turn everything that is not part of that system into a "pest", despite the fact that, according to the Sustainable Use of Pesticides Directive (128/2009/EC), it demands the use of the IPM from 2014 on.[37]

Who are the victims of metam sodium? What are the dangers involved? Everybody who eats agricultural products, in all member states, is exposed to danger:

> Based on US-EPA data Metam is a probable human carcinogen (malignant blood vessel tumours) … Independent studies show that Metam (and MITC) are developmental toxins, causing cranio-facial abnormalities (teratogen) at low doses.[38]

Thus, not only are those who use the inquinated food at risk, but also "residents and people in the neighbourhood of the treated fields are at risk" (US-EPA chronic reference exposure level cite disabling effects), but the specifics of the hazardous effects have never been seriously analysed. All information is based on the research produced by the industry that manufactures the fumigant, and no peer-review or independent assessment is required.

Of course, this is simply a single example of a widespread and ongoing attack that creates victims pretty much everywhere. Not only the effects on those victims cannot be denied, but the concomitant business advances and growth (on the part of continued operations of those industries, and of the pharmaceutical companies that produce medications for cancers and other diseases) cannot be denied. This situation continues, despite the preponderance of evidence available from epidemiology, toxicology, medicine and the WHO itself, regarding the terrible effects of industrial chemicals. All the ongoing campaigns that ostensibly try to combat various diseases such as cancer, raise funds "for the cure", through marches and fundraisers; but no marches or fundraisers are attempted to close down any of these industries, or at least restrain their noxious practices, the sources of multiple diseases and various forms of abnormal development in children. Thus both industrial chemical corporations and "Big Pharma" continue to benefit as they remain undeterred and unpunished.[39]

"Feeding the world without GMOs?"

> Globally, corn and soybeans account for about 80 percent of the land area devoted to growing genetically engineered crops and both are overwhelmingly used for animal feed and biofuels. Most of the investments in GE crops end up feeding cows and cars, not people … Moreover [investments in GE crops] mainly help line the pockets of seed and chemical companies, large-scale growers and producers of corn ethanol.[40]

Initially "corporations" were formed to serve what seemed to be desirable public good, according to the beliefs of the king or other ruler, who decided on the purpose of the corporation. For Canada, the British "need" for beaver pelts and tails for the hats of the citizens, was the basis for funding the inception of the Hudson's Bay Company in the "colonies".

The oldest commercial corporation in North America, it was incorporated by English Royal Charter and King Charles II, on 2 May 1670, as the Governor and Company of Adventurers of England Trading into Hudson's Bay. That company was intended to handle the fur trade in North America, before European States could lay claim to that land. At one time, this first corporation, which is today a well-known Canadian institution, held the monopoly over the Indian trade, especially the fur trade in Northern Canada, in Hudson's Bay.

The region it controlled consisted of 1.5 square miles in the drainage basin of Hudson's bay, known at the time as Rupert's Land, as he was the company's first director, and cousin to King Charles. The corporate mode of operation was simple. In the Spring and Summer, First Nation and Metis trappers caught the animals and treated their pelts. They travelled by foot and by canoe, and arrived either at Fort Severn in Manitoba, or at Cumberland House in Saskatchewan, where they traded the furs for "metal tools and hunting gear", often imported by the company from Germany, the centre of inexpensive manufacturing in that era.[41]

At this stage, the corporation was thriving as a single purpose organization: it was fulfilling a "need", or at least a clear "want" of society at the time, and it was operating directly under the direction and the guidance of the founding government.

We have travelled far indeed from those days, when a commercial power was only permitted to operate to fulfil a specific function, approved only for that reason by a governing body.[42] Today's corporate legal persons not only are allowed to expand their operations in any number of directions, beyond the original one, but can do so in any way that is profitable, without any consideration of public needs, or safety. These needs have multiplied exponentially, into "choices" or "desires", often in ways that are in direct conflict with the real "needs" of their stakeholders.

Today's corporate actors have acquired comparably powerful public relation departments, whose function is to "sell" as beneficial or "desirable" any number of harmful products, for profit. This corporate function is particularly relevant in regard to the present topic. With an increasing population growth, and especially with the growth of a large wealthy class in almost all countries, that suggest that "by 2050 the demand for food will be twice what it was in 2005":[43]

> One big driver of this trend is that people get richer, they buy more meat which requires huge quantities of crops such as corn and soy for animal feed. Food production occupies about 40 percent of the Earth's land area and uses more fresh water than any other human activity.[44]

Yet the desire for meat is counterproductive for the consumers: rather than providing a "good", that choice is the source of most adult diseases, from obesity to diabetes, to several cancers and numerous heart problems.[45] As well, returning to our chosen example of a corporate criminal, Monsanto, together with Dow Chemical, Syngenta, Bayer crops and other companies, have produced chemical substances, herbicides, pesticides and such, of which, Monsanto's Roundup, composed primarily of glyphosate, has contaminated the food supply of the world[46] and together with other industrial chemicals has introduced a number of childhood, adult and even old age diseases, as all these chemicals are endocrine disruptors.[47] These substances not only alter organisms in natural systems, but they also alter the predisposition of humans to a number of diseases, all of which are on the increase because of pre-birth and early exposures, starting from the embryonic stage.[48]

Hence, we have "progressed" from tightly controlled, one-approved corporate purpose, to legal persons, led only by the profit motive, whose rights are now beyond those of natural individuals, and whose powers now equal those of states and often exceed them. That corporate power represents the gravest attack on the biological integrity of all humans in various ways, and to the ecological integrity of all systems and in all regions of the world.

One Health: a hope for integrity? The Manhattan Principles

> As defined during the meeting titled "Building Interdisciplinary Bridges to Health in a Globalized World" held in 2004 … The Symposium set priorities for an international interdisciplinary strategy for combating threats to the health of life on Earth.[49]

One Health, as a set of principles, has a long history: Rudolph Virchow (1821–1902), a German pathologist, recognized the linkages between human and veterinary medicine and coined the expression "zoonosis", an infectious disease that may be passed from animals to humans. Another notable "founder" of the movement was a Canadian doctor who taught at McGill University in Montreal, where he emphasized the linkages between animals and men's health. He died in 1919. Later, Calvin Schwabe (1927–2006) was the first to use the term "One Medicine" as he worked for the World Health Organization.

In 2004 the Wildlife Conservation Society[50] published the 12 Manhattan Principles, from which the quotation above is taken. Another meeting in 2007 recommended the "One Health" approach, where the emphasis was clearly on global pandemics, and was aimed primarily at maintaining human security. In 2008, the FAO and WHO collaborated with UNICEF, UNSIC and the World Bank to combat emerging infectious diseases, and in October of the same year One Health became a "recommended approach and a political reality", after the International Ministerial Conference on Avian and Pandemic Influenza at Sharm-el-Sheik. In 2009, the Public Health Agency of Canada combined a newly formed "Centre for Food-Borne, Environmental and Zoonotic Infectious Diseases", which hosted the "One World, One Health Expert Consultation".[51]

It is significant that by 2011, the 1st International One Health Congress (Melbourne, Australia) expanded the ongoing approach of One Health from its emphasis on zoonotic disease and the human/animal interface: "In addition to understanding the interdependence of human, animal and environmental health … also considered the importance of economics … food security and safety".[52]

Thus the environment was a late-comer of sorts to the One Health movement, although it remains well-established within its principles today. In fact, the Manhattan Principles go even further, as in 2004 the opening paragraph states:

> These Manhattan Principles urge world leaders, civil society, the global health community and institutions of science, to holistically approach the prevention of epidemic/epizootic disease *and the maintenance of ecosystem integrity*.[53]

Hence, by now, the interconnectedness of the community of life is clearly recognized, and not only the need for the safety and integrity of ecosystems is acknowledged, but, at the same time, integrity is neither defined nor advocated.

As noted in Chapter 1, it was Aldo Leopold, a forester, who first spoke of the community of life; also it was Leopold who first recognized the foundational importance of the preservation of ecological integrity, not only as a scientific principle, but also as a moral necessity.[54] Agricultural giants like Monsanto, through their ongoing production of herbicides and pesticides, cause grave harm to ecosystems, hence to ecological integrity. At the same time, with the promotion and production of GMOs, they attack the biological integrity of individual organisms.

Both attacks manifest a total disregard for the right to food, now established in international law by the UN itself, which has recently termed the current food production/delivery a "broken system" in a report by its Special Rapporteur on the Right to Food, Olivier De Schutter:

> Thus, the normative content of the right to food can be summarized by reference to the requirements of availability, accessibility, adequacy and sustainability, all of which must be built into legal entitlements and secured through accountability mechanisms.[55]

The report emphasizes the interface between:

- the right to work;
- the right to social security; and
- the right to food.

Thus the first aspect that is urgently in need of radical re-orientation is the way current agricultural production and distribution are managed. The first problem that emerges is that "boosting agricultural production"[56] is totally insufficient, as the present practices increase the profits of large industrial conglomerates, without, however, increasing nutrition, especially for children. Even the FAO's *State of Food Insecurity in the World 2013*[57] provides limited and even misleading information regarding the "advances" in hunger reduction it reports.[58]

Current practices not only foster inadequate nutrition as well as poor health for children, but they also contribute significantly to the elimination of local farming communities, decimated by large agro-conglomerates. These corporations only consider the quantity, rather than the quality of their production while, at the same time, they ignore both the health and the environmental "collateral" effects of their operations, due to the overuse of pesticides and other industrial modes of agricultural production, which contribute significantly to climate change:[59]

> Globally over 165 million children are stunted – so malnourished that they do not reach their full physical and cognitive potential, and 2 billion people globally lack vitamins and minerals essential for good health.[60]

But perhaps the worst harms inflicted on large numbers of people are inflicted through climate change, because of the proliferation of meat production,[61] which projects the figures that would emerge through the expected demand for meat production in 2050, "to reach 470 million tons", which that document describes as an entirely unsustainable situation.[62]

Industrial meat production requires feeding animals cereals and grains diverted from feeding poor people who cannot afford anything else; thus, much of the desperate poverty and hunger that motivate flights from third world countries originate from the practices that enrich agribusiness, while depriving the poor of the basic necessities. Nor is meat production and availability at the current levels beneficial to those who can afford to consume it:

> in high income countries, the net health impacts of meat consumption are turning negative: at current levels, it is contributing to chronic diseases, including obesity, type 2 diabetes, cardiovascular diseases and cancer.[63]

In addition, the various chemicals used for both animal fodder, other industrial crops and industrially grown meat, use extreme amounts of water, increasingly scarce today.[64] Finally, the chemical substances used contribute significantly to a number of developmental problems and diseases for children, adults and older persons, when pre-birth exposures occur.[65] The effects of these early exposures also include irreversible diminished brain capacity in children and young adults, autism and other forms of neurotoxicity, including long-term effects and emergence of Parkinson's and Alzheimer's diseases.[66]

Finally, we cannot forget that "livestock is found to be responsible for 51 per cent of anthropogenic greenhouse gas emissions", as well as "livestock production accounted for 70 per cent of the land surface of the planet".[67] When agricultural development was essentially led by states (as in the 1960s and 1970s), the initial mistakes were made, that eventually precipitated the present situation. At that time, the farmers were not paid fair prices, and the largest producers, able to compete globally, were subsidized. The rural migrations and urban sprawls that resulted, were the prelude to both hunger and poverty in many countries, in South America, Asia and Africa.

The present situation is now based on the preferences and choices of large industrial agriculture and livestock production, supported by the governments of the countries where production occurs, but also by those who are the home bases of those operations on one hand, and of the poor countries that provide the raw material, and the necessary resources, on the other.

Once those whose given "roles" enable them to make the decisions that create and support these interconnected problems, it is easy to see who is responsible, thus who should be held accountable for the entrenchment and continuation of the complex practices that harm the health of the rich, while victimizing the poor:

> Foresight studies have suggested that, if current mandates are implemented, the price of cereals and other crops could be 35 per cent higher by 2030 than under a reference scenario where biofuel consumption remained constant at 2008 levels, putting an estimated 136 million more people at risk of hunger.[68]

Hence justice, distributive fairness, the right to normal development of human beings and poverty reduction, all require urgent radical reforms of global food systems. From the standpoint of the topic of this work, the issue of poverty reduction is perhaps the most compelling reason for seeking accountability.

Therefore, the ongoing "broken system" manifests its attacks not only on the right to food, but also on the right to health, and to natural systems and their integrity. Further, the current system also clearly manifests harmful links to both water shortages and climate change.

Water, air and climate change: integrity and one earth

> As California experiences a massive drought, we examine the overlooked link between water shortages, climate change and meat consumption. With some 98 percent of the state suffering from a water crisis, California Gov. Jerry Brown ordered residents and businesses to cut water use by 25 percent. It is the first mandatory statewide reduction in California's history. One group not facing restrictions is big agriculture, which uses about 80% of California's water. According to the Pacific Institute, 47 percent of California's water footprint is in meat and dairy products.[69]

One Health shows clearly the connection existing among all parts of nature, that is the environment and the organisms that live within it. This acknowledges the "community of life" of which Aldo Leopold spoke, and the undeniable interface among all components and aspects of that community: we can term it "One Earth". Hence it is difficult, if not impossible, to truly separate the different aspects of the global environment crises fostered by the so-called Anthropocene's various manifestations (and we will return to that concept below). For instance, to speak of water issues, *must* involve the question of food and agriculture, since the largest use of water globally, depends on industrial meat production.

As well, the same factory farming meat production contributes significantly to climate change, through methane emissions' contribution to the problem. The same is true of health itself: once again the meat industry not only engenders a number of diseases through promoting unneeded and harmful consumption, a "preference" that harms direly, but also the covert, unchosen harm that derives from the increasing use of antibiotics in meat. That use renders meat consumers unable to combat "superbugs" of enhanced infectious diseases, as their organisms are regularly dosed with antibiotics in their meat:

> The meat industry is buying up more and more medically important antibiotics, threatening human health in its quest to ramp up the factory farm model to meet the demands for pork, chicken and beef. New FDA data shows that sales of human antibiotics use in livestock jumped 20 percent between 2009 and 2013, in keeping with past trends. It's in keeping too with projections for global antibiotic use by the meat sector which experts say could increase by as much as 67 percent by 2030.[70]

Thus all aspects of the environmental crisis are also in some sense aspects of One Health, as all issues we are confronting are affected at the same time. Thus allowing the meat industry, for instance, or the pharmaceutical industry to enjoy voluntary standards without controls or binding legal regimes, affects all areas at the same time: climate, food safety and water.

Yet, some argue that the presence of specific, binding instruments that make the right to water mandatory, is not necessary: "The human right to water exists without requiring any legal recognition, if one admits that water is vital to life and the only basis for human rights is being human."[71]

These documents acknowledge it as a basic right, which includes "the right to life, the right to adequate housing, the right to food, the right to health, the right to development, and the right to work".[72]

However, these assurances are hollow: water like food and air are basic to the maintenance of life in a way that "development" and "work" are not: water and air's connection to life is far more immediate and necessary. Somewhat less explicit are the related articles in the Convention on the Elimination of all Forms of Discrimination Against Women,[73] and the Convention on the Rights of the Child.[74] Far more explicit than the language in these covenants, is the General Comment 15 which, however, is non-binding:

> [T]he human right to water entitles everyone to sufficient, safe, acceptable, physically available and affordable water for personal and domestic uses. An adequate amount of safe water is necessary to prevent death from dehydration, to reduce the risk of water-related disease and to provide for consumption, cooking, personal and domestic hygienic requirements.[75]

In addition, the earlier reference to "One Earth" indicates that the immediate necessity of humans for water is parallel to the necessity of natural systems for water, as these cannot thrive without it. Nor is the water necessary simply by itself: deserts such as the Sahel in Africa represent an ongoing climate disaster:

> Water conservation is critical, but so is reforestation and soil conservation, for without trees to help absorb the water and hold the soil in place and terraces to catch the soil, the floods wash away our water reservoirs and they will fill with silt and undo all our hard work.[76]

Nor is this the only region in Africa affected by water shortages, as part of climate disasters and droughts producing famines, starting in the early 1980s in Ethiopia, followed by more in 2003, 2004, 2008 and 2009 in Eritrea, all of which resulted in famines in that region:

> This isn't climate change, this is climate disaster and science tells us that the world should be preparing for even worse things to come. Thanks to the mainly western countries contribution to rising CO_2 levels heating up the planet, droughts will test the very ability of our species to survive.[77]

The presence of drought, recently termed "death by a thousand cuts", is the phenomenon that, more than most, manifests the necessity to recover integrity, as much as possible, as the condition for the survival of One Earth, as it combines a number of issues all at once.[78]

Droughts are not new, but at this time, they are no longer an occasional part of "nature's course", because "anthropogenic global warming is at the root of the problem...on a worldwide basis".[79] The interconnectedness of all aspects of droughts are clearly in evidence in the situation present, for instance, in California in 2015; "California is the 4th largest oil and gas producer in America",[80] thus the CO_2 produced by greenhouse gas contributes significantly to the worst drought the US is experiencing at the time. That is a clear indictment of that sort of "success" as it returns to harm.

What is required is not the continued intensive production of fossil fuels, but a worldwide divestment movement, given that in China, India and Taiwan, millions are hungry and desperately in need, but facing huge areas of desertification. In India, for instance, 25 per cent of the area is so affected. In Taiwan water is rationed several days a week already but "up to three million people will be without water on any given day".[81]

Thus, as we consider droughts, what is the main issue? Is it water scarcity? Climate change? Food deprivation? But all these problems coalesce in one major issue: the lack of integrity on earth. In fact, even One Health is insufficient as such, despite the paragraph cited above, that referred explicitly to ecological integrity. That concept should be basic to One Health, but it is not. We need to re-examine the concept of health, starting from the understanding of the term according to the WHO. Health is viewed as functionality, not as the completeness, wholeness and integrity of each individual organism. An example of the difference between a human individual being "healthy" in that sense, and one possessing her original biological integrity, might be understood as being a person, quite "healthy" in general, but having a knee replacement, and perhaps a bridge implant with several artificial teeth, after extractions.

This individual may be quite healthy, in the sense of being fully functional and not sick. But when we turn from a human person to natural systems instead, or even an individual grain, fruit or vegetable that has been altered in some way, the difference is that the alteration, whether individual or for a whole system, is not motivated by the preservation of the biology, original to the individual, or to the optimum functioning of the system, according to its evolutionary trajectory. In contrast with physical changes intended to better the general function of each human being, generally prescribed by professionals sworn to "do no harm", ecological alterations are not inspired by a similar spirit. The alterations are entirely motivated by the economic interests of those who decide on the alterations, or execute them.

In any case, integrity is not promoted. In contrast, much has been written about "ecosystem health".[82] The metaphor of ecosystem health is useful to focus public attention on environmental problems and to interject an evaluative component into scientific discourse, as health is generally taken to be a desirable state of affairs.

The opening sentence of the executive summary of the 1995 report from Working Group II of the IPCC states: "The sustained health of human populations requires the continued *integrity* of Earth's natural systems."[83] Even in a health context, the required condition for human health is described as the earth's integrity, not the "health" of its ecosystems. One might question this seeming anomaly, particularly in a document devoted to health itself. It might simply be a case of appealing to the language of most regulatory and legislative documents. But perhaps the use of *integrity* here is intended simply as a public relations ploy to evoke warm positive feelings without demanding any change in the status quo. Any such intention, I am happy to say, appears to have backfired.

Much of the material available on ecosystem health deals, as Baird Callicott justly suggests, with the areas of the Earth where humankind is actually living and actively engaged in pursuing its goals.[84] In order to survive, we need to manage and manipulate large areas of the earth, and in that sense the goals of ecosystem health in managed areas appear to be appropriate. What is less appropriate is the fact that all the material on ecosystem health tends to ignore the *foundation* of the health it advocates; that is, it ignores ecosystem integrity.

Ecosystem health may thus be a useful metaphor, but only if its basis and the necessary condition for its existence are acknowledged and supported. On the other hand, if the emphasis remains exclusively on ecosystem health, we ultimately support the status quo with possible "green" modifications of various degrees, or, as I have put it in another context, we remain wolves in "green" sheep's clothing.[85] In this sense, the metaphor is not useful, but misleading, as it draws public attention away from the conditions and the background for health.

Moreover, ecosystem health suffers from conceptual and philosophical problems of its own, not only as a metaphoric goal of public policy, but also as a practical goal. I have argued that as a goal of management, it explicitly excludes the very landscapes that support life through their services, and therefore that it cannot support "health" in a meaningful sense, but only, at best, the sustainability of certain specific production goals.[86] Dale Jamieson also shows several problems with the concept: a "weakness about the supposed objectivity of human health"; the lack of motive when the metaphor is applied to ecosystems rather than to humans and other creatures; and the instability of "our preferences with respect to ecosystems" and their composition.[87]

From our point of view, the major difficulty is that aside from its conceptual problem, the emphasis on ecosystem health as the goal of public policy is particularly hazardous to our health. Given our previous record in dealing with the environment and the production goals of our management, it is clear that to preserve, respect, and restore are not our main aims. The lesson has not been learned yet, in spite of our present precarious environmental situation: we need to stop believing that all on earth can be managed, and start to manage our own selves and society instead.[88] Whatever is "managed" for production may be plentiful, even sustainable, in itself. But if it involves any management "tools" such as chemicals, toxic substances, or intensive practices of any sort, not only is the productive area eventually affected, but also the "fragmented nature"[89] that is left; and this is not conducive to our own health, as we have seen. Further, the technological optimism that governs these management goals also excludes zoning, controls for harmful activities and the possibility of serious restraints. The human health paradigm provides examples. Why do we need to seriously restructure our lifestyles, consider our diet, and avoid excesses when we can "manage" our so-called health through chemical and technical means – say, liposuction if we are obese, heart bypass operations if our arteries are clogged, and other medical interventions? There is a plethora of medical interventions not only for the diseases caused by our natural deterioration but also for those we actively court through our inappropriate lifestyles. There are many ways of managing our health.

In contrast, as the Intergovernmental Report on Climate Changes and Human Health clearly states, the *integrity* of a largely unmanaged earth is necessary for our health, and therefore our managing expertise must be exercised where it is most needed: in ourselves and our activities. Understanding the role of integrity in the prevention of harm to all life ensures that the goal is recognized as more than a prudent, desirable choice, something in our interest. It also becomes a moral imperative.[90]

Climate change and human rights: the interface

> It is now well-understood that climate change can and does adversely affect the enjoyment of a broad range of human rights. The United Nations Human Rights Council has stated that climate change poses an immediate and far-reaching threat to people and communities around the world, and has adverse implications for the full enjoyment of human rights.[91]

We have shown that, for the most part, the jurisprudence dealing with human rights violations arises from a specific environmental condition, or hazardous environmental exposure is scarce. Hence the presence of this new document from the Office of the High Commissioner for Human Rights is highly significant, as it indicates a promising new development of environmental rights. At any rate, it will be useful to review briefly this work, in order to appreciate how explicitly human harm is linked to environmental/climate conditions, and which specific rights are judged to be under threat, starting with the right to life: the longest established human right. The right to life is termed the "supreme right", requiring "positive measures for its protection"[92] which would make the acknowledgment of the interface between climate change and the right to life the basis for a radical step forward.

However, instead of offering protection against direct and indirect environmental threats, as noted in Chapter 2, that connection has been completely ignored in the case law, despite the huge effects produced by climate change:

> Equally, climate change will affect the right to life through an increase in hunger and malnutrition and related disorders impacting on child growth and development; cardiorespiratory morbidity and mortality related to ground-level ozone. Climate change will exacerbate weather-related disasters which already have devastating effects on people and their enjoyment of the right to life, particularly in the developing world. For example, an estimated 262 million people were affected by climate disasters annually from 2000 to 2004, of whom 98 percent live in developing countries.[93]

Increases in temperature extremes result in heat-related deaths, but also in decreased food production, resulting in additional increases in malnutrition. Hence the right to Health is also under threat.[94] Of course it is not only human health that is under severe stress, but also biodiversity will be and already is significantly reduced, thus affecting the very ecosystem services upon which all life depends:

> an increase in moderate nutritional stunting, an indicator linked to increased risk of death and poor health of 1 to 29%, depending on the region assessed, compared to a future without climate change, and a much greater impact on severe stunting for particular regions such as 23 percent for central sub-Sahara Africa and 62 percent for South Asia.[95]

Those who live in poverty are disproportionally affected, as climate change fosters a decline in available water, while disease vectors (mosquitoes, tse-tse flies) will continue to spread more disease. Extreme poverty also magnifies the lack of food as all aspects of food security are potentially affected by climate change, including food access, utilization and price stability.

We have already reviewed the work of the UN Special Rapporteur on the Right to Food, Olivier de Schutter, and he clearly related how that right is affected by climate change.[96] Both the right to water and that to sanitation are also gravely affected by climate change. Finally the right to housing as well as – even more significantly– the right to remain in one's chosen place of residence:

> Rolnik also related climate change impacts to an increase in migration and substantial human mobility. She explained that, as a consequence of environmental degradation due to climate change, depletion of natural

> resources and natural disasters, many people around the world find their lives and health threatened, their houses and lands destroyed and their sources of livelihood taken away.[97]

Children are the most obvious victims of climate change, together with the poor, especially in the developing world. Hence, all aspects of human rights are under attack through climate change, nor can any one aspect of this attack be separated from the others, as the disintegrity that is basic to all forms of environmental damage unites them all.

From one health to the dynamic processes of the wild

> A more sophisticated concept of wilderness preservation aims rather to perpetuate the integrity of evolutionary and ecological processes.[98]

In the previous section we addresses a somewhat dated debate that raged in journals and books after the affirmation of the importance of biological integrity in the 1972 US Clean Water act, and particularly, after the 1988 ratification of the Great Lakes Water Quality Agreement (see Chapter l). The radical implications of embracing integrity moved many supporters of the *status quo* to promote environmental health instead. Essentially, the support of ecological integrity posed grave threats to the neoliberal economic interests that prefer to encounter no legal or scientific limits to growth.[99]

Ecological integrity is the standard that supports the need for the protection of the wild in quantities sufficient to ensure healthy conditions to the nature which includes human interventions. This reality entails that the human enterprise or, to turn to a recent buzzword, the prevalence of policies that prevail in the "Anthropocene", *must* be curtailed; it also entails that the single motive that characterizes the Anthropocene, that is the power and economic interests that provide countless consumption choices to the populations of wealthy countries, must be reversed.

There is another principle that has priority, and that is one which is dangerous for corporate/consumptive interests, the principle of integrity[100], because using integrity as a measure of the rightness or not of policies and decisions, is dangerous for the same corporate/consumptive interests, because integrity refers to the wild, to areas that cannot be mined, dug-up, plundered, or paved over. However, no matter how threatening the concept is to the preferred choices of so-called civilized, Western lifestyles, it is the absence of its protection that has proved to be the gravest danger.

In earlier times there was another ongoing dispute, between "conservation" and "preservation": the latter spearheaded by John Muir, the former, by Gifford Pinchot. Conservation is intended to protect – at best – the health of natural systems, that have been altered in part for human purposes, in order to maintain the economic viability of their products. In contrast, preservation is the fundamental value of integrity:

> Aldo Leopold famously said: "A thing is right when it tends to preserve the integrity, stability and beauty of the biotic community". He did use the word "preserve", and he evidently refers to processes or the scale of landscape planning where there is relative "stability".[101]

But stability does not entail the preservation of a specific, present *status quo* of an area. Rather what must be preserved and protected is the capacity of ecosystems to evolve naturally over time. Although there has been, so far, little emphasis on ecointegrity as an important principle of policy in law since the Great Lakes Water Quality Agreement (1978, rat. 1988), or science, with the exception of the Canadian Parks Policy or, by implication, the law dealing with Canadian First Nations (see Chapters 1 and 2), the wild has fared somewhat better.

At any rate, the preservation of the "wild" (supported as it is by several conventions and agreements, like the Convention on Biological Diversity, as we shall see in the next chapter), can be clearly contrasted with the approaches sanctioned by the policies prevalent in the "Anthropocene": the wild, or the areas minimally impacted or disturbed by human activities, can be understood as another expression to designate areas of ecological integrity. Dave Forman cites the US Wilderness Act as follows:

> An area of wilderness is further defined to mean in this Act an area of undeveloped Federal land retaining primeval character and influence, without permanent improvements of human habitation, which is protected and managed so as to preserve its natural conditions, which (1) *generally appears*, to have been *affected primarily by* the forces of nature, with the imprint of man's work *substantially unnoticeable*.[102]

There are several problems with this definition, the first of which the limited emphasis, as only American natural systems are considered, because the Wilderness Act is a US document. The second is even more problematic, as it defines human interference as "improvement", more or less permanent, which recalls the words of John Locke. Of course Locke's idea of "improvement", though often understood or explained as any sort of economic/industrial development, is no such thing. The thought underlying that position is clearly in evidence in the second treatise, as he speaks of the state of nature:

> The state of nature has a law of nature to govern it, which obliges everyone, and reason, which is that law, teaches all mankind who will but consult it that, being all equal and independent, no one ought to harm another in his life, health, liberty or possession.[103]

Hence property is based upon one's efforts, as it is a natural right such as when a man picks up an apple fallen from a tree, and that action is understood as the man's input, his "labour". Nevertheless, "The same law of nature that doth by this mean give us property does also bound that property too."[104] Furthermore:

> as much as anyone can make use of to any advantage of life before it spoils, so much he may by his labour fix a property in: *Whatever is beyond this is more than his share and belongs to others.*[105]

Hence the capitalist quest for endless growth is not justifiable, even according to Locke who is perhaps the main proponent of the theory of the right to property. No doubt we can adapt the same approach to the quest and the need for water or land, thus the intrusion of unnecessary "development" activities into the wild. Such intrusions not only harm the integrity of the wild, but also its ability to continue to develop along its own evolutionary trajectory.

Thus, what is beyond "our share", is not ours to grab, alter, make into products for sale, for our eventual profit: it simply "belongs to others". When the natural product is either water or land that had not been previously altered, we can argue that not only this or that area of nature belongs to others, but the "natural service" originating from those areas, *also* belongs to others, morally if not legally.

Perhaps, as we consider the grave impact we have upon landscapes almost everywhere, it becomes clear that beyond the interest in and respect for famous old US parks, beyond the admiration for the wonders of wildlife that needs the wild to survive, there is the question of survival in general. General consideration of the survival of all life is tied inescapably to the preservation of ecological integrity and the wild, in quantities necessary from several points of view.[106] That is the link between a scientific truth, one that has been deliberately misconstrued, even hidden for decades, and a moral obligation to preserve life, in direct conflict with our current legal regimes designed for the protection of economic interests and the states bureaucracies that are complicit with them. The laws we need to change drastically must be brought in line with the major principle on which all laws are based: the protection of the right to life. When the right to life extends to all life on Earth then the absence of a specific "victim" or even the absence of a well defined "crime", should not hold us back from insisting that clearer and more exhaustive instruments be designed to cover all attacks on life.

Survival in the battle against the Anthropocene

> By 2016, the International Commission on Stratigraphy's Working Group on the "Anthropocene" will formally decide whether or not we live in the Anthropocene literally, the epoch of humans. Many scholars with no significant knowledge or interest in geology are not waiting for permission to use that name.[107]

The overwhelming (and unchecked) human influence on all areas of the planet cannot be disputed. But, since the time of the sophists (Protagoras of Abdera, *c.*490–420 BC), the cardinal importance of "naming" has been recognized: "Of all things (chremata) the measure is man, of the things that are that they are, and of the things that are not, that they are not."[108]

Sophists were considered as clever "craftsmen", their teaching appeared to be "wisdom" or truth, but it was not: their main claim was not to argue for the truth of a matter, or for a thing that was, but, using the skills of a lawyer at the bar, their aim was to convince others to accept one opinion about something, rather than another as the truth of the matter. Thus they helped political figures to convince the citizens to accept their position, based upon the clever speeches of the sophists, as the most convincing one.[109]

Thus the sophists believed that the clever individual human being had decided what was the truth of some issue, hence "its measure" or its name, what it was. Today in public relations campaigns, particularly those initiated by governments and large corporations, similar tactics are routine. Recently the media was saturated by public relation campaigns, well-funded by the oil and extractive industries, who poured millions of dollars into the media to convince the public that climate change did not exist.[110]

Even more recently, Monsanto funded, and it is still funding a campaign aimed at discrediting no less an organization than the WHO, for finally publicly admitting that glyphosate, the main component of Roundup, was a proven carcinogen, something that has been accepted at least in Europe for several decades. In earlier times, Phillips and many other cigarette manufacturers attempted to convince the public that smoking was not harmful, and that the many diseases and early death occurrences were not originating from their products.[111]

Thus the very art of naming/defining the present period as the Anthropocene appears to acknowledge an obvious situation not only of human influence on the natural systems, but also one of power and control on the part of humankind. According to Vucetich et al., "To some the label 'Anthropocene' serves as a reminder that the condition of the world is now harmful to humans."[112] But the harm we are observing is reciprocal, humans are harmed by nature but most often this takes place because humans have already harmed nature itself. This fact should be sufficient to discourage the hubris involved in calling the whole era after ourselves. That is similar to the hubris that suggests it is our "right", even our own destiny perhaps, to follow their own short-term misguided interests, no matter how hazardous that pursuit may be to the natural environment, hence to the rest of mankind.

It is worthy of note that in an era which greatly prizes "democracy", at least in its current instantiations, in the US we see that form of government arrogates to itself Protagoras's role as being "the measure of all things". In modern times, another philosopher, Thomas Hobbes, argued that "it is the state, or more precisely the sovereign, that determines good and evil".[113]

And it is the complicity between a greedy state, eager to acquire ever increasing power, and the wealthy corporations that benefit from that power and share that greed: they jointly determine what is "right" to do, what we should avoid, regardless of consequences to either environment or humanity. Rachel Carson was one of the major scholars who made us aware of the terrible impact of pesticides, in the *Silent Spring*,[114] and accepted that humans could not "manage the planet".[115] And that is an excellent basic insight. Yet what still lingers, is the notion of "stewardship":[116] that notion implies two separate entities, that is, the steward (or stewards) and that which requires stewardship.

Once again, even with the best of intentions, "stewardship" implies the separate presence of a "caretaker" and that of nature, somehow dependent upon our "care". Aside from the dismal failure of that stance to succeed in its stated and expected aims, it is a stance that does not recognize that "care" for nature is not an optional choice, as it implies "care" for ourselves at the same time. The more we fail in our caretaking "duties" the more we fail to implement any form of self-protection, as we are an integral part of the community of life, and we have an obligation to protect it.

This is where the integrity approach, hard as it is to implement, serves humanity as it serves our natural habitat. It would make no sense to "care" for fish, unless their water was to be protected first. In fact caring for their water represents the best, the only way to protect the fish that inhabit it. Unlike fish, humans have many interests beyond safety and survival, but to be in a position where those interests are in direct conflict with the purely physical/biological "safety and survival", is a travesty not only of anything we can define a true human interest, but also, and most importantly, we must acknowledge that those interests we are attempting to defend, are *collective* interests, because what is under attack is not only the safety and simple interest of a single human, important though that is, but the common good of humanity.

Aggregate interests and collective rights

> An aggregate interest has from the outset an odd feature in that it is non-neutral in respect to potentially trivial changes in the collectivity's membership. An aggregate interest will vary based on both changes in the interests of continuing members and changes in membership. Even a very minor change in a collectivity's membership could change the aggregate interest, if for instance a new member's interests diverged in the appropriate way. This feature is arguably problematic in a *collectivity*, for the defining features of a collectivity as opposed to a set include that it remain the same collectivity even with changed membership.[117]

Once again: that is our starting point, that is, not only to support a "community of rights",[118] that is a community of agents, free to make informed and reasoned decisions for themselves as individuals, but also as components of that moral community which defines them. Our starting point also requires that the basic rights supported would be those of the universal collectivity, and that these be *basic* in the sense that only when such rights are ensured, a "moral community" is sure to be physically/biologically capable of reaching decisions, and of exercising and defending their own rights, beyond the most basic ones, intended to simply support their survival and normal capabilities.

Thus, to clarify the point further, there is no conflict between "social (better: common) good" decisions, and those that support the freedom of agents to act morally (with the full exercise of their normal faculties). It is simply necessary that the collective rights here proposed fit two basic conditions: (1) that they remain primary, both conceptually and temporally; and (2) that they should not extend beyond their basic nature, to usurp the decision-making agency of the individuals within the community of rights, such as Brownsword defines it.[119]

These conditions must be kept in mind as we consider the role that communities as such can play in relation to the notion of a collectivity. In fact, we should do something that liberal thinkers, and others, abhor, that is, we should rank the interests of individuals and aggregates, which may well be "incomparable" in the normal course of ranking them from the standpoint of law.[120] Many will resist any attempt to rank goals and preferences, the equality of which (other than those that are clearly illegal) represents both a modern trend and even the development of "rights" within the UN[121] as they appear to follow an ongoing project to support the freedom of choice.

Yet, if we consider the development of rights within international law, we will note that the extension of rights deals primarily with *individual* rights, and *individual* activities especially within the area of sexual mores. The Roman emperors used to advocate *panem et circenses* to keep the populace quiet and satisfied, no matter what else was happening in the empire. That can be loosely translated as "food (consumerism?) and entertainment" (the latter of which includes sexual preferences), and both are in fact viewed as almost sacred within Western affluent countries.

In contrast, community and collective rights are much harder to be added to the roster of conventions and other legal instruments; witness for instance the agonizingly slow pace of the ratification of the Draft United Nations Declaration on the Rights of Indigenous Peoples.[122] Collective decision-making, however, is not necessarily decision-making for the common good; it is at best a way of aggregating social preferences, unconstrained by the specific non-derogable obligation to choose one option rather than another.[123] Essentially: "Given that an interest is something that makes someone's life go better, then a collective interest is something that makes a collectivity's life go better."[124] While true, this is too mild a statement to describe collective interests, when these are understood as common good. Without some restraints placed on other choices/interests, neither survival nor moral capacities/development are ensured, when the common good of the collectivity in our sense is not given primacy. Thus it must be understood as far more basic than whatever makes "life go better", although the latter is trivially true.

This is why now we need to approach "communities" in a similar vein, and to propose ranking them as Newman proposes for individual interests. Communities are such when they are more than aggregates, or sets of individuals who may share one goal, while also holding many differences in lifestyle preferences and beliefs. However, this would be a futile exercise, given the great number of present, past and future communities, assembling an endless variety of peoples and purposes.

The best way to proceed, is to single out a specific sort of community, one which is rare, but still existing today, as it holds within it the seeds of the values and beliefs that make it unique, and its characteristics, representative of the common good aspects we require. It is a traditional Indigenous or local land-based community that can manifest the characteristics of unity of belief, practice, and respect for its habitat, and the creatures with which they share that habitat, that exemplifies the collective quest for the common good we are seeking to outline.

In addition, these communities share another major characteristic: at least in principle, they are protected by legal instruments and regimes, both domestic and international, although in practice such protection is very limited and, in many cases, non-existent, as we shall see below. By analysing the conditions that make such a community unique or – as it is described in law – *sui generis*, the characteristics that will emerge will show a community that is both inspirational on its own, and a clear constitutive part of the collectivity of humankind, because of its basic tenets.

In contrast, other aggregates or "communities" such as that of "agrochemical producers", or "petrochemical and extractive industries", are fostering choices and preferences that, whether or not supported by part of the citizenry even on a global scale, are contrary to the common good. They are, one and all, hostile to the common good as expressed by the goals of ecological integrity in general, and the aim to protect the biological integrity of individual organisms, in particular. Hence we can say that the collective interests, or the common good, are the most basic but the most necessary of support, and they are dependent on the closest possible systemic approximation or closeness to ecological integrity we can find to protect, although it is not a condition that prevails globally.

We need to rely on the interests that are truly collective and basic first, so that all humanity can be protected through practices that support the common good. This primacy must be enforced because too many other interests as represented in various "communities" only practice and attempt to motivate practices and policies that support their own interests, not those of all humanity.

Concluding thoughts

There is a little effort, even among the most obstinate, to deny the reality of the situation regarding our basic rights and the survival of nature. Most seem to accept the dangers of global warming and the many other issues that increasingly affect us uncontrollably. Nevertheless, there are few examples in the jurisprudence that actually recognize the connection between our rights and the environmental conditions. We have noted the successful climate change case in New Zealand, and there are cases in Canada regarding fracking, and perhaps the Permanent Peoples' Tribunal (PPT) or The Hague, and even more significantly, the court in The Netherlands' revolutionary judgement that forces the Dutch government to reduce the emissions that cause climate change.

This confirms the fact that, when governments do not protect human rights, it is right and just that the law should intervene and bring its power to bear in the pursuit of the common good and justice. These are minimal results indeed, given the terrible consequences of disintegrity in all its aspects.

In the next chapter we will seek to discover whether there are any instruments, beyond the expected ones in environmental law, that might be better suited to deal with the necessity to restore integrity and control the ongoing attacks on basic human rights.

Notes

1 Ari Phillips, 2015, "There are Only Two 'BigBlobs' of Forest Remaining on Earth", 27 March, available at http://thinkprogress.org/climate/2015/03/26/3638910/all-forests-not-created-equal.
2 Nick M. Haddad et al., 2015, "Habitat Fragmentation and its Lasting Impact on Earth's Ecosystems", *Science Advances* l(2), article el500052, 20 March, available at http://advances.sciencemag.org/content/1/2/e1500052.
3 Ibid.
4 Ibid.
5 Ibid.
6 Ibid.
7 Gretchen Daily, 1997, *Nature's Services*, Island Press, Washington, DC, pp. 3–4.
8 Jonathan Patz and M. B. Hahn, 2013, "Climate Change and Health: A One Health Approach", *Current Topics in Microbiology and Immunology* 366, pp. 141–171.
9 Laura Westra, 2013, "Health and Environment: The Denied Connection", in Laura Westra, Colin Soskolne and Donald Spady (eds), *Human Health and Ecological Integrity*, Earthscan, London, pp. 7–19.
10 Secretariat of the Convention on Biological Diversity and the World Health Organization, 2015, *Connecting Global Priorities: Biodiversity and Human Health, a State of Knowledge Review*, World Health Organization, Geneva, available at www.cbd.int/health/stateofknowledge.
11 Ibid., p. 1 (emphasis added).
12 Ibid., p. 8.
13 Ibid., p. 7.
14 Richard Falk, 2015, "The Mistakes of the Global Imperial State and The Mistakes of Others", available at http://richardfalk.wordpress.com/2015/03/29/the-mistakes-of-the-global-imperial-stateand-the-mistakes-of-others.
15 Joseph Dellapenna, 2008, "A Human Right to Water: An Ethical Position or a Realizable Goal?", in Laura Westra, Klaus Bosselman, and Richard Westra (eds), *Reconciling Human Existence with Ecological Integrity*, Earthscan, London, UK, pp. 183–194.
16 USRTK, Gary Ruskin Executive Director, 2015, "USRTK Calls for Investigation of Monsanto Cover Up", 30 March, available at http://commondreams.org/newswire/2015/03/30/usrtk-calls-investigation-monsanto-cover-harassment-usda scientists.
17 Ibid.
18 Richard Westra, 2012, *The Evil Axis of Finance*, Clarity Press, Atlanta, GA.
19 The Charter of the International Military Tribunal – Annex to the Agreement for the Prosecution and Punishment of the Major War Criminals of the European Axis (hereafter "Nuremberg Charter"), 82 UNTS 279, 8 August 1945, available at https://www.icrc.org/ihl/INTRO/350?OpenDocument.
20 Ibid., article 6, II, "Jurisdiction and General Principles" (emphasis added).
21 Ibid.
22 Regina A. Robson, 2010, "Crime and Punishment: Rehabilitation as a Justification for Organized Criminal Liability", *American Business Law Journal* 47(1), pp.109–144; see *United States v. John Kelson Co.*, 86 F.304, 305–6 (ND Cal 1898).

23 Countercurrents.org, 2012, "NBA Confirms Monsanto/Mayho and Others to be Criminally Prosecuted in B. T. Brinjal Biopiracy Case", 24 May, available at www.countercurrents.org/esg240512.htm.

24 Health and Environment Alliance, 2012, "HEAL Speaks at French Senate on Pesticides and Health", available at www.env-health.org/spip.php?article1462&.

25 Ibid.

26 Theo Colborn, Dianne Dumanoski and John Peterson Myers, 1996, *Our Stolen Future*, Dutton (Penguin), New York.

27 Philippe Grandjean and Philip Landrigan, 2006, "Developmental Neurotoxicity of Industrial Chemicals", *The Lancet* 368, pp. 2167–2178; also Philippe Grandjean, 2013, *Only One Chance*, Oxford University Press, Oxford; and Philip Landrigan and Ruth Etzel, 2013, *Children's Environmental Health*, Oxford University Press, Oxford.

28 Laura Westra, 1994, *An Environmental Proposal for Ethics: The Principle of Integrity*, Rowman Littlefield, Lanham, MD.

29 Le Monde, 2012, "Condamnation de Monsanto: Une premiere qui va donner des idees", *Le Monde*, 13 February, available at www.lemondae.fr/planete/article/2012/02/13/condamnation-de-monsanto-une-premier-qui-va-donner-des-idees_1642912_3244.html.

30 Euronews, 2012, "Long-Awaited Eternit Asbestos Verdict Expected Soon", *Euronews*, 10 February, available at www.euronews.net.2012/02/10/longawaited-eternit-asbestos-verdict-expected-soon.

31 PAN-Europe, 2011, "France European Backdoor Champion on Pesticides", 26 January, www.pan-europe.info/News/PR/110126.html.

32 Council Decision of 13 July 2009, Concerning the Non-inclusion of Metam in Annex 1 to Directive 91/414/EEC, and the Withdrawal of Authorization for Plant Protection Products Containing that Substance (2009/562/EC).

33 See for instance Regulation (EC) No.1907/2006 of the European Parliament and of the Council on the Registration, Evaluation, Authorization and Restriction of Chemicals (REACH).

34 Ibid.

35 PAN-Europe, "France European Backdoor Champion on Pesticides".

36 Ibid.

37 See also Regulation EC No.1107/2009 of 21 October 2009.

38 Stephen B. Pruett, L. Peyton-Myers and Deborah E. Keil, "Toxicology of Metam Sodium", *Journal of Toxicology and Environmental Health* 2, pp. 207–222.

39 Samuel Epstein, 1978, *The Politics of Cancer*, Sierra Club Books, San Francisco, CA; Debra Davis, 2007, *The Secret History of the War on Cancer*, Basic Books, New York; Grandjean and Landrigan, "Developmental Neurotoxicity of Industrial Chemicals".

40 Emily Cassidy, 2015, "Feeding the World – Without GMOs", Environmental Working Group, 15 March, available at www.ewg.org/agmag/2015/03/feeding-world-without-gmos.

41 Wikipedia, "Hudson's Bay Company", available at http://en.wikipedia.org/wiki/Hudson's_Bay_Company.

42 Laura Westra, 2013, *The Supranational Corporation*, Brill, Leyden, The Netherlands.

43 D. Tilman, C. Balzer, J. Hill and B. L. Befort, 2011, "Global Food Demand and the Sustainable Intensification of Agriculture", Proceedings of the National Academy of Sciences USA 108(50), pp. 20260–20264; Jonathan A. Foley, 2011, "Can We Feed the World and Sustain the Planet?", *Scientific American*, 1 November, available at www.scientificamerican.com/article/can-we-feed-the-world.

44 Cassidy, "Feeding the World – Without GMOs", p. 3.

45 A. Pan et al., 2012, "Red Meat Consumption and Mortality: Results from 2 Prospective Cohort Studies", *Archives of Internal Medicine* 172(7), pp. 555–563.

46 C. H. Benbrook, 2012, "Impacts of Genetically Engineered Crops on Pesticide Use in the US in the First Sixteen Years", *Environmental Science Europe* 24(1), pp. 1–13.
47 WHO, 2012, *Report on the State of Knowledge on Endocrine Disruptors*, World Health Organization, Geneva.
48 Philippe Grandjean, 2013, *Only One Chance: How Environmental Pollution Impairs Brain Development – and How to Protect the Brains of the Next Generation*, Oxford University Press, Oxford; Landrigan and Etzel, *Children's Environmental Health.*
49 "The Manhattan Principles", as defined during the meeting titled Building Interdisciplinary Bridges to Health in a "Globalized World" held in 2004, available at www.cdc.gov/onehealth/pdfs/manhattan/twelve_manhattan_principles.pdf (accessed 31 March 2015).
50 See www.wcs.org.
51 All information on the historic background of One Health is taken from the Wikipedia page at https://en.wikipedia.org/wiki/One_Health.
52 Ibid.
53 The Manhattan Principles (emphasis added).
54 Aldo Leopold, 1949, *A Sand County Almanac, and Sketches Here & There*, Oxford University Press, New York; see also Westra, *An Environmental Proposal for Ethics.*
55 Olivier De Schutter (UN Special Rapporteur on the Right to Food), 2014, *Final Report: The Transformative Potential of the Right to Food*, UN Doc. GE.14-10537, Human Rights Council twenty-fifth session, available at www.srfood.org/en/documents, p. 3.
56 Ibid., p. 4.
57 FAO, 2013, *The State of Food Insecurity in the World 2013: The Multiple Dimensions of Food Security*, FAO, Rome, p. 8.
58 Frances Moore Lappé, Jennifer Clapp, Molly Anderson, Robin Broad, Ellen Messer, Thomas Pogge and Timothy Wise, 2013, "How We Count Hunger Matters", *Ethics and International Affairs* 27(3), pp. 251–259.
59 De Schutter, *Final Report: The Transformative Potential of the Right to Food*, p. 5.
60 Ibid., p. 4.
61 FAO, "How to Feed the World in 2050", available at http://www.fao.org/fileadmin/templates/wsfs/docs/expert_paper/How_to_Feed_the_World_in_2050.pdf.
62 De Schutter, *Final Report: The Transformative Potential of the Right to Food*, p. 5.
63 Ibid., p. 6.
64 Maude Barlow, 1999, *Blue Gold*, special report issued by the International Forum on Globalization (IFG), San Francisco, CA.
65 Landrigan and Etzel, *Children's Environmental Health.*
66 Grandjean, *Only One Chance*; see also Laura Westra, 2014, *Child Law: Children's Rights and Collective Obligations*, Springer, Berlin.
67 De Schutter, *Final Report: The Transformative Potential of the Right to Food*, p. 6; see also Arnold Tukker et al., 2011, "Environmental Impacts or Changes to Healthier Diets in Europe", *Ecological Economics* 70(10), p. 1776.
68 De Schutter, *Final Report: The Transformative Potential of the Right to Food*, p. 10.
69 Democracy Now, "Cowspiracy: As California Faces Drought, Film Links Meat Industry to Water Scarcity & Climate Change", available at www.democracynow.org/2015/4/7/cowspiracy_as_california_faces_drought_film.
70 Lindsay Abrams, 2015, "While the Superbug Crisis Grows, the Meat Industry is Using More Human Antibiotics than Ever", 19 April, accessed at www.salon.com/2015/04/10/while_the superbug crisis_grows_the_ industry_is_using_more_human_antibiotics_than_ever/?Spurce=newsletter.
71 Dinara Ziganshina, 2008, "Rethinking the Concept of the Human Right to Water", *Santa Clara Journal of International Law* 6, pp. 113–128, here p. 114. Indeed, all major covenants either recognize the right to water as a separate human right; see International Covenant on Civil and Political Rights (ICCPR), 16 December 1966,

999 UNTS 1171, 6, ILM 368; International Covenant on Economic, Social and Cultural Rights (ICESCR), 16 December 1966, 993 UNTS 3 6 ILM 383.

72 John Scanlon, Angela Cassar and Noémi Nemes, 2004, *Water as a Human Right?*, IUCN, Gland, Switzerland.

73 Convention on the Elimination of All Forms of Discrimination Against Women, 18 December 1979, 1249 UNTS 13, art. 14.

74 Convention on the Rights of the Child, 20 November 1989, 1577 UNTS 3, art. 24.

75 UN Economic and Social Council on Economic, Social and Cultural Rights, General Comment No. 15, 2002; The Right to Water (arts. 11, 12 of the International Covenant on Economic, Social and Cultural Rights), UN Doc. E/C.12/2002/11, 20 January 2003.

76 Thomas C. Mountain, 2015, "Surviving Climate Disaster in Africa's Sahel", available at www.countercurrents.org/mountain310315.htm.

77 Ibid.

78 Robert Hunziker, 2015, "Drought: Death by a Thousands Cuts", 10 April, available at www.counterpunch.org/2015/04/10/drought-death-by-a-thousands-cuts.

79 Ibid.

80 Ibid.

81 Cindy Sui, 2015, "Tackling Taiwan's Water Shortages", *BBC News*, 8 April.

82 Dale Jamieson, 1995, "Ecosystem Health: Some Preventive Medicine", *Environmental Values* 4(4), pp. 333–344.

83 IPCC, *Impacts, Adaptations and Mitigation of Climate Change: Scientific-Technical Analyses*, Report of Working Group II, Intergovernmental Panel on Climate Change, Montreal, 20 October 1995, available at www.ipcc.ch/publications_and_data/publications_and_data_reports.shtml.

84 James Kay and E. Schneider, 1994, "The Challenge of the Ecosystem Approach", *Alternatives* 20(3), pp. 1–6; see also Laura Westra, 1995, "Ecosystem Integrity and Sustainability: The Foundational Value of the Wild", in Laura Westra and John Lemons (eds), *Perspectives on Ecological Integrity*, Kluwer Academic Publishers, Dordrecht, The Netherlands, pp. 12–33.

85 RIVM, 1986, *National Environmental Outlook, 1990–2010*, Rijksinstituut voor Volksgezondheit en Milieuhygiene, Bilthoven, The Netherlands.

86 Westra, *An Environmental Proposal for Ethics*, ch. 3.

87 Ibid.

88 Ibid.

89 Theo Colborn, 1996, "Plenary Address" to IAGLR (International Association of Great Lakes Researchers), 27 May, Erindale College, Toronto, Ontario; see also Colborn et al., *Our Stolen Future*.

90 Bryan Norton, 1995, "Why I am Not a Nonanthropocentrist: Callicott and the Failure of Monistic Inherentism", *Environmental Ethics* 17(4), pp. 341–358.

91 Human Rights Council, 2015, "The Effects of Climate Change on the Full Enjoyment of Human Rights", Resolution 18/22, Office of the United Nations High Commissioner for Human Rights, 30 April; see also Office of the High Commissioner for Human Rights, 2014, *A New Climate Change Agreement Must Include Human Rights Protections for All*, 27 October, available at www.ohchr.org/Documents/HRBodies/SP/SP_To_UNFCCC.pdf.

92 Office of the United Nations High Commissioner for Human Rights (OHCHR), *The Effects of Climate Change on the Full Enjoyment of Human Rights*, available at www.thecvf.org/wp-content/uploads/2015/05/humanrightsSRHRE.pdf.

93 OHCHR, 2009, *Report of the Office of the United Nations High Commissioner for Human Rights on the Relationship between Climate Change and Human Rights*, 15 January, A/HRC/10/61, available at http://ap.ohchr.org/documents/alldocs.aspx?doc_id=14880.

94 ICESCR, General Comment 14, para. 11

95 IPCC, *Impacts, Adaptations and Mitigation of Climate Change*, Technical Summary, p. 1056.
96 Olivier De Schutter (UN Special Rapporteur on the Right to Food), 2010, Report, UN Doc. A/HRC/16/49, Human Rights Council sixteenth session, 17 December.
97 Raquel Rolnik, 2009, Report of the Special Rapporteur on Housing and Adequate Standards of Living and on the Right to Non-Discrimination in This Context, 6 August, UN Doc. A/64/25.
98 Holmes Rolston III, 2015, "After Preservation? Dynamic Nature in the Anthropocene", in Ben A. Minteer and Stephen J. Payne (eds), *After Preservation: Saving American Nature in the Age of Humans*, University of Chicago Press, Chicago, IL, pp. 32–40, here p. 34.
99 D. H. Meadows, D. L. Meadows and J. Randers, 1992, *Beyond the Limits*, Chelsea Green Publishing, Pest Mills, VT.
100 Westra, *An Environmental Proposal for Ethics.*
101 Rolston, "After Preservation?", p. 34.
102 Dave Froman, 2015, "Anthropocene and the Ozymandias", in Minteer and Payne, *After Preservation*, pp. 50–58, here p. 54 (emphasis added to qualifying words in italics).
103 John Locke, 1689, *Two Treatises of Government*, Awnsham Churchill, London, available at www.gutenberg.org/files/7370/7370-h/7370-h.htm, 2, 6.
104 Ibid., 2, 21.
105 Ibid., 5, 31 (emphasis added).
106 Reed Noss and Alan Cooperrider, 1994, *Saving Nature's Legacy*, Island Press, Washington, DC.
107 John A. Vucetich, Michael Paul Nelson and Chelsea K. Batavia, 2015, "The Anthropocene: Disturbing Name, Limited Insight", in Minteer and Payne, *After Preservation*, pp. 66–73, here p. 66.
108 Fragment 1, in Joseph Owens, 1959, *A History of Ancient Philosophy Greek*, Appleton Century Crofts, New York, p. 157.
109 Owens, *A History of Ancient Philosophy Greek*, p. 156.
110 See for instance the thorough and well-argued Kivalina Case, which unfortunately was not successful: *Native Village of Kivalina v. ExxonMobil, et al.*, CV08-1138 (ND Cal 2008).
111 Westra, *The Supranational Corporation*, ch. 4.
112 Vucetich et al., "The Anthropocene", p. 67.
113 Coplestone, 1959: 57
114 Rachel Carson, 1962, *Silent Spring*, Houghton Mifflin, Boston, MA; see also Amy Seidl, 2015, "Resembling The Cosmic Rhythms", in Minteer and Payne, *After Preservation*, pp. 186–193.
115 Seidl, "Resembling The Cosmic Rhythms", p. 187.
116 Ibid., p. 186.
117 Dwight G. Newman, 2004, "Collective Interests and Collective Rights", *American Journal of Jurisprudence* 49, pp. 127–163.
118 Roger Brownsword, 2008, *Rights, Regulation, and the Technological Revolution*, Oxford University Press, Oxford.
119 Ibid.
120 Newman, "Collective Interests and Collective Rights", p. 135.
121 Margot Salomon, 2007, *Global Responsibility for Human Rights*, Oxford University Press, Oxford.
122 Draft United Nations Declaration on the Rights of Indigenous Peoples, adopted by the UN Subcommission on Prevention of Discrimination and Protection of Minorities by the resolution 1994/45, 26 August 1994, UN Doc. E/CN./1995/2, E/CN4/Sub.2/1994/56 at 105, adopted in 2008.

123 See for instance the "arrow impossibility theorem", based upon "four reasonable conditions" to provide "a transitive ranking of social states"; Newman, "Collective Interests and Collective Rights", pp. 136–137.

124 Ibid., p. 140.

5 Ecological integrity as a basic human right and the principle of the common heritage of humankind

Introduction

> It is not enough to know what you are fighting against: you must also know what you are fighting for.[1]

This is the main reason why an all-out effort to restore the fundamental value of integrity is the necessary first step. The fight for integrity is the fight to restore the conditions of survival for life in general, not only the life of humanity. But it is through the latter that we can seek a link to the right to life, that is, one that could give us the grounds to reach a non-derogable norm, rather than additional voluntary or otherwise non-enforceable legal regimes. In this chapter we will start by reviewing the effects of the present regulatory regimes that ought to protect integrity, that is, the existing environmental regimes.

When these "effects" are fully understood in all their implications, they are far more than environmental problems: they manifest their true nature as actual attacks on humanity, direct or indirect. Globalization's emphasis on economics, combined with the immunity surrounding the US's imperialism, are clearly in evidence, for instance in the decisions handed down by the tribunal of the WTO, an institution that has no open documentation available to the general public, and most of all, one which allows no open appeals and no recourse possibility for its decisions.

In Chapter 2 we discussed the incompleteness of international environmental law. But the basic reason for the flaws exhibited by those laws is the primacy accorded to the WTO and, for North America, to NAFTA, as we shall see as we consider some of the very few (and mostly inconsequential) cases decided by those tribunals.

The WTO and the conflict between trade, health and human rights

> Article XX
>
> General Exceptions
>
> Subject to the requirement that such measures are not applied in a manner which would constitute a means of arbitrary or unjustifiable discrimination between countries where the same conditions prevail, or a disguised restriction on international trade, nothing in this Agreement shall be construed to prevent the adoption or enforcement of any contracting parties of measures …
>
> (1) necessary to protect human, animal, or plant life or health; …
>
> (2) relating to the conservation of exhaustible natural resources if such measures are made effective in conjunction with restrictions on domestic production or consumption.[2]

This document, like the Agreement on the Application of Sanitary and Phytosanitary Measures (1994), is entirely oriented to trade, not to the protection of health and the environment.[3] In the *Hormones* case, as in the other cases (*Australia/Salmon* case and the *Japan/Agricultural Products* case), the government appealing the use of substances or products judged to be harmful to human health, lost their cases.

These decisions may represent violations of human rights, but they are defended purely on economic grounds, although clearly, there are other values at stake, including democratic values, such as the right to due process. For instance, Robert Howse raises the obvious question: because of their role as transnational organizations with power over individual states, what of democracy in this context? Howse claims that democracy is not implemented by responding "to widespread fears of citizens about risks"; instead, the WTO decisions "can and should be understood not as usurping legitimate democratic choices for stricter regulations, but as enhancing the quality of rational democratic deliberations about risk and its control".[4] Howse adds that "popular choices should be respected," but only "if the choices have been made in awareness of the facts".[5] But that is precisely the point raised here: the facts provided by the corporate interests who wish to avoid regulation and their hired experts may be far removed from the true facts of the case. Right decisions are only taken after all scientific sides of a debate are heard, with those affected by the decision casting the deciding vote and the precautionary principle is brought into the decision.[6]

Perhaps the basic error lies in expecting these documents, specifically and openly oriented to deal with *trade*, to also provide health and environmental protection that we all require, and that humanity should have a "basic" right to have. However, given the lack of other instruments of equal or superior enforcement and implementation power designed for our protection, it is hard to see why we should reduce our expectations of fairness and justice, principles that govern all laws, including civil laws pertaining to trade. We need to be aware of this cardinal problem: "free trade" has been described as a "Corporate Charter of Rights and Freedoms" for Canada,[7] and the notion of an "economic Constitution for North America" was proposed by then President Ronald Reagan.[8] For a country less rich and powerful than the United States, such as Canada, the effect of WTO judgments may include "trading away one's national sovereignty",[9] and may include a number of consequences far beyond "trade" issues.[10] In some sense, what is at stake is the existence of sovereignty itself.

In the seventeenth century, Jean Bodin set out clearly a view of the limits of sovereignty: "all princes and people of the world … [are] subject to the laws of God and Nature".[11] This understanding of the limits of human planning and decision-making, even in commercial relations, is still held by many today, although God/Nature are combined in one concept. For a popular understanding, the limits of liability in insurance claims routinely exclude the effects of such disasters as earthquakes, by terming these "acts of God". Nevertheless, humanity as a whole has lost most of the understanding of its own limitations.[12] René-Jean Dupuy says:

> Humankind is engulfed by the planetary environment, even though whole people tend to behave as though they were outside of nature. In antiquity all was sacred, except humankind. Mountains, spring, the winds, and the sea were deified; people did not enjoy any particular rights. With the advent of Judeo-Christian reversed, and Man alone is sacred. Nature having become secularized, has been treated as if it were at man's disposal, indeed as if it were a reservoir of riches subject to unlimited exploitation. Today, we have begun to understand that we cannot retain this dualistic vision.[13]

But we ignore and depreciate nature and its complex processes and interactions only at our own risk and peril, as we saw in the last chapter. In fact, we are placing the very continuity of life at risk, as we increasingly impose disproportionate burdens on people of colour and people in developing countries, as well as future generations and the whole environment.[14]

Part of what is at issue is the increasing dissonance between the proliferation of explicit "green" "soft law" instruments that give primacy to our habitat and to humanity, and the even greater proliferation of "trade-as-sovereign" documents. These, for the most part, express a few green sentiments in their nonbinding Preambles perhaps, but continue to view cases and issues as "business first". In the first group, we can include such documents as the UN Convention on the Moon (1979); The Convention on the Law of the Sea (1982); the Rio Declaration (1992); the Vienna Convention of the Protection of the Ozone Layer (1985); the Montreal Protocol on Substances that Deplete the Ozone Layer (1987), as adjusted and amended in 1990, 1992 and 1995; and others pertaining to forests and to the "Common Heritage of Mankind".

All these documents make explicit the principles invoked in the International Court of Justice decision,[15] that is, the principle that states do not only have obligations to one another, but they have obligations to humanity as a whole, obligations *erga omnes*, and these are particularly directed to "respect for the rights of man and the environment".[16]

Dupuy's position parallels my own but, to be fair, "the rights of man and the environment" are by no means explicitly coupled in *Barcelona Traction.*[17] Although this pivotal case will be discussed below, it is important to understand both what the judgment does say and what it does not; hence, what might be required to bridge the gap between its explicit language and the point made by Dupuy:

> (33) When a State admits into its territory foreign investments or foreign nationals, whether natural or juristic persons, it is bound to extend to them the protection of the law and assumes obligations concerning the treatment to be afforded them. These obligations, however, are neither absolute nor unqualified. In particular, an essential distinction should be drawn between the obligations of a State towards the international community as a whole, and those arising vis-à-vis another State in the field of diplomatic protection: they are obligations *erga omnes*.
>
> (34) Such obligations derive, for example in contemporary international law, from the outlawing of acts of aggression, and of genocide, as also from the principles and rules concerning the basic right of the human persons, including protection from slavery and racial discrimination. Some of the corresponding rights of protection have entered into the body of general international law ... others are conferred by international instruments of a universal or quasi-universal character.[18]

The first step to establish the linkage to the environment that Dupuy wants to establish, is the meaning of "basic right of the human person" and their connection to "fundamental rights".[19] What is at issue here is the presence of non-derogable rights, giving rise to obligations *erga omnes*, thus, not all human rights, many of which are state-specific, like the right to a nationality, a passport, or a country's free education or health care.

However, increasingly, human rights are considered to be protected by universal obligations. Theodor Meron says: "But the most interesting feature of this development is that the growing acceptance of the *erga omnes* character of human rights has not been limited to the basic rights of the human person only".[20] Meron adds that, in fact, "one of the accomplishments of the United Nations has been to consolidate the principle that human rights are a matter of concern that the international community is entitled to discuss".[21] The next step is the need to connect, explicate, and interpret the language of *Barcelona Traction*, to render explicit the intimate relationship between human rights and environment.

I believe that there are no less than two explicit concepts one can refer to in this regard: "acts of aggression" and "the basic rights of the human person". In the previous chapters I have first argued that ecoviolence is very close to other forms of violence such as the one present in armed conflicts (Chapter 1); then I reported on the ample evidence that has emerged in recent times about the dependence of the survival and normal function of the human person, on their habitat, the environment.

If my argument in Chapter 1 is found to be plausible and the evidence provided in Chapter 2 is accepted, then the connection between the right to life, implying the right to "living",[22] hence to basic health and normal function, is clear. In this case the relation between *erga omnes* obligations proscribing acts of aggression, and outlawing breaches of the "rights of the human person" is rendered explicit. Moreover, when the acts arise out of the corporate activities of the North, and these have significant impacts on whole regions and populations in the South, then even the concept of genocide may be appropriate.

Thus, this is far more than the expression of nice sentiments about the environment or about human rights: the justification for these obligations follows logically from the very arguments that corporations use to support their rights to negotiate on a level of parity with states. If there is a difference between a crowd or a mob, and a corporate body, because of their unity of purpose, represented by the corporate intentional decision-making (CID) structure, as French argues,[23] and if that difference allows a corporation to become a separate legal entity, beyond the individual existence of those who compose it, then, if we also accept Dupuy's argument that "Humankind forms a biological community" we must also accept his conclusion: "The result is that it must constitute a legal entity."[24] It is inappropriate and logically inconsistent to say that legal entities will have standing in the law, even standing and power beyond those of legitimate states, if, and only if, they represent specific economic interests, but not if they represent the basic, biological interests of that community of life. Neither appeals to economic interests, nor even to democracy, should supersede such basic concerns, as Shue, for instance, argues.[25]

In addition, present liberal democracies do not offer the conditions and circumstances in which citizens' protection and that of their habitats can be ensured through the enactment of fully protective laws, embracing the Precautionary Principle. Reed argues:

> First, no actual democracies entirely satisfy the conditions for the generation of legitimate law. Second, not all ethical concerns can be adequately addressed through the process of law (viz., they may require more immediate action, etc.).[26]

I have argued that neither present corporate approaches, nor liberal/democratic national states' laws appear to be able to defend even the most basic rights of their citizens, especially in North America.[27] Hence, the argument that emerges is not that going beyond sovereignty is, in all cases, an unmitigated evil, but that the reasons for so doing cannot and should not be purely economic.

In general a "Common Resource" includes commercial and economic rights, but it ought to go beyond these to the primacy of the public interest. The same should be said of decisions pitting economic interests against the common interests of mankind in the preservation and defence of its life-support systems.[28] When viewed in this light, our common human moral right to the protection of nature, clearly supersedes the commercial rights of any economic group or corporation: their rights exist, but they should not trump the right to life and life-support conditions for all humanity. Thus, it is clear, the protection of the common interests of all life must be found elsewhere, beyond any existing environmental regulatory regime.

A possible role for the principle of the common heritage of humankind

> The international community has developed several types of legal regimes to govern natural resources. In general terms these include … recognizing property as the common heritage of mankind – or, to use a more contemporary phrase, the common heritage of humankind (CH) – whereby all manage resources and share in the rewards of exploiting them, even if they are not able to participate in that exploitation.[29]

In this section we will consider CH as the principle which should exhibit the strongest, most protective characteristics of any international legal regime: as well, it should represent the best antidote to the principle of "economics and trade first" we saw demonstrated in the position and the decisions of the WTO. The same situation obtains in the position and the decisions of NAFTA and its tribunals. It is even more explicitly expressed in the language of the Trans-Pacific Partnership (TPP), in the "Environment" chapter,[30] which repeats the familiar language we have seen in the "Chapeau" of the WTO and in NAFTA. Consider for instance the following:

> The Parties further recognize that it is inappropriate to establish or use their environmental laws or other measures in a manner which would constitute a disguised restriction on trade or investment between the Parties.[31]

Then there is the very short article 20.8 on "Opportunities for Public Participation":

> Each Party shall seek to accommodate requests for information regarding the Party's implementation of this Chapter.
>
> Each Party shall make use of existing, or establish new, consultative mechanisms, such as national advisory committees, to seek views on matters related to the implementation of this Chapter. Such mechanisms may comprise persons with relevant experience, as appropriate, including *experience in business*, natural resource conservation and management, or other environmental matters.[32]

As in all such organizations, "consultative mechanisms", the "persons with relevant experience", include primarily "experience in business" before environmental concerns; further, there is no mention of public health concerns. Yet even the CH in the formulation cited, speaks of "natural resources" as "property", to be "managed" and exploited, so that the common aspects appear to reflect exploitation, not preservation for the future of mankind.

The integrity of natural systems, taking into consideration the irreparable damages inflicted by fragmentation (as we showed earlier regarding forests), needs to be considered a unitary, common heritage, that is, a united "heritage" of the greatest value, a value that is only such for humanity, if it is *not* "managed" or "exploited" today, without losing its value for mankind in the future.

I would argue that the CH, in its primary sense, encompasses historical, traditional value, existing in the past, but extending *as it is* into the future. Speaking of the CH, Noyes asks: "What are its component elements?", and "What is its legal status?".[33] The first clear element pertains to its range of application: it pertains to areas "beyond the limits of national jurisdiction and to natural resources found there".[34]

For that reason its clearest areas of application are to be found in the 1982 Law of the Sea,[35] and the 1979 Agreement Governing the activities of States on the Moon and other Celestial Bodies;[36] these areas, especially the one defined in the LOS, are "defined as the seabed and ocean floors and subsoil thereof, beyond the limits of national jurisdiction". These treaties incorporate the ideals by the principle and the concepts present in its development through history:

> In 1995, Malta invoked the CH principle in proposing that the UN Trusteeship Council be transformed "from a guardian of dependent territories to a body that acts as guardian and trustee of the global concerns and the common concerns in the interest of present and future generations", a proposal directed at conserving the international environment.[37]

However, without the protection of ecological integrity, neither the "interests of future generations", nor the "international environment" will be protected for the future. That is the case argued in the previous chapters of this work. Yet, the understanding which follows upon the previous remarks of the author (Noyes) who cites this important letter, include such concepts as "exploitation" although that concept appears to conflict with the language of the Letter of Malta the author also cites.

It is interesting to consider the six elements Noyes cites as "the elements of the CH principle":

- a prohibition of acquisition of, or exercise of sovereignty over, the area or resources in question;
- the vesting of rights to the resources in question in humankind as a whole;
- reservation of the area in question for peaceful purposes;
- protection of the natural environment;

- an equitable sharing of benefits associated with the exploitation of the resources in question, paying particular attention to the interests and the needs of developing states; and
- governance via a common management regime.

When we consider each element separately, it is clear that some support the interpretation here proposed as primary. For instance, the denial of the exercise of sovereignty (limited though it appears to be); the rights to the resources being vested in "humankind as a whole" (and the concept does not limit humankind to the presently existing human); the emphasis on peaceful purposes; the protection of the natural environment; but "sharing benefits" is not beneficial if the benefits in question are related to the economic exploitation of the resources, thus to their possible diminution or even elimination in relation to future.

Perhaps we need to apply our conceptual analysis more stringently to the various "elements" in order not to tacitly allow the presence of conflicting elements both within the principle and in relation to the protection of integrity. The concept of CH implies first of all (a) something of great value; and (b) something that is to be *inherited* by humankind. An example might be for instance a great artwork, such as the David by Michelangelo (presently in the Galleria dell'Accademia in Firenze), or the Mona Lisa (presently in the Louvre in Paris): it is easy to agree that such masterpieces represent part or elements of CH. But it is difficult to speak of "exploiting" them, beyond showing them in a museum or art gallery. Their "benefits" cannot be shared literally, to enrich individuals or communities, except insofar as these masterpieces enrich humanity as a whole, provided they are not tampered with.

The same understanding persists also in the "immaterial" or – better yet – the "intangible cultural patrimony of humanity".[38] What are the elements of this aspect of the CH principle? There are five elements that define the Intangible Cultural Heritage:

(a) oral traditions and expressions, including language as a vehicle of the intangible cultural heritage;
(b) performing arts;
(c) social practices, rituals and festive events;
(d) knowledge and practices including nature and the universe:
(e) traditional craftsmanship.[39]

The major masterpieces mentioned above, like major works of poetry, philosophy or music, are unitary, they continue to enrich humanity only as long as no one interferes with their integrity: dividing a painting or a musical score in many parts in order to apportion the various parts to members of the human collectivity would destroy the works.

But performances, practices and traditional events are such that different communities could "share" in the sense of participating at different times and places: they do not need the same integrity and unity as the masterpieces named above. Hence it is vital to confront what I consider to be the most basic aspect of the CH principle: its protection of the greatest values in their original form, and its supreme respect for the past, its traditions and its historical persistence into the future. As well, we cannot forget its clear defence of the rights pf humanity as a whole, against the partisan and mostly short-sighted interests of sovereign states. In this sense it is perhaps the only instrument that explicitly embraces the UN Declaration of Human Rights, in its protection of what is pre-eminently valuable for all of us, thus repeating the UN's words, "We, the people ...".

In fact, if we reflect on this brief analysis, the elements and components of the CH principle may well be more diverse than those for which we argued for ecological integrity, because they include cultural and artistic elements beyond the biological/ecological ones defended by the principle of integrity.[40] Yet these purely human aspects do not negate the primacy of those that are exclusively biological, any more than all human rights, be they political, social or cultural, depend exclusively on the existence and the primacy of the right to life, without which no further human activity or interest is possible.

Judge Christopher Weeramantry has argued for the indivisibility of the concept of human rights in all its aspects and applications[41] so that life, health and the ability to function and think like a human depend absolutely on the biological integrity of each human being.[42]

As we saw in the earlier chapters, especially in Chapter 2, there is an ongoing disconnect in law between environmental regulation and the protection of public health, that emerges in both instruments and the related jurisprudence. But the clearest connection between the two is in evidence most clearly in the recent research regarding the development of the human brain and nervous system from conception, so that the biological and intellectual/reasoning aspects of a developing human are shown to be inescapably interconnected as any harmful exposure to the former (the brain) has grave and lasting effects upon the latter (intellectual capacities and nervous system).[43]

An aside on ecological integrity, health and the development of normal function in the child

> We live in a world in which man-made chemicals have become part of everyday life. It is clear that some of these chemical pollutants can affect the endocrine (hormonal) system and certain of these endocrine disruptors may also interfere with the developmental processes of human and wildlife species.[44]

This report, belated, and deliberately inconclusive though it is, is extremely important in two senses. First, as it supports scientifically the true "right to development" that should apply to children, so that the wording of legal instruments we have cited, if modified, should manifest the true meaning of the protection of "the right to life" and of "the right to the means requisite for the child's healthy development". But industrial activities that involve countless substances known to be endocrine disruptors (EDCs), should then be controlled and possibly either eliminated or forced to comply with impartial (not in-house) testing for the safety of their products and processes.

These industries should be subject to government oversight and allowed to operate only under tight controls, as the worst period of vulnerability for the child occurs during its foetal and pre-birth life, when the affected child has no way to avoid such exposures. Second, the research and discovery of multiple hormonal exposures from EDCs also confirms without the shadow of a doubt the reasons why abortion is the deliberate, often cruel, killing of a human being.

All feminist arguments regarding the difference between the preborn and the born child, and the sharp difference between one state and the other, distinct enough to justify killing without any specific reason in the former period, while it becomes a crime in the latter, fail, once the continuity between the two periods is confirmed scientifically, by exposure in state (a), followed by consequences in state (b).

Support for abortion depends absolutely on the "discontinuity" between foetal life and the life of the born child. But all scientific evidence available long before this Report was published (see for instance all scientific research on thalidomide, from the 1950s on, and several WHO reports in later years; as well as the scientific evidence on both wildlife species and humans by Theo Colborn and colleagues),[45] contradicts sharply what I will term the "discontinuity thesis" which treats the preborn as a different creature altogether, or even by most extreme theories, as a part of the mother's body, contrary to DNA and blood type evidence.

Thus, as we review the evidence, cautiously presented as it is probably because of the participation in the Report of the World Bank and other financial institutions who participated in the editing of the document, we need to keep in mind how and why the EDC findings eliminate completely the argument that there is no child present before birth. EDC's research confirms the presence of the developing foetus from the earliest stages of gestation and demonstrates the results of exposures on various areas of the body of the developing child. The report states:

> Timing of exposures is also critical during development likely lead to irreversible effects, whereas the effects of adult exposures seem to go away when the EDC is removed.[46]

This is the most significant feature of EDCs; they target specifically foetal development, and in so doing, they exceed even the expected harm to the child, as they also play a role

> in the increased incidences of reproductive diseases, endocrine-related cancers, behavioural and learning problems, including ADHD, infectious diseases, asthma and perhaps obesity and diabetes in humans.[47]

The ubiquitous presence of EDCs indicates how many of today's prevalent diseases may be traced back to these exposures, as "many of the most prevalent diseases are associated with the endocrine system". In fact most "complex non-communicable diseases have both a genetic and an environmental component".[48] The report is extremely cautious in the presentation of its findings, as it states that "as much as 24% of human diseases are at least in part due to environmental factors".[49]

But the WHO's earlier reports paint quite a different picture with much higher percentages attributed to environmental factors. For instance, the recent research linking EDC exposure to obesity and diabetes opens a whole new world of after birth harms, including cardiovascular disease and many cancers due to the initial foetal exposures thus further aggravating the import of attack to the child.

The fact that the initial exposures during gestation generate not only immediate, but also future effects, both medium and long-term, and that these are largely irreversible as long as they occur to the preborn, irrevocably link EDC exposure to the rights of the child, and through them, to human rights in general:

> exposure to hormones or EDCs during development in utero and in infancy and early childhood (in humans) can have permanent effects if the exposure occurs when a specific tissue is developing. These effects may only become visible decades later. This is called developmental programming.[50]

Of course not all tissues stop developing at birth, as both brain and reproductive systems continue to do so for some time after birth. But it is the developmental factor of each tissue that determines its vulnerability, and the earlier period is clearly the most receptive time for irreversible harms.

These harms represent particularly grave effects as they may transcend the present individual, to continue harming future generations. A whole legacy of abnormal development and disease initiated with the "invisible" preborn, but reaching far into the future, must be stopped at its inception, hence the documents and instruments which purport to defend and support the rights of the child should be the first and most important bastions of defence.

Before continuing discussion, it is important to acknowledge that even the preambles of many international and domestic instruments which refer to the "rights of future generations", given the recent research on the role and effects of EDCs, should add protocols referring to those substances in order to protect not only the present child, but also future children and adults.

A "new branch of paediatrics": the developing field of "children's environmental health"

> Children's environmental health is based on a very inclusive definition of childhood. It is concerned with environmental exposures that occur during pregnancy as well as in infancy, childhood and adolescence. It considers prenatal exposures prior to conception that may influence the health of children.[51]

The "new brand of paediatrics" emphasizes and supports a "new" or rediscovered reality that is neither acknowledged nor considered in law, either in national or international regimes. It is from that standpoint that this work has been argued. Landrigan and Etzel state that this new branch of medicine is "highly interdisciplinary", as they acknowledge links with a number of medical specialties, but also to "architecture, urban planning, social work, education, ecology, economics and political science".[52]

The sad part about this otherwise inclusive list, is that without the presence of strong laws, the wealth of scientific discoveries that underlie the chapters listed in this textbook, in fact the very research upon which the work of Landrigan and Etzel is based, will not succeed in advancing the rights of children to health. Essentially, the early discovery that measles or rubella were contagious would not have succeeded in preventing epidemics and contagion among children, unless the quarantine of affected patients were made mandatory. Similarly, the vaccine for pertussis, polio and any number of diseases, would not promote public health, without the requirement for vaccination in almost all developed countries.

Clearly, the science, the discoveries, come first, and are basic. However, they remain the necessary first step, only insufficient without strong coercive measures to implement the protection of children. The reality is that the "epidemiological transition"[53] is starting to reverse the gains in children's health, and the decreases in children's mortality due to infectious diseases, which are now largely under control, at least in developed countries, whereas "Today the major pediatric health challenges are chronic diseases, asthma, obesity, learning disabilities, autism, attention deficit disorder and type 2 diabetes. These diseases are on the rise."[54]

The origins of the "epidemiological transition" in children's health were first noted in the aftermath of Hiroshima and Nagasaki, in the "epidemics of leukemia in the children who survived", perhaps the first example of those toxic exposures.[55] Even more obviously related to harm arising from the pre-birth exposures suffered by the foetus, were the results of thalidomide exposure,[56] and that of girl babies exposed "in utero to diethylstilbestrol".[57] Landrigan and Etzel discuss these "sentinel" cases,[58] but although some of these victims might have received some compensation eventually, the overwhelming majority of them did not.

As well, no sooner were some of these threats neutralized or ameliorated, the ongoing manufacture of new industrial chemicals, most of which are only subject to in-house testing by their own manufacturers, continued the history of damaging exposures of children with impunity. The basis for those harms had already been identified, that is, the children's special nature, biology and development which disclosed the previously unacknowledged "exquisite vulnerability of children".[59] For example:

> Organophosphate pesticides provide an example. The half-life of the widely used organophosphate chlorpyrigos in the blood-stream of an adult is about 6 hours. But in an infant the half-life of chlorpyrigos is 36 hours, which means that in an infant this biologically active molecule has much more time to cause cellular injury.[60]

In fact the "chemical environment" of children attacks them through the food they eat, the water they drink, the air they breathe: the exposure starts in utero, and continues through the earliest days as their life. But the starting point of the problem is the failure to use independent testing of those substances:

> Widespread failure to test new chemicals for toxicity before they come to market is the most worrisome aspect of recent rapid increases in chemical production.[61]

The failure to test responsibly results in no information on the potential developmental toxicity of most chemicals currently in use.[62] Nor should this failure surprise, as all industrial chemicals are not only subject to in-house testing by the very industries that produce them, and therefore gain directly from their acceptance and diffusion. But this fact also ensures that the interaction of chemical exposures is never studied, evaluated, let alone made public or legislated. The problem is rendered even worse by the presence of the most powerful pesticide manufacturers, both within democratic Western countries' governments, the US, as participants in the legislative processes of major legal regimes.

As well, their presence is active in numerous lobbies, not only in North America but also in Europe. Yet the US remains the most dangerous location from the standpoint of the protection of children's health, after President Obama enacted the Monsanto Protection Act in 2012,[63] which ensures not only that Monsanto cannot be sued right now, no matter what harms their pesticides produce, but also that they cannot be sued even in the future. It is somewhat reassuring that – in contrast – Europe does not have such laws. In contrast, France has been the first country to condemn and jail a Monsanto CEO after grave health effects produced by one of their pesticides, on Paul Francois, a farmer, in 2013.[64]

These scientific and economic realities conflict directly with children's rights. Therefore, unless they are acknowledged, rendered visible to the public and – most of all – unless laws and regulations are enacted to control the problems they create, present and future children will continue to be harmed.

The natural heritage and the *travaux préparatoire* for the UNESCO World Heritage Convention

> There is no requirement that "natural areas" be unique or one of a kind only that they be "of outstanding universal value".[65]

The *travaux préparatoires* discuss in some detail both the cultural and the natural heritage. Of course the scientific elements that confirm the irreplaceable universal value of integrity were not known in 1973, so that we must expect less specificity than we would like from this document. Nevertheless, a section titled "Goals and Scope of the Convention" attempts definitions of both the cultural and the natural heritage. For instance, "the definition of 'natural heritage' is divided into (1) natural features, (2) special formations and areas (e.g. game reserves), and (3) natural sites and parks".[66]

Meyer adds that it is unclear whether the significant area of a large region of the world could be considered "of outstanding universal value"[67] was primarily concerned with the natural heritage. Some of the areas considered worthy of protection, even whole "geographical areas or regions", were notable not only for their "natural beauty", but also for being considered "the habitat of endangered, rare … animals and plants". In all cases, the protection was to be extended for all areas under consideration, though not for the individual animals or plants.

It is worth noting that at that time the science of ecosystems, their functions and services, was only beginning to be studied and discussed, so we could not expect that the implications for the future of humanity would be fully appreciated, any more than they were at the time of the writing of the Charter of the Forest.

However, by the time the present Convention was enacted, states were in power, not just barons with feudal holdings, and it was these states that held *de facto*, as well as legal, control of the areas to be protected. Yet the Convention acknowledged that the states were not permitted to reach decisions regarding what they considered to be their own areas of "natural heritage"; article 3 of the Convention "does not permit each state to determine unilaterally that an area or site in their territory is of 'outstanding universal value' for the purpose of inclusion in the World Heritage List".[68]

Hence, only the World Heritage Committee can decide whether or not an area possesses universal value.[69] The Convention's ability to supersede state decisions and interests in favour of the common interest of humanity is the most important aspect of this document, from the standpoint of achieving an ecological form of governance, but it is not clear at this time what are the qualifications of those who make the final decisions regarding what is worthy of protection. No doubt, the state parties should have the primary obligation to protect the areas listed by the World Heritage Committee. But, if they do not, it is necessary to ensure that protection is imposed and enforced, despite the state's interests. An example might be the presence of the CH Principle's protection in an area as vital for the curbing or reduction of global warming as the Amazon rainforest. Even if we set aside the importance of the biodiversity of the region and the rights of the Indigenous communities it houses, the role and function of the area's natural systems regarding the future of humanity is undeniable, thus the existence of its "outstanding universal value", as mentioned in articles 1 and 2.[70]

The states that are parties to the convention, undertake "a duty to avoid taking measures which might damage directly or indirectly the cultural and natural heritage referred to in articles 3 and 2, situated in the territory of other state parties",[71] although "unintentional damage" caused by pollution did not impose strict liability on the offending state.[72]

The Intergovernmental World Heritage Committee governs membership, rules and procedures, as well all the tasks of

> (1) defining the criteria on the basis of which a property is selected for inclusion in the two lists [e.g. cultural or natural heritage]; (2) selecting the properties; (3) determining the order of priority for granting international

> assistance; (4) deciding on uses of the World Heritage Fund, and seeking ways and taking steps toward increasing these resources; (5) receiving and studying requests from state parties for international assistance; and (6) granting that assistance.[73]

The persons serving on this committee are "qualified" either in the field of cultural or in that of natural heritage (article 9(3)). Nevertheless the presence of two established committees was rejected in favour of the committee setting up two sub-committees instead; as well, NGOs were permitted to participate in the committee's decisions in an advisory capacity.[74] Of course given that all such decisions are in the hands of the committee, both the range and the depth of "expertise" of those specified as experts for the natural heritage sub-committee, and the selection/acceptance of participating NGOs, depend on the decisions of a committee whose openness to ideas and depth of preparation may not be the optimum standard required to ensure the natural heritage for humanity.

Thus, although the CH appears perhaps the best possible instrument with which to approach a problem that involves the whole world, the problem is too grave and urgent to leave to other non-binding regulatory regimes. However, this cursory discussion of how the document functions indicates that the CH principle is not a panacea as it stands, but that it offers some hope, even as it may need further adjustments.

The common heritage of humankind and the defence of ecointegrity

> Kemal Baslar would add the explicit requirement that only those natural and cultural resources which globally affect the survival and welfare of mankind can be exploited, conserved or protected under the common heritage regime. Others suggest that the "common concern" concept, important in international environmental law, is distinct and weaker than the CH principle, not incorporating other elements of the CH principle.[75]

But the explicit requirement cited is not something to be established once and for all time, especially by legal scholars alone: the "survival and welfare" of mankind are too vital, too grave, to allow their determination to be decided without the input of expert ecologists, biologists, epidemiologists, toxicologists, and perhaps even the input of the WHO with its experts, but without the insidious presence of corporate/state interests.

Moreover, the "common concern" is a much weaker concept: we are "concerned" about the weather on the weekend, about our children's grades in school, about the state of our investments, about any number of things that have no impact on the survival of humanity. In addition, a "common heritage" with no specific present, or even future "inheritor" is clearly intended for future generations and must retain its intrinsic value, without diminution; as it cannot be divided or altered in any way today, as that would entail it would not retain its value tomorrow.

The common survival, both biological and intellectual, can only be based on whatever will provide for that survival, not for something to be exploited today for specific, rather than common interests, especially the economic concerns implicit in "exploitation". The only necessary "management" for natural areas, is the strict control, based on recent science, of *our* self-interested economic activities, whether state-supported or not.[76]

Can the comparison with ecological integrity here proposed be sustained? Current scholarship, whether scientific or legal, simply avoids any mention of ecological integrity for the most part and for the reasons outlined in the first chapters of this work. But circumlocutions abound, as they claim novelty for their work, even hinting at a "breakthrough", while arguing for what is basically the same concept, involving the same values. According to ecologist E. O. Wilson in a recent interview:

> I'm confident we can go from 10% to 50% coverage, land and sea. A large part of my new book is devoted to where [that 50%] is, what's in it, how it can be pieced together. It could be an immense reserve that still exists, like in the Atlas mountains of Mongolia; in the Taiga, the major wilderness areas of Congo; in Papua, New Guinea, The Amazon – these can be made inviolate reserves; they can be pieced together.[77]

Is this a quest for integrity? It is, without a doubt, a plea for rewilding, but it is (a) limited in the sense that its goal is to save "the Earth", with its wild components, but without any acknowledgment of the fact that we, humans, are part of the nature he intends to save, and also depend upon the preservation of large portions of the Earth's integrity for our own survival; and (b) a total disregard not only for the copious work on integrity and rewilding published since the early nineties, but also for similar pleas, albeit encompassing only North America, published by Reed Noss, and especially by Noss and Alan Cooperrider.[78] Hence hardly a "breakthrough" in the sense of a totally new discovery, although it is a reminder of a long ago argument, based on fresh research.

But the gravest problem of this "breakthrough" can be found in the author's total lack of awareness of the law and of the political climate within which this research should unfold. We noted the situation of tribunals such as those of NAFTA and the WTO, which function, presumably, to impart justice through their decisions, regarding environmental and health issues; but without any expert in either field to discuss and direct the proceedings. The same can be said of Wilson's work, but in reverse: here we read the work of a renowned ecologist, who pronounces on matters in his own field, but without any apparent awareness of the impossibility of seeking the rewilding he advocates without seeking first a radically changed legal climate, and radically altered institutions in the present geopolitical situation.

We too need to discover the status of the principle to which we appeal: what is the legal status of the CH principle?

> Some have argued that it sets out a fundamental and non-derogable norm, constituting a *jus cogens* obligation ... some have concluded that the principle has attained the status of customary international law ...[79]

This paragraph indicates that perhaps the CH principle is "too indeterminate and too lacking in state practice and *opinio juris*" to be treated as international customary law, but that is not the claim advanced here. It is best to set out the argument this work proposes in sequence:

1. Ecological integrity reflects a fundamental value based on the historical, natural development of various areas of the Earth;
2. although human projects necessarily affect the optimum ecological conditions of many areas, a balance of wild zones and exploited ones, with the latter controlled so as not to impact gravely on the wild, is absolutely required;
3. to protect "enough" areas of ecological integrity is necessary in order to ensure that the Earth's conditions are not deteriorating to the point where the organisms it supports with its natural services (including human beings) are harmed;
4. hence, to protect ecological integrity is, essentially, to protect the best possible means to protect humanity and to defend its survival;
5. the basis of that survival is something to which humanity as a whole has a right: it is its common heritage, something to sustain it now, but which needs protecting, defending the earth's ability to continue its natural future development;
6. therefore, in conclusion, given that both the CH principle and the protection of ecological integrity are intended to protect the historically established conditions humanity needs in order to survive (including both a physical survival and that of its evolving cultural development), the CH principle appears to be the ideal vehicle for the protection of integrity in law, even though for now, the CH principle applies primarily to areas that are not under state control. However,
7. the importance of the CH principle and the defence of integrity should have a much wider reach, because to limit its jurisdiction only to the areas beyond state sovereignty, is insufficient for the protection of integrity, which needs protection both within and without state borders;
8. yet there is a precedent for the approach proposed in (7) in the "intangible heritage", which also exists primarily, if not exclusively, within the cultural enclaves of individual nations, yet the CH is expected to supersede the regulatory regimes of the state;
9. the reasons for bypassing state rule (as in (8) above) is that the intangible heritage is of irreplaceable value for humanity;
10. the same can be said *a fortiori* about ecological integrity, as the heritage in question supports both the life and the ability to be intellectually and culturally active of humankind; finally,

> 11 international law is no longer simply aimed, as the expression implies, at relation between states. After the 1948 Declaration of Human Rights, and the proliferation of multiple human rights instruments supported by *jus cogens* norms, human rights transcends state borders, hence so should the most important principles designed in defence of those rights.

The Magna Carta and the Forest Charter as the origin of legal human rights

> The Charter of the Forest was first issued on November 6, 1217 as a complementary charter to the Magna Carta from which it evolved. It was re-issued in 1225, with a number of minor changes to the wording, and then was joined too by the Magna Carta in the Confirmation of Charters in 1297. In contrast to the Magna Carta which dealt with the rights of barons, it provided some real rights, privileges and protections for the common man against the abuses of the encroaching aristocracy.[80]

The Forest Charter is without doubt the "first ecological charter in history", but it is more than an environmental regulatory regime, it is also the first document that grants "liberties … to the common man".[81] The Magna Carta was a document forced upon King John by the nobles and barons at the time, although he attempted to revoke it. After John's death in 1216, in 1217 Henry III re-affirmed it through his advisers (he was only 9 years old when he inherited the title), and it was Henry III who proclaimed the Charter of the Forest.[82]

Not only are these Charters unique in their scope, but connection is itself a breakthrough for the acknowledgment of the interface between environmental rights and human rights. The Magna Carta was written first and it encompasses a number of rights we take for granted today. For example, it put an end to litigants having to pay the King in order to have their cases heard: it fixed a specific time for the holding of courts of justice and ensured that courts were held in the counties where the involved people lived; finally it established that after securing the King's portion, the rest of a personal estate would go to a man's wife and children; it also ensured that uniform weights and measures prevailed in the land.[83]

In addition, the Charter of the Forest (the longest lived English statute, only eliminated in 1971) regulated the forests of the land:

> In many ways the Charter of the Forest was the first statute to protect the environment and to provide for the wise use of the land. Courts of the Forest were established, Courts that persist today even after the repeal as such of the Charter of the Forest.[84]

Some of the provisions of this Charter include treating the "forest" as a commons, but the forest meant also cultivated fields and villages and the green "commons" were to be used to graze pigs, as well as to make use of the products of the forest; its wood could be freely used (within reason). The English translation reads as follows:

> In the first place, all the forests which King Henry, our grandfather, made forest shall be viewed by good and law-worthy men and if he made forest any wood that was not his demesne to the injury of him whose wood it was, it shall be disafforested. And if he made his own wood forest, it shall remain forest, saving common of pasture and other things in that forest, to those who were accustomed to have them previously.[85]

Also:

> Every free man shall agist his wood in the forest as he wishes and have his pannage. We grant also that every free man conduct his pigs through our demesne wood freely and without impediment to agist them in his own woods or everywhere he wishes. And if the pigs of any free man shall spend one night in our forest he shall not on that account be so prosecuted that he loses anything of his own ...[86]
>
> Every free man henceforth without being prosecuted make in the wood or in land he has in forest a mill, a preserve, a pond, a marl-pit, a ditch, or arable outside the covert in arable land, on condition that it does not harm any neighbour.[87]

In addition, there are articles that assure free men they will be freed, if being held for an offence regarding the forest; foresters and beadles shall not exact payment for any personal/family use of forest (as above); finally no one shall "lose life or limb" because of taking venison or anything else connected with the forest.[88]

It is easy to see the importance of the charter: not only is it an environmental regulatory regime, but it is the first legal document that clearly couples the environment and human rights, perhaps the only one to do so explicitly to date, and we shall consider some other recent proposals for ecological governance in the next chapter. But this Charter remains unique in prescribing free use of natural products of the forest, but only insofar as such use does not deprive or otherwise harm others.

It is incredible that such an obvious limitation of natural or legal persons appears to have been quietly forgotten, or set aside when, in contrast, aside from environmental matters, both civil and criminal law demand such limits of all our activities. Moral theory established the limits of our freedom, as does law. If those limits were clearly perceived and accepted in 1217, it is hard to see why today legal persons and organizations can advance their economic interests without any consideration of those limits.

In fact, although ostensibly the motivation for switching from the concept of the "common heritage of mankind" to the "common concern of humanity", was said to be climate change issues and the concern expressed regarding the Convention on Biological Diversity (CBD), the lack of meaningful action which followed the Rio Convention of 1992 when those concerns surfaced for the first time, seems to suggest otherwise. Perhaps what was of "concern" was the possibility of the imposition of limits to the ongoing oil-related and other extractive activities, that suggested a weaker expression.

Nevertheless, in the UK access to the commons persisted until the "enclosure movements". In fact, capitalism arose in agrarian England as the economic motive and competitiveness replaced traditional values in the "enclosure movements". The "enclosures" provided "the most famous redefinition of property rights": they eliminated the commons, with no regard for human rights[89]. Philosopher John Locke defended the right to property above all, although he predicated his defence upon ensuring that enough would be left to be held in common. But he also espoused the defence of "improvements" as needed to impose value upon nature, an argument that supported the policies of his master, the Earl of Shaftsbury.

Through his friendship with Jefferson, the Lockean arguments filtered into the American Declaration of Independence. But these enclosure movements, brutal though they were in their effects against the people, only started what eventually became known as the "Tragedy of the Commons".[90] What we encounter today, in the primacy of the economic motive over and above human rights including the right to a safe and healthy habitat, is the final "enclosure movement": it is once again mostly the poor and dispossessed of the world who are shut out of the natural global commons.

The benefits that would accrue to them are no longer available: whatever is left of the commons has become someone's property, and is used as such. Even the simplest "natural goods" are no longer available freely: clean air, pure water, safe sunlight, safe foods, all are unavailable to the poor. Drinking water must be bought; sunscreen is needed to protect us against the sun; both travel to the few locations that can boast of "clean air", or at least housing removed from hazardous industrial operations; food in areas of famine and safely organically grown food where it is available, but it is laced with toxic substances: all are commercial goods.

As Wood points out, the very notion of "improvement" as originally conceived is problematic: "we might like to think about the implications of a culture in which the word for 'making better' is rooted in the word for making monetary profit". [91] What was at stake then, as it is now, is first and foremost the existence of the most basic human rights: that of respect for human life, for human "security and subsistence",[92] long before questions of religious or sexual rights were at issue. Dispossessed farmer/tenants in seventeenth-century agrarian England had no way of supporting themselves or their families. Today many of us, especially in developed Western democracies can – in fact – support ourselves, but our life and health are under attack nevertheless.

The language of "attacks" to describe the results of unsafe, unhealthy habitats upon us, is particularly apt as it emphasizes two main points connected to the law, one historical, the other moral. I have described the relation between what I term "ecoviolence", that is violence perpetrated in and through the environment elsewhere.[93] The "attacks" of which I speak deprive humanity of their basic rights. "Basic rights are the morality of the depths",[94] they represent "everyone's minimum reasonable demands upon the rest of humanity".[95] Subsistence rights include the bare necessities we all need, from our habitat's conditions of "unpolluted air, unpolluted water, adequate food, adequate clothing, adequate shelter …".[96] We note that although some of these subsistence rights are at least present in the language of the Universal Declaration of Human Rights,[97] neither the International Covenant on Economic, Social and Cultural Rights (1966)[98] nor the International Covenant on Civil and Political Rights (1966),[99] specifies that, beyond the right to life, the triad of air/water/food that is safe, hence supportive of life, is an actual right. The Convention Concerning the Protection of the World Cultural and Natural Heritage[100] appears to have been the next international instrument to take seriously some of the rights supported by the Forest Charter, by stating that some natural features of the world must be protected, hence the basic natural features that define ecological integrity could and should be included in that "heritage", given the fundamental value integrity presents for humanity as a whole. This position should be accepted and included although it is not at present explicitly stated.

No doubt, the most wonderful natural features in the world, such as the Niagara Falls in Canada and other such unique landscapes, merit both the "common concern" and the title of valued "common heritage": as it must be protected as unique as it is, with no alterations. But the protection of multiple areas of ecological integrity, perhaps even the 50 per cent proposed by E. O. Wilson, should be considered prior to cultural concerns, as it is basic to humanity's very survival.

Possible future developments?

> While notable achievements have been made within a few regional seas, so far there is no process that is universally accepted and could apply on a world basis to establish a network of marine environments protected in areas beyond national jurisdiction.[101]

What is at stake is the establishment of a "future global regime for marine protected areas".[102] In May 2014 Greece prepared a submission to the Working Group of the CHM on behalf of the European Union, as they suggested an evocative acronym for a network seeking to identify and protect marine discoveries: UlySSES ("Universally Selected Sites of Environmental Significance"). The emphasis remains, at best, on the equitable exploitation of rare forms of life, adapted to live under extreme conditions.[103]

The present conditions of land areas, for the most part under the control of states, as well as the existence of numerous uncatalogued and unstudied plants and animals, might represent a similar case, meriting the appeal to the common heritage as well as the rare marine resources. In fact, in 2006 State parties took contrasting positions regarding the CHM and UNCLOS:

> Several delegations reiterated their understanding that the marine genetic resources beyond areas of national jurisdiction constituted the common heritage of mankind and recalled article 140 of the convention, which provides that the activities in the Area shall be carried out for the benefit of mankind and that

> particular considerations should be given to the interests and needs of developing States, including the need for these resources to be used for the benefit of present generations and to be preserved for future generations.[104]

In contrast, other states opted for regulations that would aligned instead with the "freedom of the high seas", and for "unrestricted exploitation of genetic resources of the deep seabed".[105] The United Nations Convention on the Law of the Sea (UNCLOS), "a cornerstone in the field of codification of international law", has been rightly qualified as a constitution of the oceans.[106] Nevertheless, as Scovazzi justly points out, that treaty is a product of its time, thus, like most legal instruments related to the environment, it could not anticipate later scientific discoveries.

A prime example of the need to adjust earlier legal documents to incorporate recent and pertinent science, is the arbitration mentioned in the well-known Separate Opinion of Judge Christopher Weeramantry in the 1997 *Gabčíkovo-Nagymaros* case.[107] In fact, we have been appealing to this basic principle all along: all the damages arising from disintegrity could be mitigated or even rectified, by a timely adjustment of environmental laws and human rights law, if they could simply be altered to incorporate what current science now proves.

And this is what might perhaps happen if a "third UNCLOS implementation agreement" were to result in a "global and more coherent vision" and eventually, "move from the technical to the political and legal level and start the formal negotiations for a binding instrument".[108] This recent development, if it eventually comes to fruition, would represent a watershed decision in international law, which might form the basis for comparable developments in other aspects of environmental governance, if not as a "precedent", surely as an inspiration to true ecological sustainability. The decision to develop a legally binding instrument was strongly debated (with grave doubts expressed by Canada, the Russian Federation and the United States and a few other States). But hope for progress remains:

> Consensus was finally achieved on the development of a legally binding instrument. This means a treaty, that is something very different from a set of recommendations or guidelines. However the date of the opening of an intergovernmental conference for the drafting of the future treaty is subordinated to a decision that the General Assembly is called to take in 2018 after consideration of the progress achieved within the preparatory committee.[109]

The main obstacle to true progress remains the fact that any and all conservation measures, even considering the impact of fishing activities, are limited to areas beyond State control. However, "under art.206 parties are under an obligation to assess the effects of activities that may cause substantial pollution of, or significant and harmful changes to, the marine environment".[110] Already the present UNCLOS (article 192) speaks of protecting and preserving the marine environment, and the measures adopted for this purpose "shall include those necessary to protect and preserve rare or fragile ecosystems as well as the habitat of depleted, threatened or endangered species and other forms of marine life".[111]

The important issue remains the protection of "rare or fragile ecosystems", and just like in the case of ecological integrity in the Clean Water Act and the Great Lakes Water Quality Agreement, water cannot be completely circumscribed by state borders, nor can the fauna that lives within their natural systems. Hence, in some sense, the state obligations and the related "borders" are fluid, incapable of being totally circumscribable, even if the intent is to say that this area should be protected, because outside state jurisdiction, and perhaps the next one ought not to benefit from the same protection.

Thus, even understanding the slow development anticipated before achieving a binding instrument, and the delay and uncertainties expected, it is in this future instrument that we can place our best hopes for the future and for the possible recovery of the primacy of integrity. No doubt, this is an overly optimistic statement, and countless difficulties may intervene. Nevertheless, it is the most hopeful signal that some things may change and improve international law. In the next chapter we will consider some of the other proposals for ecological governance that have emerged in the recent literature, as this work is by no means the only one concerned with the desperate conditions of most of the world's environments.

Notes

1 George Monbiot, 2015, *Feral: Rewilding the Land, the Sea and Human Life*, University Press of Chicago, Chicago, IL, p. xxi.
2 General Agreement on Tariffs and Trade (GATT), signed by 23 nations in Geneva, 30 October 1947, took effect 1 January 1948; still in effect under the WTO framework, subject to the modifications of GATT 1994. Article XX is referred to as its "Chapeau".
3 See, for instance, Appellate Body Hormones Decision, EC Measures Concerning Meat and Meat Products (Hormones), AB-1997-4, WT/DS 26/AB/R,WT/DS48/AB/R.
4 Robert Howse, 2000, "Democracy, Science, and Free Trade: Risk Regulation on Trial at the World Trade Organization", *Michigan Law Review* 98, pp. 2329–2357.
5 Ibid.
6 Joel Tickner, 1999, "A Map Toward Precautionary Decision Making", in Carolyn Raffensperger and Joel Tickner (eds), *Protecting Public Health and the Environment*, Island Press, Washington, DC, pp. 162–186; Nicholas Ashford, 1999, "A Conceptual Framework for the Use of the Precautionary Principle in Law", in Raffensperger and Tickner, *Protecting Public Health and the Environment*, pp. 198–206.
7 Maude Barlow, 1999, *Blue Gold*, special report issued by the International Forum on Globalization (IFG), San Francisco, CA, p. A25; Stephen Clarkson, 2003, "Global Governance and the Semi-Peripheral State: The WTO and NAFTA as Canada's External Constitution", in Marjorie Griffin Cohen and Stephen Clarkson (eds), *Governing Under Stress: Middle Powers and the Challenge of Globalization*, Zed Books, London, pp. 153–174.
8 James Laxer, 1991, *Inventing Europe: The Rise of New World Power*, Lester Publications, Toronto, p. 209.
9 Stephen McBride and John Shields, 1993, *Dismantling a Nation: Canada and the New World Order*, Fernwood, Toronto, pp. 161–187.

10 L. Wallach and Michelle Sforza, 1999, *Whose Trade Organization? Corporate Globalization and the Erosion of Democracy*, Public Citizen, Washington, DC, ch. 2 and 3.
11 Jean Bodin, 1962, *Six Books of a Commonwealth*, trans. R. Knolles and Kenneth D. McRea, Harvard University Press, Cambridge, MA, p. 92.
12 William Rees, 2000, "Patch Disturbance, Ecofootprints and Biological Integrity: Revisiting the Limits to Growth (or Why Industrial Society is Inherently Unsustainable)", in David Pimentel, Laura Westra and Reed F. Noss (eds), *Ecological Integrity: Integrating Environment, Conservation and Health*, Island Press, Washington, DC, pp. 139-156.
13 Rene Jean Dupuy, 1991, "Humanity and the Environment", *Colorado Journal of International Law and Policy* 2, pp. 201–204.
14 Laura Westra, 1998, *Living in Integrity*, Rowman Littlefield, Lanham, MD; Laura Westra and B. Lawson, 2001, *Faces of Environmental Racism*, Rowman Littlefield, Lanham, MD.
15 *Barcelona Traction, Light, Power Co. Ltd. (Belgium v. Spain)*, 1970 ICJ 50, 54 (5 February).
16 Dupuy, "Humanity and the Environment", p. 202.
17 *Barcelona Traction.*
18 Ibid.
19 Theodor Meron, 1986, *Human Rights Law Making in the United Nations*, Clarendon Press, Oxford, pp. 184–185.
20 Ibid., p. 187.
21 UN press release (Geneva) HR/1/1733, 6 August 1985, p. 2; see also UN Doc. A/40/348, 6-7 (1985).
22 Cancado-Trindad, 1992, "The Contribution of International Human Rights Law to Environmental Protection with Special Reference to Global Environmental Change", in E. Brown-Weiss (ed.), *Environmental Change and International Law*, pp. 244–312.
23 Peter French, 1984, *Collective and Corporate Responsibility*, Columbia University Press, New York.
24 Dupuy, "Humanity and the Environment".
25 Henry Shue, 1996, *Basic Rights: Subsistence, Affluence and American Foreign Policy*, Princeton University Press, Princeton, NJ.
26 D. Reed, 1999, "Three Realms of Corporate Responsibility: Distinguishing Legitimacy, Morality and Ethics", *Journal of Business Ethics* 21, pp. 23–35.
27 Westra, *Living in Integrity*, ch. 3 and 8.
28 James Karr and Ed Chu, 1995, "Ecological Integrity: Reclaiming Lost Connections", in Laura Westra and John Lemons (eds), *Perspectives on Ecological Integrity*, Kluwer Academic Publishers, Dordrecht, The Netherlands, pp. 34–48; James Karr, 2000, "Health, Integrity and Biological Assessment: The Importance of Measuring Whole Things" , in Pimentel et al., *Ecological Integrity*, pp. 209–226; Westra, *Living in Integrity.*
29 John E. Noyes, 2012, "The Common Heritage of Mankind: Past, Present and Future", *Denver Journal of International Law and Policy* 40, pp.447–471, here p. 447.
30 Trans-Pacific Partnership Agreement, Environment Chapter, consolidated text, 24 November 2013, available at https://medium.com/the-trans-pacific-partnership/environment-a7f25cd180cb#.h7v3bkd95
31 Ibid., article 20.2, "Objectives", para 3.
32 Ibid., article 20.8, "Opportunities for Public Participation", paras 1–2 (emphasis added).
33 Noyes, "The Common Heritage of Mankind", p. 448.
34 Ibid., 449

35 United Nations Convention on the Law of the Sea, 10 December 1982, 1833 UNTS 397 (LOS Convention).

36 1979 Agreement Governing the activities of States on the Moon and Other Celestial Bodies, 5 December 1979, 1363 UNTS 3 (Moon Treaty), article 11.

37 Noyes, "The Common Heritage of Mankind", p. 450; citing the Letter from the Permanent Rep. of Malta to the United Nations to the secretary General (2 June 1995), UN Doc. A/50/142, at 3 (16 June1995).

38 This change of language is explained by Tullio Scovazzi: the French expression "immatériel" should not be translated literally as "immaterial" given the connotation of that term as "unimportant" in the English language; Tullio Scovazzi, 2011, "La Convenzione per la Salvaguardia del Patrimo nio Intangibile", in Tullio Scovazzi, Benedetta Ubertazzi and Lauso Zagato (eds), *Il Patrimonio culturale Intangibile nelle sue Diverse Dimensioni*, Giuffrè Editore, Milan, pp. 3–27, here p. 4.

39 Tullio Scovazzi, 2011, "Prefazione: La Dimensione Interdisciplinare del Patrimonio Culturale e Intangibile", in Scovazzi et al., *Il Patrimonio culturale Intangibile nelle sue Diverse Dimensioni*, pxvii.

40 Laura Westra, 1994, *The Principle of Integrity*, Rowman Littlefield, Lanham, MD.

41 *Gabčíkovo-Nagymaros Project (Hungary/Slovakia)*, Judge C. Weeramantry Separate Opinion, at www.icj-cij.org/docket/index.php?p1=3&p2=3&case=92.

42 Alan Gewirth, 1982, *Human Rights Essays on Justification and Applications*, University of Chicago Press, Chicago, IL, esp. pp. 5–7; see also Laura Westra, 2004, "Environmental Rights and Human Rights: The Final Enclosure Movement", in Roger Brownsword (ed.), *Global Governance and the Quest for Justice*, vol. 4, Hart Publishing, Oxford, pp. 107–121.

43 Philippe Grandjean, 2013, *Only One Chance: How Environmental Pollution Impairs Brain Development – and How to Protect the Brains of the Next Generation*, Oxford University Press, Oxford.

44 WHO and UNEP, 2013, *State of the Science of Endocrine Disrupting Chemicals – 2012*, an assessment of the state of the science of endocrine disruptors prepared by a group of experts for the United Nations Environment Programme (UNEP) and World Health Organization (WHO), edited by Åke Bergman, Jerrold J. Heindel, Susan Jobling, Karen A. Kidd and R. Thomas Zoeller, available at www.who.int/ceh/publications/endocrine/en, p. v.

45 Theo Colborn, Dianne Dumanoski and John Peterson Myers, 1996, *Our Stolen Future*, Dutton, New York.

46 WHO and UNEP, *State of the Science of Endocrine Disrupting Chemicals – 2012*, p. 6.

47 Ibid., p. 7.

48 Ibid., p. 9.

49 Ibid.

50 Ibid., p. 12.

51 Philip Landrigan and Ruth Etzel, 2013, *Children's Environmental Health*, Oxford University Press, Oxford, p. 3.

52 Ibid., p. 4.

53 Ibid.

54 Ibid.

55 R. W. Miller, 2004, "How Environmental Hazards in Childhood Have Been Discovered: Carcinogens, Teratogens, Neurotoxicants, and Others", Pediatrics 113: 945 51

56 Lens, W., 1963, "Chemicals and Malformations in Man", in Fishbein, M. (ed.), *Second International Conferenced on Congenital Malformations*, International Medical Congress, New York, NY, pp. 263–271

57 A. Herbst, M. M. Hubby, F. Azizi and M. M. Makii, 1981, "Reproductive and Gynecological Surgical Experience in Diethylstilbestrol Exposed Daughters", *American Journal of Obstetrics and Gynecology* 141, pp. 1019–1028.

58 Landrigan and Etzel, *Children's Environmental Health*, p. 5.
59 Ibid., pp. 18–27.
60 Ibid., p. 221.
61 Ibid., p. 29.
62 Ibid.
63 Laura Westra, 2014, *Revolt Against Authority*, Brill, Leyden, The Netherlands, ch. 6.
64 Laura Westra, 2013, *The Supranational Corporation*, Brill, Leyden, The Netherlands, pp. 87–88.
65 Robert Meyer, 1976, "Travaux Préparatoires for the UNESCO World Heritage Convention", *Earth Law Journal* 2, pp. 45–81.
66 Meyer, "Travaux Préparatoires for the UNESCO World Heritage Convention", p. 49.
67 Ibid.; UNESCO Doc. SHC/MD/18 Annex II at 11 (1972).
68 Meyer, "Travaux Préparatoires for the UNESCO World Heritage Convention", p. 50.
69 Ibid.
70 Ibid., p. 51. Pope Francis's Encyclical of 18 June 2015 calls the climate "un bene commune dell'umanita" ("a common value for humanity").
71 Meyer, "Travaux Préparatoires for the UNESCO World Heritage Convention", p. 52; see also article 6/3.
72 See UNESCO Doc. 17C/99 at 45 (1972) for further clarification regarding one state "directly or indirectly" damaging the heritage of another state.
73 Meyer, "Travaux Préparatoires for the UNESCO World Heritage Convention", p. 53; see also articles 8,9,10,11(2), (3) and (4); 13(4),13(6),15(1) (2) and (3).
74 Meyer, "Travaux Préparatoires for the UNESCO World Heritage Convention", p. 54.
75 Noyes, "The Common Heritage of Mankind", p. 454; citing Kemal Beslar, 1998, *The Concept of the Common Heritage of Mankind in International Law*, Brill, Leyden, The Netherlands.
76 James Kay and E. Schneider, 1994, "Life as a Manifestation of the Second Law of Thermodynamics", *Mathematical and Computer Modelling* 19(6–8), pp. 25–48; James Ray, 1991, "A Nonequilibrium Thermodynamic Framework for Discussing Ecosystem Integrity", *Environmental Management* 15, pp. 483–495.
77 Jonathan Mingle, "E.O. Wilson on Saving Half the Earth", available at http://nature.berkeley.edu/breakthroughs/spl5/eowilsonon-saving-half-the-earth.
78 Reed Noss, 1992, "The Wildlands Project: Land Conservation Strategy", *Wild Earth*, Special Issue 1992, pp. 10–25; Reed Noss and Alan Cooperrider, 1994, *Saving Nature's Legacy*, Island Press, Washington, DC.
79 Noyes, "The Common Heritage of Mankind", p. 455.
80 "Forests and Chases: Henry III's Charter of the Forest" available at http://info.sjc.ox.ac.uk/forests/Carta.htm.
81 Guy Standing, 2015, "Magna Carta: What Prospects for a Precariat Charter?", available at www.opendemocracy.net/ourkingdom/guy-standing/magna-carta-what-prospects-for-precariat-charter.
82 Allen E. Shoenberger, 2015, "Magna Carta: The Charter of the Forest and the Prerogatives of Kings", Faculty Publications and Other Works, Paper 517, Loyola University of Chicago, School of Law, Chicago, IL.
83 Ibid.
84 Ibid.
85 "The Charter of the Forest of King Henry III", available at http://info.sjc.ox.ac.uk/forests/Carta.htm, article 1, p. 3.
86 Ibid., article 9, p. 4.
87 Ibid., article 12, p. 4.
88 Ibid., article 10, p. 4.
89 Ellen Meiksins Wood, 1998, "The Agrarian Origins of Capitalism", *Monthly Review Press* 50(3), pp. 67–94, available at monthlyreview.org/1998/07/01/the-agrarian-origins-of-capitalism.

90 Garett Hardin, 1968, "The Tragedy of the Commons," *Science* 162, pp. 1243–1248.
91 Wood, "The Agrarian Origins of Capitalism", p. 81.
92 Shue, *Basic Rights*.
93 Laura Westra, 2004, *Ecoviolence and the Law*, Transnational Publishers, Ardsley, NY.
94 Shue, *Basic Rights*, p. 18.
95 Ibid., p. 19.
96 Ibid., p. 23.
97 UNGA Res. 217(LII), UN GAOR, 3rd Sess., Supp. No. 13 at 71, UN Doc. A/810 (1948), A.25.
98 International Covenant on Economic, Social and Cultural Rights (ICESCR), 16 December 1966, 993 UNTS 3 6 ILM 383.
99 International Covenant on Civil and Political Rights (ICCPR), 16 December 1966, 999 UNTS 1171, 6, ILM 368.
100 Convention Concerning the Protection of the World Cultural and Natural Heritage, adopted 16 November 1972, UNESCO, Paris, available at http://whc.unesco.org/en/conventiontext.
101 Tullio Scovazzi, 2015, "The Conservation and Sustainable Use of Marine Biodiversity, Including Genetic Resources, in Areas beyond National Jurisdiction: A Legal Perspective", available at www.un.org/Depts/los/consultative_process/ICP12_Presentations/Scovazzi_Presentation.pdf, p.20.
102 Ibid.
103 Ibid., p. 21.
104 Report of the Ad Hoc Open-Ended Informal Working Group to Study Issues Relating to the Conservation and Sustainable Use of Marine Biological Diversity beyond areas of National Jurisdiction U.N.Doc.A/61/67 of 20 March 2006, para. 71.
105 Scovazzi, "The Conservation and Sustainable Use of Marine Biodiversity …", p. 22.
106 Ibid., p. 23.
107 *Gabčíkovo-Nagymaros Project (Hungary/Slovakia)*.
108 Opening Statement made on 20 January 2015 before the Working Group by Tullio Scovazzi on behalf of the European Union and its Member States; Scovazzi, "The Conservation and Sustainable Use of Marine Biodiversity …", p. 3.
109 Scovazzi, "The Conservation and Sustainable Use of Marine Biodiversity …", p. 3.
110 Ibid., p. 4.
111 UNCLOS, article 194, para. 5.

6 Ecologically based governance and the future of integrity

Introduction

Although I can rightfully claim that the scholars within my group and I have been the most committed and vocal supporters of integrity, we certainly are not the only ones seeking to propose a radically new form of ecological governance, given the lacunae and weaknesses existing in international environmental law, and the corresponding problematic domestic laws. Hence this chapter will survey some recent proposals for ecologically based legal regimes and governance in general.

As noted, the major present problems include not only the lack of enforcement, but also the presence of legal instruments that use some of the weakest, least specific language to be found in international law. Some of the major problems at this time, include (a) the fact that environmental legal regimes are not binding; that (b) infractions are still not considered breaches of *jus cogens* norms; (c) that there is no acknowledged connection between environmental issues and human rights and public health; and finally that (d) the primacy of environmental rights are not acknowledged (as Weeramantry proposed), nor do they follow his recommendation to ensure that present laws and conventions be updated with the latest scientific knowledge.

Hence, what emerges is a clear need for a radical re-organization of the way international environmental law is designed, administered and enacted. Some approach the possibility of achieving ecological governance by appealing to traditional principles, presently forgotten in the ongoing race to supplant them with innovations, uncritically accepted, and the pursuit of convenience or profit. Others instead focus on a major changed approach, based on some concept, the importance of which is seen as sufficient to effect changes. This work uses both approaches: a central concept, biological integrity, and principles found primarily in natural law and Kantian morality.

It will be useful to review briefly other concepts and approaches, in order to show whether the ones here proposed should prevail. Actually the simplest way to effect some environmentally desirable changes, are the ones proposed by David Boyd in his early work,[1] as the author exposes the lies, inconsistencies and inadequacies of environmental law, both Canadian and US, before proposing a turn to Northern Europe, where Sweden, Norway and the Netherlands are governed far more sensibly, from the standpoint of environmental harm and human health.[2] Nevertheless, while valuable, Boyd has no answer for the ongoing harms and lack of regulations that persist internationally, as does the ongoing basis of all regulatory regimes, on the tenets of the market, and globalized trade, both of which cannot be remedied by single state decisions.

Thus the local changes he cites represent slight improvements, band-aid solutions that do little to dispel the gravity of today's situation overall. This example indicates the self-contradiction inherent in the very concept of "global governance", from its inception, when it emerged as "a key term in the discourse on world politics at the dawn of the 21st century".[3]

Frank Biermann admits the term itself is "vaguely defined", but he suggests that "Generally, the term implies notions of self-regulation by societal actors, of private–public cooperation in the solving of societal problems, and of new forms of multilevel policy, especially in the European Union."[4]

Somewhat later, among a wide variety of proposals, discussions and analysis we can see a non-European attempt at definition of global governance by Michael Jeffery:

> The concept of environmental governance encompasses the relationships and interactions among government and non-government structures, procedures and conventions, where power and responsibility are exercised in making environmental decisions. It concerns how the decisions are made with a particular emphasis on the need for citizens' interest groups and communities, generally, to participate and have their voices heard.[5]

However, although some of the major claims present in these definitions have some merit, in the one proposed by Biermann for the EU, one thing is a lot more difficult to accept than it is when the same is applied to Australia: that is, the need for citizens' involvement. It is certainly true for Europe that

> Carefully orchestrated campaigns of environmentalists have proven to be able to change foreign policy of powerful nation-states – markedly against the dumping of the Brent Spar – or to initiate new global rules such as the global campaign on banning anti-personnel land-mines.[6]

These successes are not necessarily duplicated in other continents, and they are especially hard to envision in North America, even in Australia: in those regions, states are far more resistant to public pressure. For North America, for instance, it is sufficient to cite the power of industrial agriculture[7]:

> Industrial agriculture is supported and largely created by corporate agribusiness after WWII and some of the largest and most detrimental corporate agribusiness companies today include the pesticide and GMO corporations known as the Big 6.[8]

The "citizens" that ought to get together to correct the government industrial rule, not only have no power to fight against them, but for the most part, have been convinced that there is no reason to fight and, finally, primarily in the US, have been termed "ecoterrorists" should they retain their understanding of the situation and attempt to stand on their position. The present Canadian administration is only slightly better in that regard.

Thus, while in Europe the fight against GMOs and pesticides – for instance – is ongoing and somewhat successful, in North America that battle has been lost a long time ago, although the war continues. It is for this reason that the main ingredient cited by several authors, that is the presence of citizens' participation in environmental regulations, is not a success so far, and cannot be viewed as an unqualified plus. Often citizens associations, many of which bear some responsibility for the status quo, are simply industry-funded think tanks, the role of which is to disseminate disinformation.[9] The same is true of other "Characteristics of global environmental governance" as listed by Biermann, such as the "new role" of scientists providing highly technical information in uncertainty.[10]

But the most ominous aspect is the one Biermann cites as the third novel aspect: "Business has taken a more prominent direct role in international decision-making" which, despite the positive input and the "increasing influence of intergovernmental organizations",[11] counters the valiant efforts of citizens and communities to defend themselves and nature. Biermann concludes by stating correctly "The role of international courts in environmental policy remains yet to be seen".[12] Eleven years after his assessment things have neither clarified nor improved regarding the role of international courts.

This brief review shows the grave problems inherent in the very concept of "global environmental governance" as originally (and perhaps even presently) understood. It is self-contradictory to put together elements which are inherently conflicting: for the most part corporate interests are not aligned with the interests (and the rights) of affected citizens and communities. The Australian analysis of the issue highlights the positive role played by the Indigenous peoples regarding environmental issues.[13] We noted the same results in relation to the role played by the Canadian First Nations in Chapter 2.

However, the first step to analyze the possibilities present in the quest for global environmental governance is to retain a critical approach. We need to see whether the governance we advocate does not include the very systemic flaws we are seeking to combat. Even in Europe the only acknowledged clear proclamation of environmental rights, that is the Aarhus Convention, is entirely procedural in its recommendations.[14]

In fairness, the Convention states in its Preamble "that every person has the right to live in an environment adequate to his or her health and well-being", and it has been ratified by 45 European States.[15] The right "to participate", however, does not ensure that the result of the participation will be favourable to environmental rights, anymore that the general right to vote in free elections does. In Canada, with the exception of the Green Party, which has no real standing or chance to succeed in a general election, no other party has a platform that protects environmental rights, let alone nature as such. The Conservatives, who have been in power since 2006, have consistently enacted policies that are in conflict with all human rights,[16] as the July 2015 UN Report states.

Particularly daunting and clearly related to the environment is Prime Minister Harper's position regarding mining companies, admittedly the worst kind of "development" in all areas of the world, inflicting harm with impunity to both environment and Indigenous peoples.

Harper's negative position on the environment was in evidence as well in his support of the exploitation of the tar sands, his inaction/opposition regarding climate change, and his enactment of "anti-terror" legislation that criminalizes dissent, including that directed to environmental issues.[17]

Hence it is clear that the bare "right to participate" is no more conducive to an ecologically desirable result, than the right to vote in a "democratic" country is. The multiple environmental/human rights failures present and ongoing in the United States, centred primarily on environmental racism,[18] or in Southern Italy where waste disposal is organized and managed by "'Ndrangheta", while carcinogenic and other toxic exposures affect severely the area's inhabitants, especially the women and children, are just some examples of the reality we need to resist. It is the reality that forces us to reconsider the true impact of the present "democratic" governance, worldwide. It also forces us to face the urgent need for a radical revision not only of all food-related operations, as noted, but also all the other aspects of a governance that combats rather than respects the integrity of nature, and the rights and dignity of all organisms, including our own.[19]

In the following sections of this chapter we will focus primarily on the recently published new proposals that appear most significant, as they suggest alternatives for green governance, to the approach proposed in these pages.

Towards a middle path: an attempt to moderate and control ecosystem harm

> [The meaning of resilience] as it was first defined by Holling, is concerned with the magnitude of disturbance that a system can experience before it shifts to a different state. A more recent explanation of this property also emphasises the ability of an ecosystem to "re-organize", while undergoing change so as to retain essentially the same function, structure, identity, and feedbacks.[20]

The work of Olivia Woolley attempts to use science to support law as I have been doing with my work on integrity since 1992 and the publishing of my first work, *The Principle of Integrity*.[21] It has been difficult to continue to uphold integrity outside of the disciplines of forestry (given the influence of Aldo Leopold), and in some exponents of conservation biology, hence Woolley is right in starting her quest for ecological governance by an examination of the scientific concepts that might support it.

For this purpose, "structural integrity" might be more significant than functional integrity since it facilitates the execution of "integrity" from notions of health, continued existence, or stability. Structural integrity may then form the basis for both the "dignity" of the environment, and the obligation of respect in regard to it. This appears to imply that "structural integrity" might relate to some kind of phenomenon that is both cultural and natural, even if no longer pristine. According to this model, one would need a further distinction between "pristine structural integrity" and "transformed structural integrity", and an example of the latter might be a restored ecosystem, supporting sustainable development. Yet "structures" may be understood as "slow processes or functions", and processes (functions) as "rapidly changing structures". Clear separation of the two concepts may not be as easy as it may first appear. When dealing with policy and social issues, "pristine structural integrity" will be termed I_a, or "true pristine ecosystem", whereas "transformed structural integrity" will be termed I_b. Robert Rosen discusses the concept of "function" in a chapter entitled "Entailment without States: Relational Biology", in his work *Life Itself*.[22] He speaks of "heterogeneous systems", wherein "one part looks different, or behaves differently from another part". He continues:

> If we leave the system alone, some autonomous behavior will ensue. On the other hand, we can ask a question like: if we were to remove or change, one of these distinguishable parts, what would be the effect of that behavior? This is a pregnant question. It involves a new element, not merely observation, but willful active intervention. The result of that intervention is, in effect, the creation of a *new system*, which can be regarded as a kind of perturbation or *mutilation* of the original one.[23]

The natural, "autonomous" behaviour of a system is contrasted with that of a system after "willful, active intervention". The intervention's result is *another* system, a "mutilation of the original one". It is not necessary to totally qualify, quantify, and define the former, to be able to say the latter is "mutilated", thus at best a health ecosystem (or I_b area), and at worst, a measurably degraded one. "Mutilation" is a pejorative term, although the ensuing ecosystem might be supported/manipulated for desirable human goals. Integrity (as I_a) refers instead to the ecosystem in its unmutilated condition.

To seek a possible answer to these difficulties, it is worth returning to the science of ecology and its main current paradigms. The ecosystem approach is by no means the *only* available "window" through which these can be studied. At any rate one major approach views individual organisms, aggregates, and communities as the main basic units of study, thus reducing ecosystem to "relatively constant backgrounds".[24] Another views ecosystems (however defined) as primary and considers the relevance of succession and change first, thus reducing individuals and communities to the role of members/parts of the ecosystems. Both approaches are valid and in fact necessary for better comprehension of both composition and functioning of ecosystems.

The latter could be defined as "any system that … [is] open to the flow of energy and matter and (contains) at least one living entity",[25] yet this offers no answers to persistent questions of time and scale, without which ecosystems cannot be understood properly. Ecosystems can also be defined as "the smallest units that can sustain life to isolation from all but atmospheric surroundings", although there is no "simple method for specifying the size of an ecosystem unless recognizable boundaries exist".[26]

Hence, those who are accustomed to more easily identifiable objects of study, such as organisms or communities (although the latter may not be totally precise themselves), tend to downplay the ecosystem approach, as based on entities too ephemeral and imprecise to support a scientific theory. Aside from such debates, it is clear that different scientific projects may well require different approaches. On the other hand, the concept of "integrity" may well provide an "umbrella" under which both aspects, that is, that of function and that of structure, retain their relevance. Integrity (as I_a) takes into consideration both organisms and communities within an ecosystem, as both additions and subtractions of species. The addition of species alien to the ecosystem under consideration is viewed as inappropriate – at least *prima facie* – from that point of view, and the introduction of exotics appears even less recommendable.

The functions and processes taking place within an ecosystem, therefore, need to be understood through careful consideration of its structure; and the organisms and species that inhabit and form it also cannot be understood in isolation.[27] The same is true of human organisms: a human being's physiology can be studied as such, but stresses and disturbances, that is its pathologies, require additional investigation of its environment. Viruses and bacteria, for instance, interact with and within the human system, and so do food, water, and air that sustain its life, as well as the toxins, pollutants, and man-made chemicals that might be ingested, absorbed through outgassing of chemicals in its surroundings.[28]

In this sense, some of the problems concerning the precise definition and boundaries of ecosystems may need to be rethought as requiring too limiting and reductionist a view. Taking the example of the human organism once again, the same question can be raised: what are our "limits"? Is it simply our skin that limits the individual a scientist or doctor needs to understand? What of genetic background, medical history, lifestyle, present surroundings, and possible exposures, as well as emotional attachments or isolation? A doctor attempting to understand an organism without an understanding of these factors, would be just as handicapped as the blind men were, feeling only one part of the elephant.

But an ecosystem is not just a plurality of interacting processes and functions through which organisms and communities affect one another in various ways. It is also a unity, a whole, as I am, in spite of my temporal and geographical interconnections; and this is true to some extent, whether or not one can tell precisely when and where it starts and ends. Of course there is no claim made here that individuals and ecosystems are analogous in all respects. It simply appears that their status as developing and changing entities containing life, renders them similar to each other in some relevant respects. It is their complex, changing, developing unity that is addressed by the concept of integrity.

A basic disanalogy between a single organism and an ecosystem lies in their respective time scales; an individual organism is born, reaches maturity, then ages, and eventually dies. The organism will dissolve into its chemical components and give rise to other life-forms (grasses, plants, worms, and the like). On the other hand, the ecosystem integrity views ecosystems in their continuing, though sequential, development. It might help to use C. S. Holling's "figure eight", which inspired the definition, together with its modified version manifesting the environmental position defended there (Figure 6.1).[29]

The first point to note is that James Kay's work makes use of the "figure eight" view of ecosystem functioning through time; Holling's detailed presentation of that figure, based on his own theory on "extensive comparative field studies", led him to postulate four principal "revisions" of existing ecosystem theories. The result represents a way of understanding, through the figure eight design, through which "devaluation or evolution" are viewed as "revolution", and where the concepts of release or "creative destruction" and "reorganization" must be added to the traditional functions of "exploitation" and "conservation".[30]

For our purposes, the "figure eight" has the following notable characteristics: it does not ultimately lead anywhere, except back to the beginning; it does not "culminate" in either harmony or stability, and its paths are not entirely predictable.

Against this background and framework of understanding, several points emerge. For the sake of clarity, these points can be listed under four major headings, although they cannot be completely separated from one another: (a) the

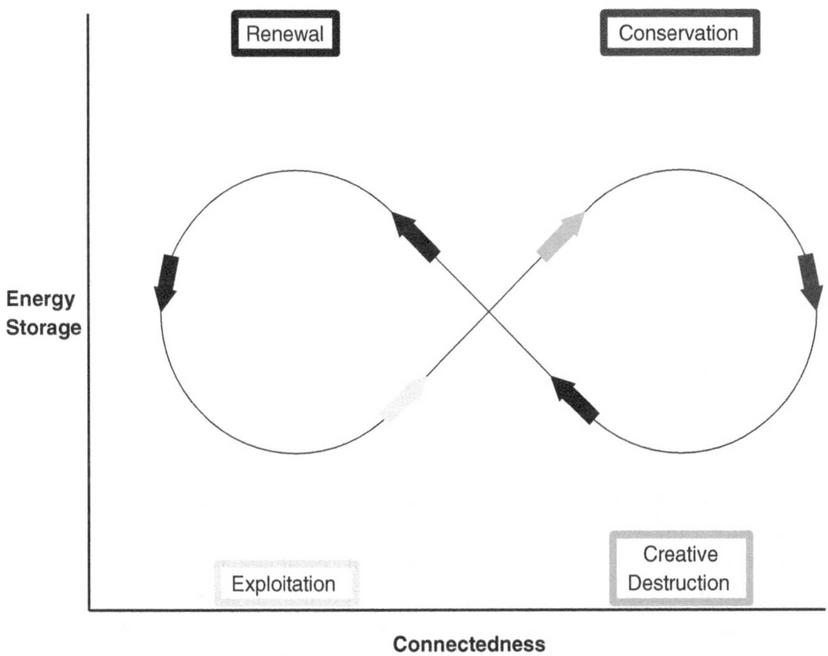

Figure 6.1 A representation of C. S. Holling's "figure eight" concept.

concept of "well-being"; (b) the concepts of "optimum functioning" of an ecosystem, and the possibility of using ranking terms in that regard (e.g. "better" or "worse"); (c) the teleological aspects of Kay's perspective; and (d) the difference between "health" and "integrity" in ecosystems.

It is worth noting that ecosystem "health" is not identical to "health" in a human organism. It does not represent the "absence of disease"; rather, it is the capacity to remain self-organizing in spite of changes, such as the addition or subtraction of species (see "health", earlier in this chapter). Yet several analogies persist between organisms and ecosystems. Some individuals claim that "the health paradigm can be applied to ecosystems" and that it is "a useful strategy for dealing with society's concern about environmental degradation and the susceptibility of natural resources".[31] Further, some may argue in support of human and other single organisms also being viewed as "ecosystems", because of the existence of bacterial colonies and other species within such organism. Kay advances the suggestion that the concept of "well-being" might be a better choice to describe the optimum state of an ecosystem.

Is resilience a sufficient theoretical and practical goal to direct policy?

> The inescapable conclusion is that, on this and other counts, we are far from being able to control development by the accurate assessment of its propensity to move ecosystems closer to failure or to trigger tipping points.[32]

Woolley concludes that a "capacity-based approach to ecological protection" only offers a "flimsy defence against developmental pressures",[33] after citing three major issues: first, the extremely complex relation between resilience and ecosystems' ability to maintain their "functionality"[34]; second, "resilience is not amenable to quantification";[35] third, no indicator of resilience has been developed, and it is extremely problematic that any could be designed, given "the non-linearity of ecosystems".[36]

In contrast, the Index of Biotic Integrity or IBI (see Chapter 1) has existed for some time and, because it is more demanding than a possible resilience indicator, forces an even more serious consideration of any and all "development" and industrial activities. These must be judged a priori to be guilty until proven innocent, contrary to the rule governing the operation of justice regarding individual actions.

We can start by reconsidering resilience: because of various forms of pollution, the ecosystem becomes weaker, "simplified" as it lacks its previous capacities. But when ecosystems are so undermined by the depletion of their "biotic community", the very possibility of support for life is diminished.[37] This very affirmation indicates the theoretical poverty of resilience as a basic concept: the goal posed by the quest for resilience is insufficient to direct policy, as the author herself states; at the same time, it is less than an appropriate ultimate goal for which we should aim, as it is only the utility of ecosystems, their functionality regarding our interests that is at stake.

In contrast, integrity includes all the biotic aspects of the system so that the protection of integrity represents a far stronger, thus worthier goal of policy: as a comparison, perhaps it is similar to justice as a goal, whereas resilience may at best be compared to fairness instead. Aside from this superficial comparison, resilience, even if identified as an ecological situation that requires an "urgent precautionary response" for its protection, cannot guarantee that governmental responses will ensue, or even that it would be economically feasible at that time,[38] although, no doubt that is a problem it shares with integrity itself.

The major problem is that resilience counsels scientific guidance, which is a strong plus, but it still appears to leave both the policy decision-making aspect, and the goal desired, entirely on the side of human interests (however enlightened ones), with no serious consideration of the diverse biotic aspects of the system, *their* survival and *their* continued ability to function. Even more problematic is the fact that, unlike integrity, resilience is not an endpoint, a standard, thus it puts the responsibility to decide at what point of a process human interests can continue to be served, while ecosystem function is not irreparably damaged.

Because the standard is not the full structural/functional composition of the ecosystem in its optimal state, the decision-making process, normally not undertaken by conservation biologists and ecologists, is bound to be weighted on the side of human interests. This means still trying to judge how far one can go without creating a disaster, something that is ongoing at this time with obvious dire results, especially in the case of climate. Hence it is not a significant enough change from the way decision-making functions in democratic countries today.

Woolley counsels community participation and deliberation: "Whilst the appeal of deliberation in the abstract is widely recognized, it has been questioned whether its putative advantages can be realized in practice."[39] She argues that while "deliberative democracy" is extremely desirable[40] the realities of political everyday situations including "existing power imbalances and unequal capacities to participate",[41] show the necessity for further means to test the validity of its decisions.

However, the belief that we must keep trying, hoping that even informed deliberations regarding grave environmental decisions, based on the scientific understanding of resilience, will simply add a "greener" addition to our present approach is a real danger, which leaves little hope for changed results. Any change would be based on "transforming preferences" in society, "internalising environmental considerations", "catalysing value formation" and "enhancing the acceptability of ecological governance".[42] Further, she adds that while the ideal and the actuality "are too far apart": "I adopt this approach as some means must be found of altering popular attitudes, if ecological governance is to take hold."[43]

We must respect Woolley's belief in humanity's general ability to change for the good, and to internalize ecological concern well enough to reach the right democratic decisions, even against general opinion and personal and group interests. But, when we add to these difficulties the further realities to which we alluded above, that is the overwhelming presence of disinformation campaigns regarding environmental matters, coupled with the prevalence of junk (or prostitute) science, affecting all aspects of decision making as well as providing "expert" witnesses for the judiciary, it seems that perhaps citizens face insurmountable difficulties as they attempt to chart a different course.

Global ecological governance and "the law of the commons"

> [T]he worldwide commons movement is demonstrating a range of innovative, effective models for assuring diverse expressions of the right to a clean and healthy environment.[44]

This statement, I fear, assumes what it is attempting to prove: namely, that there exists a "Worldwide commons movement". The authors are correct in stating that there are many groups and communities restating the urgent need to set aside what I have called "the final enclosure movement".[45] In other words, many individuals, groups and communities in today's world would like to change the course of history and disown capitalism and its control of the commons for profit. I am not sure that these disparate associations can be easily joined together as a category, as a unified "movement".

Some have age-old traditions to support their view of the commons: Canada's First Nations and other Indigenous Peoples are prime examples of that approach.[46] Then there is the overlapping case of what the authors term "Subsistence Commons",[47] a designation that includes all traditional agricultural works, and all traditional workers working on fields and forests, water, fisheries, and other natural resources. But these are not "commons" in the sense of being held in common as First Nations reserves are: however, they do indicate the most important and basic right of humanity as a collective, as I have argued elsewhere.[48]

Beyond these two "communities", who truly can be said to live (or to want to live) in the "commons" and to believe in both concept and goal, the other "commons" movements, according to Weston and Bollier that is the "internet commons",[49] the "Social and Civic Commons",[50] let alone the "Businesses Embedded in the Commons",[51] even the "State Trustee Commons",[52] are all clever elaborations, but none of these is co-natural with what the "commons" are, were, and perhaps should be.

The problem is that we have moved from real, life-supporting "commons" based upon natural resources, to considerations of citizenship.[53] However, the existence of "transnational citizens", and of global communities which may or may not give primacy to ecological concerns (although they all transcend state allegiances), does not fit the patterns the authors are attempting to trace, any more than "Social and Civic Commons", let alone the "Businesses Embedded in the Commons" do. They are, for the most part, unconnected though similar phenomena that testify to the transcendence of state-committed citizens, as they indicate global interests far beyond the local ones.

Nevertheless Weston and Bollier's work is extremely valuable in that it brings the concept of "commons" to the centre of their quest for global governance. The "Commons" as a concept, includes opposition to capitalism, as it was the emphasis on it and private property that brought the original instantiation of the "commons" to an end. Hence the concept also emphasises the failure of the states to align themselves with environmental human rights.

It seems clear that "modern state law" conflicts with the very premises and aspirations embedded in the real "commons" and their supporters:

> The idea of recognizing collective rights for non-market interest is alien to the very premises of Western liberal polity and law which, for the most part, favors the worldview and interests of unregulated markets.[54]

Incidentally, this statement confirms the fact that, in contrast, the "commons" that are not basic rights/ecologically based, may well be compatible with the present legal regimes of states, as they coincide with market-based interests (for instance, in the diffusion of the Internet).

The commons as a project for law and policy

> It should be obvious that long standing policies of the State/Market will thus need to be changed to recognize and advance communing. Astute strategies that can successfully validate, protect and support clean and healthy ecological commons for all must be devised.[55]

Beyond that which Weston and Bollier declare is needed, the "commoners" will need the will to pursue radical change as the ineffective commons "manifest" suggests, according to the authors. That will need to pursue with "social cooperation, trust reciprocity, without which they simply cannot succeed".[56] Yet, after the acknowledged commonality of intent between industry and the state, and the ongoing complicity of the media to ensure that the spin put on all ecological issues exonerated the state, for the most part, we confront the apathy and disinterest of the citizenry, which is ready to escape into the numerous congenial communities provided by the internet, rather than embrace committed conflict with the state's unwillingness to acknowledge their environmental rights. The state should be rehabilitated as "a trustee of common assets"[57] but it is hard to see how that "new architecture of law" can be achieved.[58]

Some of the proposed strategies include "localism" and the use of "municipal law",[59] and this re-echoes the regionalism proposed by William Rees in his argument against "production" as it ignores humans' unsustainable ecofootprint and integrity, as well as the second law of thermodynamics.[60] This approach is particularly significant in the case of agriculture, where the interests of those who live on the commons are actively opposed by both State and Industry, and whose efforts to resist are usually unsuccessful.

Far less clear is the possible role of "federal and provincial governments" as capable of supporting the commons and its defenders:[61] it cannot be denied this is a desirable result, but the likelihood of that actual conversion, on the part of such governments remains, to say the least, remote. Governments even if democratically chosen have a limited time-span, and normally have no desire to engage in difficult battles that might alienate voters.

Far more accessible as a project may well be the "expanding and strengthening public trust doctrine",[62] and I have defended that approach as well as the *parens patriae* doctrine,[63] and it is particularly important because of the case law based upon these principles,[64] although these precedents are no longer valid as such. This option will be discussed in more detail as we turn to another important work, that of Mary Christina Wood.[65]

The rest of the wish-list of strategies are re-elaborations of some of the ideas developed thus far. The ultimate result is sought with great passion, as the authors argue that,

> Indeed the road ahead will not be unlike the nineteen century struggle to abolish slavery, and render it illegal, against the full weight of deeply engrained powerful, yet also powerfully contentious moral and economic worldviews.[66]

In fact, it is the argument of this work that the urgent need at this time for radical ecological governance, goes further than even the basic rights/environmental rights platform supported by the "commons" as a goal: it is the actual survival of life, which depends on giving primacy to biological integrity.

Nevertheless Weston and Bollier, while they only advocate "common governance regimes for large scale and planetary resources",[67] also justly state that there is an ongoing movement toward green governance and a recognition of the role of the commons, visible through the multiplication of INGOs, associations and communities, primarily working through the internet toward that goal. No doubt, the undisputed presence of increasingly visible climate change extremes with all the consequences that ensue, contribute significantly to this picture.

What is missing is the recognition of the deepest need, that for integrity, a goal which is far more difficult to accept as a goal to motivate any community to become active for ecological reasons.

Capra and Mattei: ecological transformation in law

> The most important structural solution to the rush toward final disorder is to restore some harmony between human laws and the laws of nature, by giving law back to networks of communities.[68]

The authors note the most significant aspect of the current crisis, the connection of law "with power and violence",[69] as could be expected from the participation of Ugo Mattei, author of *Plunder*,[70] a work that some define as a "masterpiece". The present legal system is "owned by the state",[71] yet that acknowledgment, while necessary, is not sufficient: the reality is that the "power and violence" the authors acknowledge, is the institutions of globalization, beyond the power and the state.[72]

Hence, not only do we need to transcend the power of the state, but somehow we must expect communities to take on and defeat multinational organizations, who today are the ultimate power holders. The authors are right: horrors like the Rana Plaza tragedy should evoke resistance and boycotts, and they have done this.[73] But revulsion and boycotts unfortunately do not result in global policy changes: the clearest case in point is the persistence of the ongoing illegal and immoral occupation of Palestine by Israel, accompanied by a host of illegal activities, ranging from the targeting of civilians including children in their assaults, the imposition of cruel and unusual punishment, including collective punishment to revenge Israeli deaths, and the ongoing practices on colonization and apartheid. Boycott and Divestment campaigns are ongoing, but the US/Israeli "exceptionalism" persists with impunity.

With respect to ecology and law, Capra and Mattei state:

> Obviously transforming this established view is not easy. A first, necessary step is to challenge the dominant professionalized version of the legal order as being separate from its community of users and makers.[74]

Yet one wonders how communities who are, as Capra and Mattei acknowledge, "disconnected from nature, mired in ecological illiteracy and alienation", a condition particularly present in the overwhelming majority of urban dwellers today, can achieve their goal.[75] The authors come close to advocating areas of integrity, with their suggestion "to create and protect areas that ban ownership and exclusion from forests and other natural spaces",[76] and to increase the presence of "community law trusts".[77]

Capra and Nader contrast the "extractive institutions" that result in death within the community, with the community-run factories and organizations that represent a "radical review of property" instead.[78] However, the community would, in this case, have the power to "revoke private property"; governed as they are by community concerns, it seems this would exclude, or at least significantly delay, the urgent concerns of the global commons. The "governing activity known as commoning", the authors acknowledge, means that "some needs, such as those satisfied by culture and knowledge, share an important global dimension".[79]

This is the point that defines my gravest concern. One can understand a group, a community working harmoniously for a common interest. But some of the greatest needs of humanity today, are vested in the work of major institutions: great universities, great libraries, museums and art galleries, great research hospitals. These are all supported by global institutions, supported by global capitalist organizations. We need universities to continue to produce major scholars, doctors, teachers, researchers in all fields; we need museums and art collections and libraries to maintain and continue the basics of our civilizations; we need the research hospitals to help correct and redress the many harms globalization has inflicted upon us. All are needed, and all need more than community efforts, they need expensive equipment to continue to treat ill people in hospitals, and to research and find new medicines and equipment for the future, as well as the immediate present.

We are suffering and have suffered the ongoing onslaught of agricultural and industrial chemicals, starting long before birth in many cases, such as that of exposure to endocrine disruptors.[80] Justice demands that we continue to support and fund the great institutions that are necessary now, beyond even the best locally funded medical community clinics, and the universities that foster the formation of new doctors and scientists.

Richard Westra who advocates complete delinking from all global institutions, no matter how important, tells us to face facts, in the sense that there are costs to reaching this decision: "you cannot have your bourgeois cake and eat it".[81] Yet it seems truly extreme to jettison the accumulation of knowledge and expertise that these institutions may have to help redress the results of unbridled corporate exploitation lasting decades, when the victims are innocent and for the most part could not avoid their exposures, or the deprivations they have suffered. Capra and Mattei say:

> Regenerating the commons, challenging capitalist accumulation, reshaping the law from the bottom up, and eventually changing the whole of our common understanding requires a robust theory and the daily widespread political resolve of individuals.[82]

Mattei has been personally involved in organizing some of these community-based operations, such as "Acqua Bene Comune" (water as a common good), where he succeeded in making the water system of Naples into one that is owned and managed by the people "in the interest of the whole community".[83] This and many other successes of organizing communities are to his credit and support the validity of his insights. But, in contrast, there are in Naples itself issues that require an independent, separate, well-organized institution, and even that is insufficient to limit transnational criminality, such as the Camorra, the Mafia, who control toxic wastes near Naples, and whose power was made evident to the world in the recent Casamonica funeral organized by the Mafia families in Roma (where Rome's mayor was forced to resign on 12 September 2015). The authors do acknowledge that, in order to achieve "ecolaw now": "We need a new narrative to make ecological behaviour appealing, and a new legal system created by widespread community resistance and networking."[84]

As for the other "commoning" strategies we have discussed, this passage emphasizes the gravest problem they face, that of transforming consciousness and beliefs of citizens, which represents a huge stumbling block, even if Capra and Mattei do not expect the total delinking from the globalized economy Richard Westra advocates. Still, the question of the relation between the centralized powerful institutions we consider necessary and helpful, even to ensure that top notch research on ecological problems continues, and the regional/community associations remain insufficient.

I admire Capra and Mattei's vision, optimism and faith in a just ecological future, but I remain concerned about the necessary postponement required before achieving the desired results, while we wait patiently for enough citizens in all countries to give primacy to ecological concerns in the third world and globally.

Perhaps the answer they acknowledge is the right one after all, but I prefer to take a different road, although what I propose is not hostile to their position but could be reconciled with it, when it comes to fruition.

Green governance and "nature's trust"

> If indeed the body of public trust law aims to protect society and safeguard the natural infrastructure necessary for the citizens' survival and prosperity, courts can no longer tether it to artificial categories defined by courts two centuries ago. Nature's Trust recognizes a full ecological *res*. Ecological integrity rather than navigability, forms its talisman.[85]

The approach suggested by Mary Christina Wood is one with which I concur fully, although I might perhaps disagree with her exclusive reliance on state trust doctrine. Unlike the position of Weston and Bollier on "the commons", which included "informal, socially negotiated values, principles and values a given community develops"[86] thus including much that is beyond the "natural objects" governed by the laws of nature,[87] a critique that is well taken.

In fact, Wood's argument in support of Nature's Trust is well-worth a detailed discussion, because it offers a North American counterpart to the international ideal I propose as a basis for governance. The starting point is what Wood terms "the Illusion of Environmental Law", intended to protect the environment, but instead it permits environmental agencies "to legalize *destruction* of the environment",[88] as "most agencies today" are aligned "all too closely with the industries they regulate".[89] In addition, "the judiciary has largely relinquished its role as an institutional check on environmental agencies, regularly invoking the administrative defense doctrine". However, "environmental law scholarship ignores these systemic problems".[90]

As we saw, at best legal scholars address each problem in isolation, while new and emerging legal instruments are – at best – procedural in content,[91] while the old "notify-permit-destroy cycle of environmental law"[92] persists: that must be the first focus of radical change. That is the main focus of integrity as well, as all systemic components, biotic and abiotic, function together, and the removal of even one species may have grave and unexpected consequences.[93] Ecosystems include physical and chemical components, such as soils, water, and nutrients that support the organisms living within them. These organisms may range from large animals and plants to microscopic bacteria. Ecosystems include the interactions among all organisms in a given habitat.

The clearest example of trust principles enacted by governments, can be found today in their legal position regarding Indigenous peoples, Native Americans in the US, First Nations in Canada, Aboriginals in Australia. In Canada, the fiduciary duty of the Crown is undisputed, and it and it alone trumps even economic interests in the case law regarding their lands and traditional pursuits. We saw an example of this "defence" in Chapter 2 (see Wood Buffalo case), but it remains a recurring theme throughout the jurisprudence that characterizes First Nations rights, specifically, rights to hunting and fishing, established since the proclamation of King George III of 1763.

The public trust, beyond police powers and regular statutes, can indeed "limit the scope of government action":

> A sovereign property interest arises from government's control over a particular territory (just as private title to property comes from an individual's association with a particular parcel). The trust defines the character of this sovereign property ownership, recognizing rights held perpetually by the people. Weaving together two civic strands of power and obligation the trust embodies: (1) the people's delegation of authority to their government to control and manage resources; and (2) the people's assertion through a fiduciary obligation of limits on that authority to ensure that it functions to benefit the public rather than special interests (who may have greater sway over the legislative process).[94]

However, invoking the fiduciary relation between Indigenous peoples and the government in power where they reside is enlightening in principle, but it does not fully fit the model of "trust for humanity", in the sense that in Canada, for instance, the First Nations rights may not coincide with the rights of the majority, except insofar as ecological protection is concerned, given their commitment to the land, according to the seven generations rule.[95]

Thus, not "public trust" in general, but the ecological trust specifically, as it unites Wood's understanding of the concept and the ongoing fiduciary obligation of states. In fact Wood specifically addresses the "ecological res", that is, the ecological assets, the natural wealth that must sustain all foreseeable future generations of humanity.[96] In contrast, the protection of integrity, while recognizing the role of ecosystems, nature itself, in human survival, also proposes respect and concern for all forms of life, for their intrinsic value as well as for their role in ensuring human survival (see Chapter 1).

However, Wood is certainly correct in emphasizing human survival as a non-derogable obligation of states, and as the basis for "public concern",[97] so that public trust should not "surrender to statutory law in case of conflicts".[98] The major differences between public trust and statutory law lies in the fact that although common law is intended to be both flexible and adaptable, special interests render it either flexible enough to fit such interests, or at times, too fixed to incorporate the changes necessary to reflect ongoing scientific discoveries.

Weeramantry's eloquent plea to the effect that an agreement should not and could not contradict environmental human rights when enacted, if the scientific information available at t_2 should differ substantially from that present at t_1, remains among the most important legal opinions ever uttered.[99] This necessity for change is becoming increasingly obvious: "humans need all of ecology"[100], which includes all ecological processes, hence all aspects, all components of natural systems.

And here lies the crux of the problem, whether we consider "nature's trust", or whether we want to protect biological integrity: all human enterprise requires use, and often privatization, of some areas of nature, so that *all* forms of commodification cannot be proscribed. But, starting from the current "scientific understanding"[101] is basic to both nature's trust arguments and those in support of principle of integrity. Wood cites the Ecological Society of America:

> Ecosystems include physical and chemical components, such as soils, water, and nutrients that support the organisms living within them. These organisms may range from large animals and plants to microscopic bacteria. Ecosystems include the interactions among all organisms in a given habitat.

Thus, once science establishes equally the relation between human survival and ecosystem services, it is only the perverse clinging to the industrial/economic interests arising from globalization that can allow the ongoing overconsumption of "resources", the plunder and destruction that govern today's permissible, legal corporate activities. In addition, the approach employed by regulatory regimes is – at best – an attempt to "save" one species or another at a time, "evaluating each asset in isolation to determine whether it merits protection".[102] However, the opposite is necessary, as I argue in defence of integrity, that is, of the wholeness of each functioning system.

At any rate, the differences between Wood's understanding and ours in this work are not too grave: her reference to the "unique and irreplaceable common heritage", though more limited, is another connection.[103] Before turning to a further consideration of the differences between Wood's work and mine, we need to note her basic plan for the trustees:

> The six substantive fiduciary duties require a public trustee to: (1) protect the res; (2) conserve the natural inheritance of future generations (the duty against waste); (3) maximize the societal value of natural resources; (4) restore the trust res where it has been damaged'; (5) recover natural resource damage from third parties that have injured public trust assets; and (6) refrain from alienating (that is privatizing) the trust, except in limited circumstances.[104]

The integrity project, the parens patriae doctrine and nature's trust

> Development, in short, became denationalized; indeed globalization can be aptly understood as development without nation states.[105]

But "without nation-states" implies without the restraint of political organizations whose principal obligation is the protection of their citizens. Hence "development's" potential for harms runs largely unchecked at this time, without the limits imposed by previous "sovereign" states, but also without the necessary restraints from a powerful "sovereign" but international organization, whose responsibility is to the human collectivity, not to procedural and economic issues related to trade.

We will return to issues, concepts and principles below; but before leaving domestic jurisprudence, we must first consider a successful case against polluters, from September 2009, which also occurred in the US, in the New York Courts.

Connecticut et al. v. General Electric et al.: ***new hope in old doctrines***

The tone of the discourse changes radically with the case that is the focus of this section, *The State of Connecticut, et al. v. America Electric Power Company, Inc. et al.* First, several "Trusts", that is the Open Air Institute, Inc., Open Space Conservancy, Inc., and the Audubon society of New Hampshire in this case, join with the State of Connecticut, New York, California, Iowa, New Jersey, Rhode Island, Vermont and Wisconsin, as well as the City of New York, against several electrical power companies. Second, these States and Trusts, jointly claim "the ongoing contributions to the public nuisance of global warming" are causing "and will continue to cause serious harms affecting human health and natural resources".[106]

Third, although Defendants claimed the whole issue was a "non-justiciable political question", or that they "lack[ed] standing", or that they attempted to displace "federal common law" – the Court of Appeals rejected all these arguments. Fourth, the States itemize singly and collectively the harms of climate change, which will produce "substantial adverse effects on their environments, residents, and property", and all of which will cost each State billions of dollars to respond. As an example, "the reduction of California's mountain snowpack, the single largest freshwater source critical to sustaining water to the State's 34 million residents during the half of each year, when there is nominal precipitation".[107]

In addition, in the fifth place, the States list several significant cases of "increased illnesses and deaths caused by prolonged heatwave", the harms from smog, and poor air quality, as they couple explicitly the impacts on "property, ecology and public health".[108] In the sixth place, the Land Trusts add "how the ecological value of specific properties in which they have an interest, will be diminished or destroyed by global warming".[109]

Hence the emphasis on the connection between ecological values and public health, for instance, is particularly relevant, as is the argument presented to the courts. Well beyond the expected focus on economic impacts and property values (although these are also a significant part of the States and Trusts' argument), is the rejection of the "political question" doctrine, and especially in the use of the *parens patriae* doctrine. This doctrine, I believe, provides the first new approach to the problems we have discussed, although it is a *principle*, rather than a legal instrument, either domestic or international. That will be the topic of the next section.

The **parens patriae** ***doctrine: an old principle and a novel application***

> *Parens patriae* is an ancient common law prerogative which "is inherent in the supreme power of every state … [and is] often necessary to be exercised in the interests of humanity and for the prevention of injury to those who cannot protect themselves".[110]

There is a history of protective jurisprudence, dating back as far as the Middle Ages. In its most recent instantiations, the *parens patriae* doctrine has been used to support judicial decisions that deal with the protection of those who cannot speak for themselves, especially in the case of health issues.[111]

The language of these judgments is extremely suggestive and well worthy of attentive study. But before turning to the cases, it might be best to review briefly the history of the doctrine. The doctrine of *parens patriae*, despite its Roman name, is entirely a common law doctrine, and while, for instance, the Canadian Supreme Court makes use of it, it does not exist in Quebec law.[112] It is perhaps an anomaly that a doctrine with a Roman name and origin is presently only found in the common law, as Morin indicates in his description of the doctrine's historical background.[113]

Until 1873 a fundamental dichotomy prevailed in Britain's legal system. From the Middle Ages, royal tribunals used the "communeley", but the great majority of cases were heard by the lords and the local courts. Only rarely did the King, as "fountain of justice" participate in decisions of the courts through the person of his Chancellor, who until the sixteenth century was, at the same time, the King's confessor, hence perhaps the use of the Latin phrase.[114]

The Chancellor's aim was the promotion and the triumph of equity principles, learned in his study of Roman law. The rules guiding these judgments and their results eventually became codified, hence "precedent" was born.[115] The doctrine was used for custody and guardianship matters involving the relation between the lord and a minor, perhaps one whose father might have been a tenant of the lord before his death, so that guardianship was required until such time as the child could be recognized as a tenant in his stead, at age fourteen.

Eventually the "Court of Wards and Liveries" was instituted by Parliament, after 1540,[116] and this court remained in operation for some time. The concept of royal protection was substituted in the fifteenth century by a Court of Chancery, which kept the concept of wardship alive, and was able to introduce a novel move by 1792, when it forbade a violent father to interrupt his son's schooling and continue with his guardianship.[117]

Although the Court of Wards was abolished, the concept of "wardship" remained as an aspect of its *parens patriae* jurisdiction: "In time wardship became substantively and procedurally assimilated to the *parens patriae* jurisdiction, lost its connection with property, and became purely protective in nature."[118]

The inception of the use of the doctrine thus explains both its Latin roots and its evolution from the protection of a minor's economic interests, to the protection of children's interests, *simpliciter*. Without any further effort to trace its antecedents, we will now turn to its development use, in order to see whether its development renders the doctrine applicable to the protection of human beings in general. The classic statement of the modern principles that govern state intervention in the best interests of the child, can be found in Rand, J.'s judgment:

> The view of the child's welfare conceives it to lie, first, within the warmth and security of the home provided by his parents; when through a failure with or without parental fault, to furnish that protection, that welfare is threatened, the community, represented by the Sovereign, is, on the broadest social and national grounds, justified in displacing the parents and assuming their duties.

> This in substance, is the rule of law established for centuries and in the light of which the common law Courts and the Court of Chancery, following their differing rules, dealt with custody.[119]

La Forest, J. ties recent cases to their British background:

> It will be obvious from these provisions that the Supreme Court of Prince Edward Island has the same *Parens Patriae* jurisdiction as was vested in the Lord Chancellor in England and exercised by the Court of Chancery there.[120]

A further point worthy of note: the increasingly wide reach of the doctrine, giving the courts the ability to protect children from injury. In *Re X* (a minor),[121] Latey, J. cited "a passage from Chambers on Infancy (1842) that indicates that protection may be accorded against prospective as well as present harms".[122]

With this statement we come a lot closer to the possibility of protecting health, in the sense we have been seeking to find explicitly, in legislation, without much success. If "prospective harm" is explicitly a part of the *parens patriae* doctrine, then it is not only a juridical tool to be used after some crime has been committed or to prevent some obvious injustice. It could be instead especially powerful when there is an unconsented medical treatment at issue, as there it can be used "to prevent ... damage being done". A similar approach exists in the US.[123] In another American case, *Matter of Sallmeier*,[124] the Court said:

> The jurisdiction of the Court in this proceeding arises *not by statute*, but from the common law jurisdiction of the Supreme Court to act as *parens patriae* with respect to incompetents[125] (emphasis added).

Essentially there are two possible approaches included in the doctrine: the "best interest" approach, and the "substituted judgment" approach.[126] What is relevant from our point of view, is the fact that *neither approach* needs a "person", in order to protect. In fact *parens patriae* only comes into effect when the rights of the individual needing to be protected are not those of a "person", able to think and decide or even to protect her own interests.

We noted the use of the doctrine/principle in the case of "incompetents" or – in general – for those who are not able to protect themselves from harm. Hence the doctrine is particularly appropriate for the protection from harm of future/unborn generations, as well as those who are first harmed by any exposure, that is children and infants as the research of the WHO and other epidemiologists and scientists indicates.[127] Essentially, the particular physical configuration and growth pattern of children makes them particularly vulnerable to all forms of pollution, whether chemical or air/water based, and the WHO research supports this fact.

Temperature variability is also particularly hazardous for infants and children, as are the droughts and floods that are endemic to climate change, together with the spread of vector-borne diseases that follow global warming.[128] However, even a cursory consideration of the general "collective" of humankind indicates that all citizens are affected in varying degrees although pregnant women, infants and children and the elderly are sure to be the first to suffer grave effects from climate change as are the poor and other vulnerable populations.

In *Georgia v. Tenn. Copper Co.*[129] the Supreme Court affirm that "the state has an interest independent of and behind the titles of its citizens, in all the earth and air within its domain. It has the last word as to whether … its inhabitants shall breathe pure air".[130] The second seminal case for *parens patriae* standing in the US is *Snapp*,[131] which noted that there had been a "line of cases … in which States successfully sought to represent the interests of their citizens in enjoining public nuisance",[132] where a "test" for *parens patriae* standing is identified:

> A state: (1) "must articulate an interest apart from the interests of particular private parties, i.e., the State must be more than a nominal party";
>
> (2) "must express a quasi-sovereign interest"; and
>
> (3) must have "alleged injury to a sufficiently substantial segment of its population."[133]

In addition, the Court in this case identified two kinds of "quasi-sovereign interests" as follows:

> (1) "protecting the health and well-being … of its residents" and (2) "securing observance of the terms under which the state participates in the federal system".[134]

From our perspective only the health and well-being are relevant as we seek a possible future application of this doctrine to protection of basic collective human rights anywhere.

At any rate, here we encounter the first possible difficulty to advocating a wider use of the *parens patriae* doctrine. These are "quasi-sovereign states", which must acquire the parental standing necessary to legislate or use for the protection of all, or even a "significant segment" of their people. If the doctrine were to be used elsewhere for the protection from environmental harms, especially in the global setting and for international effects of climate change, it should be incorporated within international law, and, when collective human rights breaches occur, it should be used in international courts.

The problem that arises is, which entity could, logically and legally, take the place of the "parent" whose responsibility for its "dependent' children would indicate the applicability of the doctrine. Perhaps for the EU, it could be said that all the citizens of the state within it are in a position similar to that of citizens of individual states. But it is much harder to envision a similar "parental" role for the UN, even aside from the fact that – to my knowledge – this doctrine has not been appealed to by either the UN or the EU in any environmental case thus far.

Nevertheless, the self-appointed task of this chapter was to seek out not only what might be already available to protect basic collective human rights, but also to propose any doctrine, principle or instrument that *might*, in the future, be involved to fulfil that role. For that purpose, *parens patriae* has now been used domestically to protect these rights, by acknowledging the state's responsibility to ensure that its citizens are not exposed to the health hazards that are the inescapable result of environmental exposures.

The public trust doctrine: a discussion

> In the case of the equation of the public trust doctrine and the police power, were the state purports to act pursuant to police powers but rests its powers on the property rights of the public, the fallacy is not well concealed, and the potential for state intrusion upon the private rights of individuals is limited only by the vision of those who would extend the reach of the public trust doctrine.[135]

Perhaps it is this position and the apparent ongoing debates regarding the public trust doctrine that suggested, in the previous case, the use of a different (albeit related) tool, the *parens patriae* doctrine, instead, to better protect the rights of the collective. James Huffman sees the public trust doctrine as "property law"[136] as he argues against Joseph Sax.[137] His main point is that the "public trust" doctrine is traditionally and explicitly part of property law, so that legal scholars who seek to extend it to other fields such as "trust, constitutional, administrative and police power law" are mistaken.[138]

However, it is interesting to note that Huffman acknowledges "its birth in English common law".[139] In that case, like *parens patriae*, the doctrine originated when the King and other noblemen held rights and power, and the common people needed to protect their own rights to the "commons", such as land and waters from the sole discretion of the King. Public Trust implied that the king could not alienate the public rights in the use of those waters and lands[140]; in that case, *pace* Huffman, it seems appropriate to understand the doctrine as a form of restraint on private rights, particularly the private rights of legal persons, but also those of democratic decisions that might consider majoritarian preferences to be the ultimate word on the use of the commons, to the detriment of minorities or distant peoples affected by those decisions, as well as all future human beings.

In fact, in *Illinois Central*[141] the US Supreme Court decided that the grant of "submerged lands" to the railroad violated "a trust for the people that they may enjoy the navigation of the waters, carry on commerce over them, and have liberty of fishing therein freed from the obstruction or interference of private parties".[142]

Of course, at that time, the full impact of the interference of private property on public rights to the commons was not fully appreciated and future scientific research could not have been anticipated. But today it would be even more appropriate to invoke the doctrine to protect basic collective human rights. Nevertheless, given the debate about its true meaning, use and the procedural issues that surround it, one can perhaps appreciate why the drafters of the case of the State of Connecticut chose not to employ it, and use a doctrine whose connection to "property" has long since been abandoned, as it includes instead values like life and health, in its stead.

From the standpoint of this work, whether or not the doctrine is interpreted correctly in US case law, is not determinant. What is more important is the historical basis of "public trust" which, like *parens patriae*, indicates that even an all-powerful sovereign's policies and decisions may be limited by some of the basic needs of his people, long before the modern emphasis on legal human rights. Hence, common law offers two possible options for the protection of collective human rights, that is, for the general welfare,[143] as discussed in Chapter 1. At least in principle either could be used to support and defend basic collective human rights.

At any rate, and still within the ambit of US law, Mary Christine Wood defends a very different position on the issue, as she

> proposes a paradigm shift away from the current system of natural resource management, a system driven by political discretion, to one that is infused with public trust principles and policies across all branches of government and at all jurisdictional levels.[144]

The first step needed is not to think of the public trust doctrine simply as another form of property right. As Wood has it, speaking of environmental laws, laws regarding the "commons", "we have won many victories, but we are losing the planet".[145] In support of her position, she cites a number of familiar statistics similar to the ones cited throughout this work, including chemical and other pollution exposures affecting people from the womb on, as well as the "loss of life and ecosystem on the planet", all of which she terms "ecological bankruptcy".[146]

Despite the global reach of the "ecological bankruptcy" of which she speaks, it is not only the US law that suffers from "administrative dysfunction", such that the severity and number of grave difficulties she cites are such that they indicate a similar "dysfunction" at the international level. The latter should be the most appropriate level from which to address global problems that affect basic collective rights. Wood notes the following:

1 "The modern environmental administrative state is geared almost entirely to the legalization of natural resource damage."[147]
2 "[A]gencies have created a regulatory complexity that is mind-boggling … the complexity – legal baklava so to speak – carries several perils for environmental policy. It distracts agencies from seeing the macro picture of resource health."[148]
3 Agencies regularly confront and succumb to political pressure to issue permits and sanction other harmful actions[149]: "In theory, governments are supposed to police corporate greed, channeling it away from corner-cutting that threatens public health and safety … Corporations are constants pressuring governments to relax environmental regulations, if not to eliminate them altogether."[150]

4 The public has become disenfranchised within this system of environmental laws. While NEPA and other statutes provide for ample public notice and comment in order to promote environmental democracy, these protections often amount to a sham … standard environmental analyses contain acronyms, technical findings and conclusions that are unduly complex and incomprehensible to the average citizen.[151]

5 "[T]he judiciary has lost its potency as a third branch of government speaking in the environmental realm. This is primarily due to the tendency of courts to invoke the administrative deference doctrine."[152]

As in international law, political discretion and deference to the most powerful states and to powerful corporations trumps scientific research and moral obligation: it is not inappropriate to term this situation a form of "institutional decay".[153] Hence, despite the acknowledged difficulties in isolating "a firm source of legal obligation",[154] aiming for a fiduciary obligation, one resting on the historical foundations of the public trust doctrine, appears to be a good move, and one that ought to prevail in some way in international law as well.

For the latter, however, it would be necessary to start by securing an appropriate understanding of who would be "king", or the entity on whom the legal obligation may rest. The United Nations appears to be the only candidate for that role. But, as is well-known, the UN is both an "actor" and a "stage", and it is the latter designation that indicates most clearly the difficulty the UN would face in fulfilling that role.

Nevertheless, if the UN is to represent the global community, not only all states, but also all people, then the expected allegiance and compliance with its mandates including its Declaration and the findings of special Commissions and Rapporteurs, needs to rest on the assurance of protection and the respect for global collective rights. Without the latter, it seems unrealistic to assume the legitimacy of the international legal order headed by the UN. Perhaps we would assume the presence of a fiduciary obligation on the part of the UN based international legal regimes, somewhat similar to that owed by the Canadian government (as well as some other governments) to its First Nations. Their protection, individually and collectively (as a community), provides the most solid "last word" in cases where their welfare is at stake. Thus, like the *parens patriae* doctrine, to understand the fiduciary basis of the public trust doctrine, appears to provide desirable and possible first steps toward the protection of the "commons, and of basic collective rights".

Hence we can conclude that the trust doctrine is and should be a solid companion to the CHM Principle, which represents an international global instantiation of the state-based fiduciary relation, between governed and governing powers.

Other proposals for green governance and sustainability: major obstacles

> Increasingly, the narrow economic ideology, devoid of ecological wisdom and lacking human compassion, was spreading around the world in the policies of the Washington Consensus, and I feared, if not challenged by other more inclusive values and ethics, globalization, driven by such "neo-liberal" economic ideology, would undermine other vital human values and over exploit every local social system and ecosystem on the planet.[155]

The seriousness of our present predicament, based upon the multiple failures of our governments to protect natural systems and all organisms within them, is demonstrated by the wide variety of scholars who engage with this topic, as they write and publish on the topic of the need for changed forms of governance. It is no longer just legal scholars who decry the weakness and insufficiency of present legal regimes, or conservation biologists who produce chilling statistics about loss of biodiversity, while ecologists warn about impending climate disaster.

It is telling that even economists are joining in, proposing changed systems to avert catastrophe. However, most are not ready to abandon the "sustainable development" paradigm, although they tend to alter its terms somewhat in ways that include moral and social considerations:

> Sustainable development is a way to understand the world as a complex interaction of economic, social environmental and political systems. Yet it is also a normative or ethical view of the world, a way to define the objectives of a well-functioning society, one that delivers well-being for its citizens today and for future generations.[156]

Sachs also admits that "humanity has become a serious threat to its own future and well-being",[157] and that the effects of such "development" are now affecting both rich and poor, as Sachs mentions "Superstorm Sandy", drought in the US Midwest, and drought and fires in California.[158] The harms, especially in so-called "developing countries", affect the poor disproportionally. He adds:

> Indeed, the reshaping of the Earth's physical systems, including climate, chemistry and biology, is so dramatic that scientists have given our age a new scientific name: the Anthropocene.[159]

We have discussed the hubris involved in that appellation in Chapter 2; it is also not a name based on "scientific fact". We are indeed responsible for all the disintegrity-causing circumstances we face, but that suggests a better appellation for the age: the age of disintegrity. Sachs acknowledges the need for "good governance" but he still views sustainable development as an "alternative path", one that aims not only for economic growth, but also for "social inclusion and environmental sustainability" something that, on the current understanding of the terms, has been repeatedly proven to be the major contribution to present disasters.

In fact, the fate of Sustainable Development Goals (SDGs), unsuccessful and/or poorly conceived, indicates the impotence of that idea. All recommendations to ameliorate inequality and poverty are based on maintaining the current systems, perhaps with minor changes, that simply ignore ecological concerns altogether. The very interest in public health, is limited to a consideration of the poorest countries in Sachs's work although he acknowledges that in the US still that sector does not function well (in contrast to the Canadian system):

> Why is the US health care system so expensive compared to others? … One of the many reasons the US system is so expensive, is that it is a privately oriented health delivery system … The US system is characterized by substantial fraud, excessive care, waste and monopoly power of local health providers.[160]

If the all-important public right to health is in such difficulties in the richest country in the world, the strongest proponent of neoliberal globalization, that fact gives further support to the common thread running through the critique of current corporate/state practices, including the generally accepted version of sustainable development included among those practices.

Even a well-meaning economist like Sachs, who researches and writes seriously about the "Age of Sustainable Development", as his book is titled, seems unable to acknowledge the depth of denial, corruption and politicizing that characterizes his government's relation with scientists, business leaders and others, Thus even the most concerned scholars attempting to ameliorate present forms of governance, seem unaware of the depth of interpenetration between corporate interests, all layers of government, and even those realms that should remain beyond private interests, that is, science and law.[161]

Concerned, well-meaning and morally committed citizens, especially in North America, find it hard to face the truth. Perhaps the only comparable situation to that existing primarily (but not exclusively) in the US, is that which exists in Southern Italy, from the Mafia in Sicily, to the 'Ndrangheta in Calabria and which can be found almost everywhere in Italy.

The tentacles of this perversion of justice and morality have penetrated all levels of government, municipal, regional and central powers, so that some ongoing outrages appear unstoppable, such as the toxic dumping and the "control" of garbage in and around Naples, often present in European news, beyond the local media. Some recent events show the powers of organized crime, not only in the South, but also, as recently as 20 August 2015, in the eternal city, Rome. In Sicily and the South it is common to organize processions at religious holidays, and these pass through the city and are followed by much of the population. Around Easter 2015, one such procession deliberately detoured from the expected and policed route, to pass by the home of the most powerful Mafia boss in the city, in order to pay him homage (or bow to him, with the "*inchino*"). That created a furore, especially since the procession's route had to be approved by the local police, and was followed by police officers.

That episode took place in a town in Sicily, hence it was viewed as regrettable, but almost as something to be expected. However, this was not the case for the lavish funeral of Mafia boss Vittorio Casamonica in Rome itself. The solid gold casket was carried away from church in a baroque carriage, drawn by six black horses throughout the funeral procession, while a Dixieland-style band played music from the film, *The Godfather*, and placards were placed along the route, with the effigy of Casamonica depicted as floating over Rome's Colosseum, and other famous monuments, inscribed: "you conquered Rome, now conquer paradise!" or "Re di Roma" (King of Rome). The final touch was provided by a red helicopter flying overhead, following the procession dropping rose petals on the mourners and the street.

Some of the main questions raised by the scandal that followed, and involving everyone in the Italian bureaucracy, were who gave permission for that vulgar display of wealth; further, why were several persons in the family freed from their house arrest at the time; and finally, why the many lavish houses in the Roman compound occupied by the many members of the family contained rich furnishings and were flanked by numerous high-priced cars, which further attested to that family's power. Eventually the family's total holdings and wealth were estimated around 900 million euros, although family members were all apparently unknown to the Italian tax authorities.

Even a cursory overview of this shameful episode, one which, according to a Sicilian magistrate from Catania, was responsible for turning Italy's relations with the Mafia (and the Calabria 'Ndrangheta) back several years, changed significantly Europe's and the world's perception of Italy and organized crime.

Of course, this is no more than anecdotal evidence, and a loose comparison, but it indicates the incredible power the Mafia possesses in Italy, as it has infiltrated almost all aspects of Italian governance. It is the contention of several of the works cited, as well as my own, that corporate industrial interests have so penetrated most Western governments, especially that of the US, home of the major multinational corporations, as to be essentially identified with such governments.

Corporate power against cosmopolitan democracy

> [N]ow as then, no world executive power exists. As a result, at the world level a huge gap exists between the solemn statements of principle and bleak daily reality. The violation of human rights, conditions of extreme poverty, periodic recourse to war, and environmental degradation are but a few of the many problems facing humankind today.[162]

Carl Boggs's point about "colonizing corporations",[163] while correct, does not go far enough today. Indeed citizens rightly place the blame on corporate power, as they see dominant economic interests replacing any possible social interest that might move them to return to political concern and dialogue. But, after 2000, the most dangerous development yet in the growing trend of overwhelming, ubiquitous corporate presence, is the infiltration of that power right into the government elites intended to protect the citizens, via the presence of "embedded science". These corporations now have complete confidence in their immunity from the legal consequences of any and all crimes they might commit, especially after the advent of the Terrorist Act of 2006, where the practical identification of large corporations with the US government itself is clearly enshrined.[164]

The huge spread of corporate power transcends the global limits as well as those of the US domestic Constitutional law.

Daniele Archibugi notes the vast gulf between the affirmation of principles and the bleak – and I would add paraphrasing Philippe Sands – "lawless" reality we face. He proposes "cosmopolitan democracy", based loosely on the West's vision of democracy. He proposes a cosmopolitan democracy transcending the democracy he believes exists in the West. He says, "The West is an entity composed of countries that have a market economy and consolidated democratic institutions. With the sole exception of Japan, the West involves Europe and its ancient settlements."[165] He thinks that – in addition – beyond the material power, we can observe the domination of the US and its ideology. Yet "freedom and democracy" are no longer the values that once carried basic universal connotations. Increasingly, these high-sounding concepts, "have been turned into ideological screens to defend vested interests and attack enemies".[166]

Hence that "world power" ought not to be the sole (or the greatest) source of power as often the West "claimed to have values [e.g. freedom and democracy] for itself and denied them to others".[167] Democratic regimes are not the only ones unworthy of carrying on the torch of civilization , as autocratic regimes may be equally, or even more likely to be, aggressive and to disregard human rights.

This is not the appropriate place to follow Archibugi's sophisticated analysis of all aspects of the possible achievement of a real global democracy, while evolving "meta-state law".[168] But we should consider the effect on "the West" of corporate persons, given the power these ubiquitous legal entities possess in the international community. Archibugi is correct as he says that "no world executive power exists", at least if he refers to an officially sanctioned or elected "executive power".

The questions we are raising in this work refer to the possibility that a supranational power does exist, especially in the West, but ultimately affecting the whole global community, which does not represent either "democracy" or "freedom". This power does not possess a true political ideology or a democratic mandate: it is only unashamedly limited to the aggressive pursuit of its own interests. As we continue to examine the corporate legal persons' power, together with their influence on public policy globally, we should keep in mind what institutions and organizations might have a legitimate claim on a true cosmopolitan democracy instead.

The US is "governed by a type of 'democratic elitism'"[169] but the secret institutions of the corporate-directed second constitution "have marked antidemocratic authoritarian tendencies".[170] Miller does not discuss the actual detailed results of this duality, but he does state that the separation between the economy and the polity is only functional, as they are complementary instead. Hence a truthful understanding of the situation would be to term it the "corporate state".

This intimate relation entails that the most important aspects of democratic citizenship are eliminated. Mark Kesselman notes:

> The hidden face of power is exercised not so much by the suppression of specific issues from the political agenda as by the exclusion of the most fundamental matters of public concern form the political sphere.[171]

The corporate control here acknowledged, could not persist without an additional control, one we have neglected in this work given its wide reach and the public awareness of its results: the corporate control of the mass media. That is the final form of supranational control: neither the control of the law, of governance, nor of the markets exerts such widespread power. It is the ultimate social control of people's wants and preferences, so that unhealthy and even injurious choices become the "real" preferences of US citizens to begin with, but of people everywhere, eventually, as the "better way" is spread, from harmful McDonald's hamburgers and Coca-Cola, to mind warping computer games and other such "necessities", promoted to the public from childhood on.

Thus corporate control is not simply tolerated and accepted by the law. In contrast, again primarily in the US, the home base of most MNCs, the identification of corporate interests and legal regimes completes the structure of a "lawless world",[172] which explains and amply justifies public apathy and disinterest in what is left of "politics", while the mass flight to other, more reliable social movements and groupings attract the interest and allegiance of disenchanted transnational citizens, trying to recapture elsewhere the significant public "good" that has long since eluded them in their Western democratic national homes.

Politics, "in modern society", is conceived "in terms of elite action",[173] and "The result was an impoverishment of the public sphere and political discourse that lingers on in many parts of the world even today."[174] The withdrawal of the state, both as a purveyor of public goods and as a referent of traditional principles and national values, left the citizens adrift. The void created was quickly filled by various social movements, presented and promoted through the internet. However, like the rest of the plethora of information that is found in the internet, not everything there is either truthful or valuable, and it is extremely hard to discriminate among the multiple offerings one can find, in order to be sure that one is truly in touch with a principled organization, rather than yet another "greenwashed' or otherwise altered version of the same corporate colonizers the citizen is attempting to escape.

Carl Boggs[175] deplores the absence of political debate in the US, where "political colonization",[176] has taken the place of real debate between the parties that are almost indistinguishable, except perhaps from the respective amounts of corporate funding they manage to attract.

Ecological economics for green governance?

> The goal of this paper is to advance a precautionary transformational approach to sustainability planning. This framework recognizes that, despite a half century of alarm over "the environmental crisis" and 20 years of political rhetoric on "paradigm shifting" and "sustainable development", action to date has been mere reform at the margin, not fundamental transformation. Indeed it is arguable that no real progress is possible while the beliefs, values and assumptions of capitalism remain entrenched.[177]

The world, says Rees, "is in ecological overshoot", thus, "the human enterprise exceeds the long-term carrying capacity of the Earth".[178] Of course, as our work and the work of numerous scholars, including those discussed in this chapter, have clearly shown, the "solution" proposed by mainstream thinkers, supported mainly by corporate interests, is growth, increased GDP with its concomitant activities, such as "deregulation, globalization, expanding trade, competition and freer markets" with no concern for the mounting environmental problems, sure to be "fixed by clever new technologies".[179]

But the results of this "recipe" have become obvious to all now, we can now confirm that these business as usual (BAU) policies are just a recipe not only for disaster, but for multiple disasters instead. Rees does more than simply recite the familiar litany of grave ecological issues: he is prepared to propose solutions that range from "socially constructing a no-growth alternative", citing the wisdom of John Stuart Mill, who advised societies to reach a "stationary state" based on just distribution of property.[180]

Among other novel strategies proposed, are "fixing broken markets", which include ending "perverse subsidies to the private sector"; "reregulate the private sector as necessary to protect the public interest"; "enforce an adequate minimum (living) wage".[181] Further, he advocates rebalancing "the global and local economies", which entails "deglobalizing to reduce dependence on foreign sources and sinks" and, most of all, "to reverse WTO rules, NAFTA" and the like and it will also be necessary to "redefine the commons" as "a fundamental goal of any socially just and sustainable steady state".[182]

However worthy these goals are, Rees himself acknowledges that "Contemplating wholesale relocalization after decades of rhetoric on the inevitability of global integration makes it appear the most daunting of tasks."[183] Indeed. I can admire Rees's clarity and commitment. But in the light of the ongoing wrongheaded pursuit of power with no concern for human dignity or human rights, as we see the desperate hordes of migrants, products of globalization and the imperialism primarily fostered by the two rogue states, Israel and the United States, whose immediate concern is survival, while those who fostered the conflicts through their power play look the other way, we can only despair. As well, when we consider the impunity of the powers that control global food supplies, sanctioned by Obama's 2012 "Monsanto's Immunity Act" (expired in 2013, but representing a dangerous precedent),[184] while too many in the world live on less than $2 a day and are exposed to constant harm, rather than reached by serious attempts to reduce hunger … again I despair about the possibility of radical change.

I don't trust that there will be sufficient freedom of information, freedom of movement, sufficient respect for humanity and for the rule of law, to implement the desirable moves Rees advocates. Rees's strategies cannot be faulted, but he does not tie their implementation to any existent or even possible legal regime. I also find it hard to share his belief in the transformative capacities of human beings, their ability for cooperation and benevolence, and, most of all, I doubt their ability to regain the committed critical thinking necessary to overcome many decades of media disinformation campaigns and self-serving lies from corporate interests.

Rees presents us with a well-articulated ideal, as he argues convincingly for each of its component parts, while he admits humanity may not be up to the task of saving itself. However, aside from the immense difficulties arising from corporate and state interests opposing all aspects of such plans, we must acknowledge that one of the results of globalization and of the withdrawal of state functions, that is, of states as purveyors not only of services, but also of ideals that merit citizens' commitment, is the formation and multiplication of transnational citizens,[185] who, having transcended state borders with their allegiance to international associations, communities and INGOs, would be hard-put to return not only to their original state, but even to their villages or communities.

That aspect of globalization, fuelled by the internet, I fear is and remains irreversible, and while it offers some hope for commitments to the commons or the common good, unfortunately also works in favour of the status quo.

In the final chapter I will try to add some legal components to the quest for a survival based on the ideal of ecological integrity, as I believe, with Ugo Mattei, that although laws and their abuse have brought us to this point, it is also true that only through law might we be able to overcome the immense dangers that face us.

Notes

1 David Boyd, 2003, *Unnatural Law*, University Press of British Columbia, Vancouver, BC.
2 Boyd, *Unnatural Law*, pp. 291–306.
3 Frank Biermann, 2004, "Global Environmental Governance", GLOGOV.org, Global Governance Working Paper, 12 November.
4 Ibid.
5 Michael R. Jeffery, 2005, "Environmental Governance: A Comparative Analysis of Public Participation and access to Justice", *Journal of South Pacific Law* 9(2), pp. 1–21, here p. 1.
6 Biermann, "Global Environmental Governance", p. 9.
7 Heather Gray, 2015, "Comparing Nuclear War with Industrial Agriculture", available at www.counterpunch.org/2015/07/23/comparing-nuclear-war-with-industrial agriculture.
8 BASF, Bayer, Dupont, Dow Chemical Company, Monsanto and Syngenta; ibid., p. 2.
9 Donald A. Brown, 2014, "Norms for Scientific Claims Made in the Face of Scientific Uncertainty: Lessons from the Climate Change Disinformation Campaign", in

L. Westra and M. Vilela (eds), *The Earth Charter, Ecological Integrity and Social Movements*, Routledge, London, pp. 50–60.

10 Biermann, "Global Environmental Governance", p. 9; see also Colin Soskolne, 2015, "Public Health and Environmental Health Risk Assessment: Which Paradigm and in Whose Interest?", in L. Westra, J. Gray and Vicky Karageorgou (eds), *Ecological Systems Integrity*, Routledge, London, pp. 191–200.

11 Biermann, "Global Environmental Governance", p. 10.

12 Ibid.

13 Jeffery, "Environmental Governance", pp. 11–15.

14 UNECE Convention on Access to Information and Public Participation in Decision-Making and Access to Justice in Environmental Matters, 25 June 1998, 2161 UNTS 447, UN Doc. ECE/CEP/43, 38 ILM 517 (1999), "The Aarhus Convention".

15 Burns H. Weston and David Bollier, 2013, *Green Governance: Ecological Survival, Human Rights and the Law of the Commons*, Cambridge University Press, New York, pp. 35–36.

16 Marie-Danielle Smith, 2015, "Scathing UN Report a Rallying Cry for Civil Society Opposition", 24 July, available at www.embassynews.ca/news/2015/07/23/scathing-un-report-a-rallying cry-for-civil-society.

17 Bill C-51 passed into law as the Anti-Terrorism Act, 18 June 2015, widely acknowledged as a blatant attack on civil liberties.

18 R. D. Bullard, 1994, *Dumping in Dixie*, Westview Press, Boulder, CO; Laura Westra and Bill E. Lawson, 2001, *Faces of Environmental Racism*, 2nd edn, Rowman Littlefield, Lanham, MD.

19 Franz-Theo Gottwald, 2016, "Bioeconomy", in Laura Westra, J. Gray and A. d'Aloia (eds), *The Common Good and the Role of Ecological Integrity in Support of Life*, Routledge, London (in press).

20 Olivia Woolley, 2014, *Ecological Governance*, Cambridge University Press, Cambridge, p. 27.

21 Laura Westra, 1994, *The Principle of Integrity*, Rowman Littlefield, Lanham, MD; the summary discussion that follows has been influenced by my conversations with the late James Kay, who had worked with Holling and was kind enough to help myself and other non-scientists in the group, to better understand the interface between Holling's theory and ecological integrity.

22 Robert Rosen, 1991, *Life Itself: A Comprehensive Inquiry into the Nature, Origin, and Fabrication of Life*, Columbia University Press, New York.

23 Ibid., p. 116.

24 Robert V. O'Neill, Donald Lee Deangelis, J. B. Waide and Garland E. Allen, 1986, *The Hierarchical Concept of Ecosystems*, Princeton University Press, Princeton, NJ, p. 3.

25 Ibid., p. 4.

26 Ibid., p. 5.

27 Ibid., pp. 16–17.

28 William Vayda, 1992, *Psychonutrition*, Lothian Publishing, Port Melbourne, Australia.

29 C. S. Holling, 1992, "The Resilience of Terrestrial Ecosystems; Local Surprises and Global Change," in W. C. Clark and R. E. Munn (eds), *Sustainable Development of the Biosphere*, Cambridge University Press, Cambridge, pp. 292–317.

30 Ibid.

31 N. O. Nielsen, 1991, *Ecosystem Health and Sustainable Agriculture*, The Science Council of Canada, University of Guelph, Ontario.

32 Woolley, *Ecological Governance*, p. 161.

33 Ibid.

34 Ibid., p. 160.

35 Ibid.

36 Ibid., p. 161.
37 Ibid., p. 28.
38 Ibid., p. 30.
39 Ibid., p. 189.
40 Ibid., p. 188.
41 Ibid., p. 189.
42 Ibid., pp. 190–198.
43 Ibid., p. 199.
44 Weston and Bollier, *Green Governance*, p. 123.
45 Laura Westra, 2000, "Environmental Rights and Human Rights: The Final Enclosure Movement", in Roger Brownsword (ed.), *Global Governance and the Quest for Justice*, vol. IV, *Human Rights*, Hart Publishing, Oxford, pp. 107–120; Laura Westra, 2011, *Human Rights: The Commons and the Collective*, University of British Columbia Press, Vancouver, BC.
46 Weston and Bollier, *Green Governance*, pp.160–162; see also Chapter 2 of this work.
47 Weston and Bollier, *Green Governance*, pp. 159–160.
48 Westra, *Human Rights*, pp. 7–48.
49 Weston and Bollier, *Green Governance*, pp. 162–167.
50 Ibid., pp. 167–168.
51 Ibid., pp. 168–170.
52 Ibid., pp. 170–173, which is perhaps the most worthy of consideration.
53 On the role of the Internet in this regard, see for instance Saskia Sassen on "transnational citizens": Saskia Sassen, 2006, *Territory, Authority, Rights: From Medieval to Global Assemblages*, Princeton University Press, Princeton, NJ.
54 Weston and Bollier, *Green Governance*, p. 173.
55 Ibid., p. 180.
56 Ibid., p. 184.
57 Ibid., p. 179.
58 Ibid.
59 Ibid., p. 233.
60 William E. Rees, 2008, "Confounding Integrity: Humanity as a Dissipative Structure", in Laura Westra, Klaus Bosselmann and Richard Westra (eds), *Reconciling Human Existence with Ecological Integrity*, Earthscan, London, pp. 293–302.
61 Weston and Bollier, *Green Governance*, p. 236.
62 Ibid., p. 238.
63 Laura Westra, *Globalization, Violence and World Governance*, Brill, Leyden, The Netherlands, pp. 92–101.
64 *State of Connecticut et al. v. American Electric Power Company, Inc. et al.*, 2 September 2009 decided; see also *Minors Oposa v. The Philippines*.
65 Mary Christina Wood, 2014, *Nature's Trust*, Cambridge University Press, New York.
66 Weston and Bollier, *Green Governance*, p. 263.
67 Ibid., p. 266.
68 Fritjhof Capra and Ugo Mattei, 2015, *The Ecology of Law*, Berrett, Koehler Publishers, San Francisco, CA, p. 131.
69 Ibid.
70 Ugo Mattei and Laura Nader, 2008, *Plunder*, Blackwell Publishing, Oxford.
71 Ibid., p. 132.
72 Laura Westra, 2013, *The Supranational Corporation*, Brill, Leyden, The Netherlands.
73 Mattei and Nader, *Plunder*, p. 133.
74 Capra and Mattei, *The Ecology of Law*, p. 134.
75 Ibid., p. 136.
76 Ibid., p. 137.
77 Ibid.
78 Ibid., p. 139.

79 Ibid., p. 144.
80 Philip Landrigan and Ruth Etzel, 2014, *Children's Environmental Health*, Oxford University Press, New York; Philippe Grandjean, 2013, *Only One Chance: How Environmental Pollution Impairs Brain Development – and How to Protect the Brains of the Next Generation*, Oxford University Press, Oxford.
81 Personal communication, September 2015.
82 Capra and Mattei, *The Ecology of Law*, p. 156.
83 Ibid., p. 164.
84 Ibid., p. 179.
85 Wood, *Nature's Trust*, p. 164.
86 Ibid., 162; discussing Weston and Bollier, *Green Governance*, p. 104.
87 Wood, *Nature's Trust*, p. 163.
88 Ibid., p. 9.
89 Ibid.
90 Ibid., p. 10.
91 Ibid., p. 119.
92 Ibid., p. 120.
93 George Monbiot, 2015, *Feral*, University of Chicago Press, Chicago, IL, p. xx.
94 Wood, *Nature's Trust*, p. 129.
95 Jack Manno, 2014, "Sharing the River of Life: the Two Row Wampun Renewal Campaign", in Westra and Vilela, *The Earth Charter*, pp. 159–168.
96 Wood, *Nature's Trust*, p. 143.
97 Ibid., p. 144.
98 Ibid., p. 145.
99 *Gabčíkovo-Nagymaros Project (Hungary/Slovakia)*, Judge C. Weeramantry Separate Opinion, at www.icj-cij.org/docket/index.php?p1=3&p2=3&case=92.
100 Wood, *Nature's Trust*, p. 146.
101 Ibid., p. 149.
102 Ibid., p. 156.
103 Ibid., p. 159.
104 Ibid., p. 167.
105 Wolfgang Sachs, 2009, "Preface to the New Edition", in his *Development Dictionary*, Zed Books, London, pp. vii–xv.
106 *State of Connecticut, et al. v. American Electric Power Company, Inc. et. al.*, 2009.
107 Ibid., p. 8.
108 Ibid., p. 9.
109 Ibid., p. 10.
110 Late Corp. of the Church of Jesus Christ of Latter Day saints v. United States; *State of Connecticut, et al. v. American Electric Power Company, Inc. et. al.*, 2009: 38
111 *E. (Mrs.) v. Eve* 1986; *Winnipeg Child and Family Services (Northwest Area) v. D.G.F.* 1997
112 Michael Morin, 1990, "La competence parens patriae et le droit privé", *Revue de Barreau Tome* 50(5), pp. 827–924.
113 Ibid.
114 Ibid., p. 830; J. H. Baker, 1979, *An Introduction to English Legal History*, 2nd edn, Butterworth, London, p. 273.
115 Morin "La competence parens patriae et le droit privé", p. 830; Baker, *An Introduction to English Legal History*, p. 273.
116 Morin "La competence parens patriae et le droit privé", p. 32.
117 *Skinner v. Warner, Dickens* 799, 21 ER 473 (Ch.1792).
118 La Forest, J., 1986 (Case *E. (Mrs) v. Eve*, 1986).
119 *Hepton v. Maat* 1957 (case cited in case above).
120 La Forest, J., 1986: 39 (Case *E. (Mrs) v. Eve*, 1986).
121 [1975] 1 All ER 697, [1975] Fam. 47.

122 Re Eve, La Forest, J. at para. 44.
123 *Stump v. Sparkman* 1978.
124 378 NYS 2d 989 (Sup. Ct., 1976), at para. 991.
125 *Moore v. Flagg*; Matter of Weberlist, 79 Misc. 2d 753, 360 NYS 2d 783.
126 La Forest, J. at para. 64 (Case *E. (Mrs) v. Eve*, 1986).
127 Licia Licari, Linda Nemer and Georgia Tamburlini, 2005, *Children's Health and the Environment*, World Health Organization for Europe Office, Copenhagen, Denmark; Philippe Grandjean and Philip Landrigan, 2006, "Developmental Neurotoxicity of Industrial Chemicals", *The Lancet* 368, pp. 2167–2178.
128 Jonathan Patz, 2005, "Impact of Regional Climate Change on Human Health", *Nature* 438, pp. 310–317.
129 *Georgia v. Tenn. Copper Co.* 1907.
130 Ibid., p. 237.
131 *Snapp v. Puerto Rico* 1982
132 Ibid., p. 4 n. 10.
133 Ibid., p. 41, and n. 11.
134 Ibid.
135 James L. Huffman, 2003, "Fish Out of Water: The Public Trust Doctrine in a Constitutional Democracy", Article 6, Joseph Sax and the Public Trust, *Issues in Legal Scholarship*, available at www.bepress.com/ils/iss4/art.6, p. 21.
136 Ibid.
137 Ibid., p. 2.
138 Ibid., p. 3.
139 Ibid., pp. 4, 22, n. 146.
140 Ibid., p. 22.
141 *Illinois Central R. V. Illinois* 1892.
142 Ibid., p. 23.
143 Dwight G. Newman, 2004, "Collective Interests and Collective Rights", *American Journal of Jurisprudence* 49, pp. 127–163.
144 Mary Christina Wood, 2009, "Advancing the Sovereign Trust of Governments to Safeguard the Environment for Present and Future Generations. Part I: Ecological Realism and the Need for a Paradigm Shift", *Environmental Law* 39, pp. 43–89, here p. 43.
145 Ibid., p. 56; James Gustave Speth, 2008, *The Bridge at the End of the World: Capitalism, the Environment and Crossing from Crises to Sustainability*, Yale University Press, New Haven, CT.
146 Wood, "Advancing the Sovereign Trust of Governments ...", p. 47.
147 Ibid., p. 55.
148 Ibid., p. 57.
149 Ibid.
150 Mark Hertsgaard, 1999, *Earth Odyssey: Around the World in Search of our Environmental Future*, Broadway Books, New York, p. 273.
151 Wood, "Advancing the Sovereign Trust of Governments ...", p. 61.
152 Ibid.
153 Ibid., p. 62.
154 Ibid., p. 63.
155 Hazel Henderson, 2011, "Reforming Markets Globally and the Role of Social Innovation for Sustainability", in Patrick U. Petit (ed.), *Earth Capitalism*, Transaction Publishers, Piscataway, NJ, pp. 7–22, here p. 9.
156 Jeffrey D. Sachs, 2015, *The Age of Sustainable Development*, Columbia University Press, New York, p. 11.
157 Ibid., p. 34.
158 Ibid., p. 35.
159 Ibid., p. 37.

160 Ibid., p. 307.
161 Philippe Sands, 2006, *Lawless World*, Allen Lane, London; Mattei and Nader, *Plunder*; Arthur S. Miller, 1987, "Corporations and Our Two Constitutions", in Warren J. Samuels and Arthur S. Miller (eds), *Corporations and Society*, Greenwood Press, New York, pp. 241–262; Karin Mickelson and William Rees, 2003, "Environmental Law: Social Myth or Ecological Reality?", in E. Hughes, A. R. Lucas and W. A. Tilleman (eds), *Environmental Law and Policy*, 3rd edn, Edmond Montgomery Publications, Toronto, Canada; Martha McClusky, 2006, "The Substantive Politics of formal Corporate Power", *Buffalo Law Review* 53, pp. 1453–1501; Steven M. Druker, 2015, *Altered Genes, Twisted Truth*, Clear River Press, Salt Lake City, UT; Westra, *The Supranational Corporation*; to mention just a few of the many works addressing this topic.
162 Daniele Archibugi, 2008, *The Global Commonwealth of Citizens*, Princeton University Press, Princeton, NJ, p. 2.
163 Carl Boggs, 2000, *The End of Politics*, Guilford Press, New York, p. 119.
164 Westra, *The Supranational Corporation*, ch. 4.
165 Archibugi, *The Global Commonwealth of Citizens*, p. 3.
166 Ibid., p. 4.
167 Ibid., p. 5.
168 Ibid., p. 228.
169 Miller, "Corporations and our Two Constitutions", p. 246.
170 Ibid.
171 Mark Kesselman, 1982, "The Conflictual Evolution of American Political Science: From Apologetic Pluralism to Trilateralism and Marxism", in J. Greenstone (ed.), *Public Values and Private Power in American Politics*, University of Chicago Press, Chicago, IL, p. 571.
172 Sands, 2004.
173 Boggs, *The End of Politics*, p. 119.
174 Ibid., p. 118.
175 Ibid.
176 Ibid., p. 11.
177 William E. Rees, 2014, *Avoiding Collapse: An Agenda for Sustainable Degrowth and Relocalizing the Economy*, Climate Justice Project, Canadian Centre for Policy Alternatives, British Columbia, p. 4.
178 Rees, *Avoiding Collapse*, p. 1.
179 Ibid., p. 2.
180 John Stuart Mill, 1848, *Principles of Political Economy and Some of their Applications to Social Philosophy*, 7th edn (1909), ed. W. J. Ashley, Longmans Green & Co., London, ch. 4.
181 Rees, *Avoiding Collapse*, p. 11.
182 Ibid., p. 13.
183 Ibid., p. 15.
184 Druker, *Altered Genes, Twisted Truth*; Philip Landrigan and Charles Benbrook, 2015, "GMOs, Herbicides, and Public Health", *New England Journal of Medicine* 373, pp. 693–695.
185 Sassen, *Territory, Authority, Rights*.

7 The "integrity of the earth"

A moral and legal imperative for survival

Introduction: *Laudato Si'*, the May 2015 papal encyclical

> Patriarch Bartholomew has spoken in particular of the need for each of us to repent of the ways we have harmed the planet … "For human beings … to destroy the biological diversity of God's creation; for human beings to degrade the integrity of the earth by causing changes in its climate, by stripping the earth of its natural forests or destroying its wetlands; for human beings to contaminate the earth's waters, its land, its air, and its life – these are sins". For "to commit a crime against the natural world is a sin against ourselves and a sin against God".[1]

We need not follow Pope Francis in speaking about sin, perhaps, but we can concur with the understanding of a crime,[2] committed against both the natural world and the poor (para. 16), because both are equally fragile and equally under attack. Both the symptoms and the "deepest causes of this planetary attack" (para. 15) are based on "constant and rapid change" (para. 18), which is in conflict with the common good and with any hope of true sustainable development (para. 18).

You need not be religious to appreciate the "inherent value" of nature (para. 33) and the importance of the "ecosystem services" it provides (para. 34), while the "plunder of diversity" (para. 32) and the deprivation of water (para. 27), which is "a basic human right" (para. 30), clearly indicate what happens when "ecosystems are modified" (para. 42) and they lose their integrity as a "result of exploitation" (para. 38). We also find in that letter "the appeal to integral ecology" (paras 135–162); the reference to climate as a "common good" (para. 23); the repeated critique of "anthropocentrism" (paras 115–136) and of "consumerism" (para. 9), all themes I have proposed in this work.

What renders this Encyclical so outstanding, is the repeated and deliberate connection between the attacks on integrity and those on the poor: disintegrity fosters "global inequality" and the "premature death of the poor" (para. 48). For this reason, the "true ecological approach always becomes a social approach" (para. 49), a connection only generally acknowledged, at best, by economists and others who joined with the Pope in decrying what is here called "the ecological debt" (para. 51).

Economists do not recognize that the concern for the poor, for inequality, laudable though it remains, cannot be corrected by single environmental regulatory remedies, not without returning to the necessary basis, that is, ecological integrity, as Pope Francis clearly recognizes. That "basis" cannot be separated from the injustice that plague the world, as "foreign debt controls poor countries", as "the ecological debt fuels the development of the richer countries" (para. 52).

Every part of the "material universe" working together indicates a common functioning, even if we prefer to avoid the religious implications of Francis's own "common purpose" (para. 84 and para. 86, respectively). In fact, we need only recall Aldo Leopold's exhortation regarding natural systems, that we respect their structure, and not throw out parts whose roles, and functions, we may not accurately know.[3] Leopold's position is one of biocentric holism, as supported also by Albert Schweitzer and his work on respect for life.

I think "biocentric holism" captures the core sense of the doctrine in a better way. It is not meant to imply that "biocentric holism" advocates absolute respect for all life, as Albert Schweitzer, for instance, did. I find Schweitzer's position hard to adopt, though easy to admire. I term "holism" "biocentric" because that seems to emphasize the centrality of life to the doctrine that is indeed "ecocentric". Whether we are speaking of "ecosystems" or "wholes", we are speaking essentially of life support.

In essence, the "whole" is not the same as the sum or aggregate of individuals, in that no single individual member of the biota (except humans of course) can affect life in a general way other than its own, or perhaps that of another organism that depends upon it. An ecosystem, however, does support life in a general sense. Hence, I believe it is appropriate to emphasize this function in the way we define holism.

Whatever definition is used, for many holists Leopold's "land ethic" has been a major source of inspiration, and there is no comparable major philosophical doctrine that can be traced back to intraspecific (human) ethics, as its starting point. In fact, the only possible human "analogy" is that of sociobiology, a paradigm so fraught with problems that it offers little help to anyone attempting to ground biocentric holism on an established moral doctrine. So, those who are inspired in varying degrees by Leopold's work are often dismissed in a cavalier fashion or, at the very least, viewed as upholding an undefensible position, one which – if accepted – would lead to conclusions that are "socially absurd" and "morally paradoxical". There have been both philosophers and scientists that have focused in various ways on "the integrity of the earth", as there have been many who have worked primarily on social justice and the plight of the poor.[4]

The papal encyclical, however, states unequivocally that you cannot have respect for the dignity and the rights of the poor, and pursue social justice, without starting from the basic requirement of all humanity: their habitat.

Laudato Si' not only advocates more environmental concern, or proposes some minor changes ("changes at the margin", as described by Bill Rees), but a radical reorganization of global policies, a complete overhaul of life as we have been living it. As evidenced of this overhaul, is the position he holds regarding property, as "the right to private property is not absolute or inviolable" (para. 93) and technological advances are not always "progress". The "crisis of modern anthropocentrism" (para. 115) requires "the idea of promoting a different cultural paradigm, and employing technology as a mere instrument", a position which seems "inconceivable" today (para. 108).

Such a reversal represents an imperative because, at present, the "technological paradigm also tends to dominate economic and political life … without concern for its … negative impact on human beings" (para. 109). In fact, Pope Francis is not the only person to acknowledge the "tremendous power of technology" (para. 100), leading to the current "globalization of the technological paradigm", as Hans Jonas in 1984 suggested that nature has "a dignity of ends", and that its ends were also our ends:[5]

> Granted that we can take our own evolution in hand, it will slip from that hand by the very pulse it has received from it: and here more than anywhere else applies the adage that we are free at the first step but slaves at the second and all further ones.[6]

The "ecological culture" advocated in *Laudato Si'* should "generate resistance to the assault of the technological paradigm" (para. 111) and it should force us to recognize the need to protect "integral ecology" (para. 124), and one of its implicit requirements is the right to work, the respect for animals as part of the "integrity of creation" (para. 130), and the negative impact of GMOs (para. 136). The basis for all the requirements of "integral ecology" (para. 137) is the "interconnectedness between the networks of living organisms" (para. 138), as not only "ecosystems have inherent value independent of their usefulness" (para. 140), but we are "part of nature … and nature is not separate from us" (para. 139).

Hence the "Principle of the Common Good" (para. 156) entails fostering "intergenerational justice" (para. 159), as well as defending "cultural ecology" (para. 143), that is "preserving cultures", especially "indigenous cultures and their cultural traditions" (para. 146). Even this cursory overview of the papal encyclical shows the closeness between its understanding of the present situation and the aetiology that has led to it, and this work. Hence, although this is a religious document, rather than a legal or other scholarly discussion, its importance is incalculable, as it is at the same time the declaration of a head of state.

We cannot fully follow Pope Francis in his suggestions to remedy the current impasse, because some, though not all, have a strong religious content. But we should acknowledge the variety of almost unanimous positions we have reviewed, between our work and that of the Pontiff, so we can acknowledge that our assessment of the gravity of today's environmental conditions and the many ramifications that ensue are beyond question, and neither is the acknowledgment of the multiple causes that led and are still leading to these conditions.

In contrast, it is much harder to assess which might be the best approach to achieve the urgent progress that is needed. In the following sections in this chapter, we will review some of the proposals of the other scholars we have studied, then return to what we are tentatively proposing in this work.

Overview of positive findings for ecologically based governance

> In summary, ecosystem services are vital for human survival and well-being. Biodiversity in turn is vital· for healthy ecosystem functioning. Yet biodiversity is under unprecedented threat as the result of thoughtless, unknowing human activity. We are undermining the very support structures for our biological survival and cultural vitality.[7]

Economists, ecological economists, activists, ecologists, conservation biologists, legal scholars and even Pope Francis, appear to agree on this assessment of the current situation, regarding both this issue and climate change. Thinking people everywhere agree on the diagnosis, while still holding highly divergent positions on the possible cure, or the solutions that might work.

Each time we discussed one of these positions, we acknowledged the difficulties that accompanied each one, and we'll return to a summary of these difficulties in the next section. For now, we need to focus on the positive aspects present in each strategy, although none of them appears to offer a solid solution as it stands. Thus the question that arises is, leaving aside for now the problems and obstacles that plague each proposal, what is the most promising aspect of each: the first is the rediscovery and revaluing of the commons, the "tragedy" of which started, according to Hardin, with the enclosure movements in England,[8] but gained an important rebirth recently.[9] Klaus Bosselmann says:

> The point is to recapture the narrative about our shared wealth in the community of life and shed the instrumental approach to nature, by including more ecological, social, democratic and moral value.[10]

He adds, speaking of Hardin's "tragedy of the commons": "Rational self-interest gives rise to an irrational outcome."[11] When we consider the rise to attention of the concept of the commons, as we saw it in The Charter of the Forest, it included not only the necessary space for grazing sheep, but the forest, the woods, the rivers, the peasants' abodes and the animals in "the commons", or rather, as it was called at the time, the "forest".

One wonders why, if an absolute medieval monarch could be persuaded that he could not exploit "the forest" for himself, and have guards and "beadles" to punish trespassers or those who questioned his supreme power over those aspects of his domain, today's democratic states cannot seem to understand the urgency of the people's needs and their rights. The reason for this lack of understanding, is that any nobleman or king at least realized that peasants had to be kept alive and fit to work, minimally, even if he had little concern for their specific interest.

In contrast, the only concern of today's Western states and the corporations that support them is to increase their joint economic and geographical power. The physical fitness of their workers is no longer all-important, because the functions they perform, for the most part, require cleverness, technical expertise, not brawn. Further, should they become ill because of the lack of a healthy/safe environment (see Chapter 2), some major powers have no social medicine, and in most countries citizens must purchase medicines at the outrageous prices Big Pharma enforces, often for diseases they could have avoided, if appropriate concern for the state of the commons had been practised.

When we speak of the commons in this context, we exclude deliberately the technically manufactured "commons", such as the commonalities to be found through the internet, which include some that are in direct conflict with the biocentrism we embrace, as we shall argue in the next section. The second positive strategy we noted, was that of viewing states as "trustees", not sovereigns controlling the natural commons in their own interest, rather, holding them in trust for the public good, the common interest of humanity, at least each state for their own citizens. We will return to this concern below, as it is just an aspect of an otherwise excellent ecological strategy.

Bosselmann expresses this concern as well: "The appetite of states to exploit the global environment is greater than the interest in preserving it."[12] Yet the strategy of trusteeship, proposing a fiduciary relation to what exists presently between states and citizens, has a powerful appeal. It seems obvious that the allegiance of citizens, at least insofar as carrying their country's passports, embracing the main obligations of citizenship (paying taxes, obeying the law, respecting police and state functionaries) has as its counterpart, the state's own obligation to protect. However, it is precisely the meaning and extent of that protection that is and remains in question.

We noted in Chapter 2 the Canadian "fiduciary" obligation to its First Nation, a consideration that transcends their obligations to the general public. It is significant that it is an obligation that obliges the Crown with respect to the FNs, while at the same time, it forces upon it a corresponding obligation of ecological protection. Hence this is a prime example of fiduciary obligation on the part of a state, and it is originally based on the peremptory declaration of King George III, the head of another state of which Canada is no longer a part or a colony, although it has been retained as part of the Canadian constitution, perhaps thus maintaining an international connection.[13]

Unquestionably, the most significant aspect of the trust doctrine is to recall explicitly governments to their obligation to citizens, as the protection of their life is the governments' first obligation, an obligation not often acknowledged in the jurisprudence.[14] The obligation to protect seems to be indisputable and easy to support in law, although its reach and full meaning is in question and may need some serious re-examination. This is another difficulty to which we will return in the next section.

We are committed to reaching a regime that would support global ecological integrity, hence any legal regime that is limited to a state's own citizens is at best necessary, but not sufficient for our purpose.

Hence what is necessary is to apply the positive aspects of "nature's trust", as it applied to states, to a global situation. Wood asserts that "once a natural resource becomes identified as a planetary trust asset, legal principles evaluate its management according to measures of *asset health and functionality*", which she views as basic, a first step so that "the trust formulation creates a uniform and principled approach to global ecological responsibility".[15] Such a situation should ensure that "citizens should pursue enforcement of global trust obligations against their own governments in domestic courts".[16]

We will consider below, whether such a suggestion is feasible, based as it is on a "holistic approach to defining government obligation".[17] In fact, it is this "holistic approach" that led to a further consideration of the common heritage of humankind (CH) principle, not presently applied to global ecological responsibility, but perhaps representing the best potential for such a novel application of an existing regime.

The best potential may be found in the most recent attempt to "develop an internationally legally-binding instrument … on the conservation and sustainable use of marine biological diversity of areas beyond national jurisdiction".[18] The potential outcome is that, after acknowledging the grave importance of protecting biodiversity wherever it is, in one context, it seems hard to limit it to areas below the sea, and only beyond the reach of states.

The other important aspect from the standpoint of ecological integrity, is the fact that the proposal to the UN, the possible development of the binding instrument, is the result of the considerations of a learned group of scholars, not simply of an open "democratic" vote. It is worth noting that this approach is characteristic of every positive element we have identified, from the presence of "resilience",[19] which requires learned scientific assessment of the specific point which renders ecosystems no longer resilient, or functional. The work of George Monbiot[20] relies to a great extent on personal experience, but it's also based on the scientific assessment of the need for conservation. A science-based understanding of what is required in order to avoid ecological disasters is necessary to establish the trust Wood recommends.

Thus, each one of the most positive strategies suggested, has a clear established scientific basis, as does ecological integrity as a principle. However, each of the suggestions we have discussed also, and perhaps primarily, requires both informing and transforming the public, the citizenry on whose democratic decisions each proposal relies. And it is here that I must take an unpopular stance: the situation now is so urgent, so dire that, although both informing and even "transforming" is possible, and when applied to citizens everywhere it is important and even necessary, waiting to take action based on that hoped-for transformation is both dangerous and irresponsible. We will discuss this problem as well as other obstacles to the full adoption of the many well thought-out proposals we have examined in the next section.

Review of problems and obstacles in the best strategies reviewed

> He who demands that law should rule may be regarded as commanding that God and reason alone should rule; he who commands that a man should rule adds the character of the beast ... Law [as the pure voice of God and reason] may thus be defined as reason free from all passion.[21]

It is not encouraging to turn from the positives in the previous section to acknowledging the grave obstacles besetting any of the otherwise well-thought out strategies we have examined. For instance, when we return to a consideration of the commons, we are struck by a difficulty inherent in an otherwise highly desirable approach. Weston and Bollier point to the complex and extended meaning of "commoning" today. While the basis for their argument is indeed the natural commons in the original sense of the concept, in order to support the claims for the current acceptance and even the spread of the interest in the commons and commoning worldwide, they include the acceptance of many common interests and causes, facilitated by the internet, which contribute to unify and promote many groups.

While this is certainly true, this reality works both for and against their argument. We noted that, with the "retreat" of the states, the commitment of today's transnational citizens[22] is found far more in the various associations and INGOs proliferating through the internet. This forces us to face that, while the common interest is the engine that moves forward and encourages new communities, it is, at the same time, equally present in any number of associations whose well-paid "experts" push and promote messages in contrast with the commons. They may promote GMOs, consumerism, war and gun ownership, violent games, and messages that are generally hostile to what the "commoners" aspire to.

This recent turn to transnationality is equally hostile to the return ecological economist William Rees proposes to local centres and communities, small towns perhaps, away from globalization. It is hard to believe that most citizens who have already transcended the state barriers to move into the internationality of the globalized internet, would be willing to give primacy to even smaller units, instead. It seems that, for the most part , since the international communities we find may or may not foster the ideals of "communing" in order to support the basic rights of humanity as they relate from and are founded on the natural world, we need to transcend special communities (perhaps with the exception of those of Indigenous peoples) and reach out first to what is absolutely basic to the collectivity as a whole, viewed as "the community of life", whose collective, aggregate interests may transcend those of many globalized "communities", as I argued in Chapter 4 (see section on "Aggregate interests and collective rights" in that chapter).

Therefore, with the exception of Indigenous peoples, the fact that some groups are "commoning" may not necessarily help the goals of green governance. This is a bottom-up approach; that is, one that starts with the "earth democracy" proposed by Klaus Bosselmann.[23]

The next strategy proposed by M. C. Wood[24] comes instead from the side of governance. Nature's trust, in the hand of states, suggests a non-derogable, fiduciary mandate on the part of States, based on solid legality, but without the acknowledgment of the close connection between global economic interests and the States themselves. That connection indicates that, especially in the case of wealthy countries and their satellites, state interest and the public interest are in direct conflict.

Yet Nature's Trust is a strategy that is highly desirable: the previous chapter discussed the only US case that used that strategy successfully, at least until the appeal (see Chapter 6). But the problems we are discussing are global hence, even if States were able to somehow shake their dependence on corporate support (not a likely scenario, in any case), it is doubtful how this highly desirable situation could be enacted globally. The only global institution that might be available to hold this fiduciary mandate, would be the UN, or some significant and powerful organ of that organization, but the present situation is not encouraging in that regard.

A global trust for collective security?

> With all the convulsions of global society, only one power is left that can impose order on incipient chaos. It is the power of principles transcending changing perceptions of expediency.[25]

The Secretary-General Boutros Boutros-Ghali was indeed prophetic in his words to the Security Council. Today's situation, combining multiple unjust and unprincipled ongoing conflicts, is a clear demonstration that, failing the imposition of principled restrains, the alternative is a violent and lawless world. Yet the Security Council, even after its recent restructuring (2005), is still firmly bound by the "expediency" of interests of its own major powers, with no regard for the moral or philosophical basis that should govern its activities, or even by the basic principles and foundational aims of the UN.

Global security and the very aims of the United Nations, for instance, are totally dependent on the return to the principles of *jus ad bellum* and *jus in bello*, and the peremptory norms governing human rights.[26]

We are seeking a "world law" capable of redressing the present "unfairness" and illegalities, as well as the lack of principled action globally. The United Nations appears to be the most likely candidate to provide a centralized focus for such principled action, and as the locus of a "world law" however designed. But the Security Council clearly has the final word on any practical application of any UN declaration, instrument, or report.

The Role of the Security Council prevents the presence of fairness in UN institutions. Many different conclusions have been reached as to whether the ICJ has powers of judicial review over acts of the Security Council … If what is meant is an automatic constitutional process review with compulsory effect, both the UN Charter and the Statue of the International Court are silent in this respect.[27]

Thus, although our argument leads to the need for a centralized organization, with ultimate powers, as the locus for a "world law", and that the UN is the only present actor able to fulfil that role, the organ with overarching authority, that is, the SC, is not subject to final review of its decisions, nor is its power based on the will of a strong majority of States. However, the fact that there is no "automatic review" of its decisions, together with the reason of its limited "democratic" presence, renders such an authority suspect as the ultimate locus of power. As well, the SC may reach decisions beyond its procedural limits and, at least in the 1995 ICJ case, it was viewed as subject to the possibility of review:

> The Security Council is an organ of an international organization, established by a treaty which serves as constitutional framework for that organization. The Security Council is thus subject to certain constitutional limitations, and neither the text nor the spirit of the Charter conceives of the Security Council as unbound by law.[28]

Another important aspect of the SC powers can be found in articles 24–26 of the charter. Article 25, for instance, which "functions to give Chapter VII resolution their binding force"; however, the SC is "bound by the Purposes and Principles of the Organization, so that it cannot, in principle, act arbitrarily and unfettered by any restraints".[29] Member States are obliged to accept and carry out the decisions of the Security Council in accordance with article 25 of the Charter. But the language here is somewhat ambiguous, as it may imply the primacy of the Charter principles regarding the mandates of the SC, or it may simply refer to the obligations of the member states of the UN.

At any rate, one would think that as the UN is the matrix of the SC, the UN principles ought to prevail. Yet there is no specific mechanism, to my knowledge, to either support the decision of the SC to confirm it, or to challenge it. This lack of supervisory authority appears to apply to what the SC does and what it does not do, and it is the latter aspect of the exercise of its powers that can be found to be most at fault. In fact, despite the language of Article 2 of the Charter, which states that the "purposes and principles of the UN Charter shall bind the Organization and its members",[30] the omissions of the SC often contrast with the UN purposes and principles.

The primacy of the Charter includes the "Principles of International Law and Justice", according to Article 1, hence the SC should be obliged to prescribe and enforce certain measures in response to any instance of aggression on the part of a state, something that does not appear to occur in all cases. But the SC "discretionary powers" are not unlimited, at least according to Ian Brownlie,[31] hence the determination that there is a "threat of aggression", must still remain "within the broad framework of the UN Charter".[32] *A fortiori* then, all the determinations of the Security Council, including the decisions that certain situations do not, of themselves, constitute a threat to peace, must (or should) observe closely the Charter Articles that refer to such situations. Hence it is hard to understand why so many ongoing conflicts, as well as other obvious breaches of *jus cogens* norms (such as the prohibition of the practice of apartheid for instance), remain unremarked and, even when condemned by Advisory Opinions or other UN Declarations, unpunished for years.

The principal organs of the UN "are empowered under the Charter, to establish subsidiary organs which then, both by design and in practice, possess a high degree of autonomy from the parent bodies".[33] Thus the ICTY could exercise its judicial functions after having been established by the SC.[34]

At any rate, the possible misuse of the powers of the SC have been acknowledged by well-known scholars. For instance, speaking of possible limitations to the SC powers, Judge Fitzmaurice said:

> Without these limitations, the functions of the Security Council could be used for purposes never originally intended … [such as where] there was no threat to peace and security other than such as might be artificially created as a pretext for the realization of ulterior purposes.[35]

The argument of this work has tended to focus on the opposite danger, that is, the possibility of special "purposes", which might produce the opposite result, that is, convincing the SC not to recognize a "threat to peace and security" that is obvious, or even an ongoing situation of conflict, for political motives. To my knowledge, the SC has not been formally questioned for its omissions. Lamb recognizes that for states, organizations and even UN organs, "the legal regime is primarily one of self-limitations".[36] She adds:

> the inherent and fundamental difficulties in subjecting the Security Council to legal controls are not diminished and in this regard … the identification of the problem is easier than the prescription of a cure.[37]

Thus the only or best source of a global trust, that is the United Nations, is neither fully impartial nor entirely capable of embracing a fiduciary obligation of the needed magnitude. It seems hard to trust the survival of humanity to such a weak and conflicted institution, although it is hard to identify a substitute: we'll return to this question after we consider briefly yet another difficulty that emerges.

Earth democracy and democratic faith

> People form governments for their common defense, security and welfare. The first thing that public officials owe their constituents is protection against natural and man-made hazards.[38]

Gostin indicates what should be the foundation of the relation between any government and its citizens: complete protection from harm, on the part of governments, and citizens' support and allegiance based on trust in that common defence. When people's existence is under threat from a number of different sources, and for most of them either the government has no defence to offer, or it is even complicit with the risk/harm imposers, then the democratic social contract appears to be in danger.

Are people prepared to coalesce and join together to fight for the Earth, forcing their governments to alter their basic goals and practices? This is the main problem. Each and every author who has proposed new strategies of governance, wants to inform the public, but somehow they go from their ability to inform, which is undisputable, to their assurance to *transform* other citizens through that information, so that they fully accept the need for radical change based on ecology, and are committed to bring about that change in action through their governments.

There are two unwarranted moves in this sequence, desirable though it might be. The first is the fact that once we are informed in a credible and convincing manner, "transformation" will automatically follow. Bill Rees used to think this will happen because we are basically too intelligent to allow extinction to overtake us, while we continue to follow our "social myths", far from ecological reality, but we will soon realize that "The functional integrity of the ecosphere is not something that can be indefinitely bargained away or 'traded off' against other economic benefits."[39] However, recently he has argued that "Despite considerable grassroots activity and the proliferation of sustainability-oriented NGOs, preferred lies and shared illusions may hold sway over discomforting facts until it is too late to engineer a prosperous way down".[40]

In contrast, Olivia Woolley supports "deliberative democracy" as an integral aspect of liberal democracy,[41] as she states: "I adopt this approach as some means must be found of altering popular attitudes if ecological governance is to take hold."[42]

Yet she acknowledges that "consultation" has "obvious limitations for promoting changes in attitudes" and in fact, it "may not increase acceptance of following decisions significantly".[43] Another approach is that of M.C. Wood, who proposes a fiduciary relationship between states and citizens, based on "nature's trust". This approach should be based on a "top-down" form of governance instead. However, it is not simply so, as the author acknowledges, as "some agencies use technical discretion as free rein to contravene statutory intent":

> While the public may assume agencies implement regulations in a formulaic, objective fashion, requiring very little judgment, in fact agency behaviour can be highly politicized and even corrupt.[44]

But modern democratic governments also need environmentally concerned citizens,

> because the industries have concentrated interest in regulations, they devote the resources necessary to gaining favorable permit approvals. They pay lobbyists, consultants, and lawyers to game the process at every turn.[45]

Of course there are many, many concerned citizens who attempt to include some form of activism in their busy lives. Most often they are unwilling or unable to join others in the "trenches" of environmental protest, so they join environmental groups, which Wood terms “middlemen of democracy”.[46] These middlemen enable citizens to participate in “environmental democracy” by accepting information about ecological threats, which helps members “participate [albeit indirectly] in the current process” with the least possible effort of commitment, often through campaigns that only involve “one click email messages”.[47]

For the most part, these groups play safe “within the rules of the game” while ignoring all the “systemic causes” of the present impasse, as they practice “relentless accommodation”, while pursuing “minimalist goals”: “What is missing from virtually all these groups is an expression of the rage they feel.”[48] This modest effort based on ecological and moral beliefs of those who are already committed, however, contrasts with the disinterests of the great majority of people who continue to believe propaganda and to be driven by self-interest. It is not that the information is not available; but the “transformative powers” it is intended to produce, appear to be less than effective. Wood remarks:

> Humanity cannot hope for a livable planet if government agencies continue to license industries to pollute and destroy the remaining natural resources. Environmental law becomes profoundly relevant to the daily life and future well-being of every citizen alive today. In words that now reverberate the truth in nearly every nation, Ansel Adams once said: “It is horrifying that we have to fight our government to save the environment.”[49]

This passage summarizes the present situation primarily in North America, and in the US. But the US is a country that promotes some of the most illegal and immoral activities that promote their interests, from “counter-terrorism” to multiple conflicts described as ways to “promote democracy” abroad. They are also the country that, although its tradition is based on a vibrant citizenry, committed to civic virtues and to respect for all, is now battling a resurgence of racism and violence in almost every state.

One can understand Wood’s outrage as she considers the history of the United States, and the defence of human rights that was enacted there, as fights against the law were motivated and won by supporting justice. The civil rights movement is a shining example of citizens’ involvement, civic virtues, and the fight for justice, as such, it is clearly an encouraging precedent for those who believe in “earth democracy” and the renewed ethical commitment to ecological global governance.

The eventual triumph of the civil rights movement, a striking example of justice restored in the history of the US, however, should not blind us to the fact that it was the economic interests of the south, which initiated the sordid story of Black slavery in that country.

Hence a long history of justice denied preceded the eventual movements of labour and communist workers that initiated the hard-won eventual (though partial) success of civil rights. Yet, as late as 1960, the *Yale Law Journal* published learned papers on “The Lawfulness of the Segregation Decisions”,[50] aside from the legal opinions of the early 1950s, perhaps an anecdote may add context. The author recalls travelling from New York to Texas on a Greyhound bus, in order to rejoin her (then) US army husband, only to be faced with segregated drinking fountains at restaurant bus stops; also, being told by a benevolent bus driver, that "a nice girl like you should not be sitting in the back of the bus with those coloured soldiers", a friendly group that was singing country music accompanied by a guitar. Both events were utterly incomprehensible for a young woman freshly arrived from northern Italy.

One needs not review the historical development of the civil rights movement, something that has engaged many different scholars over the years. What is significant is the fact that a social and human rights movement was initially reviewed as a revolt against the government's position against such rights. That stance was predicated upon the economic interests of certain states, that is on a position that is repeated today in almost all protest cases, that is human rights versus economic interests.

What can actually be seen as a threat to the US government? Any speech which may "tend to subvert or imperil" the present day government was sufficient to be defined as a "clear and present danger" and states were not required "to measure when a defendant's conduct would actually lead to revolt, if it ever did".[51]

When we consider the present situation, when simply distributing leaflets at the corporate offices of companies contravening animals rights, or environmental regulations, can be construed as an act of terrorism,[52] the historical continuity becomes clear.

In fact it is the social history of the civil rights movement, that the phenomenon we are studying first developed. Kenneth Mack terms it "a new model that emerged" and which "trained its sights on community-level protests and reorganizations".[53] The interesting point is the interplay of law and activism, as often local movements were not supported by the law: the central focus of the latter was "the NAACP, the Supreme Court, Congress, Martin Luther King Jr, and the Congress of Racial Equality (CORE)".[54]

The question that arises is whether courts and legal regimes could, on their own, bring about social change.[55] In addition, Nancy MacLean has written on these questions.[56] Her starting point is former US President Lyndon B. Johnson, whose speech at Howard University in 1965 stated clearly that "freedom is not enough".[57] Racial equality requires far more than formal equality. That question was raised and sometimes answers were attempted in the years that followed. But it is still a live question today, and one that is thoroughly controversial in the US.

Thus, we can understand the motivation of those who have faith in democracy and who believe in the possibility that people everywhere may change their convictions and social attitudes, as they become convinced of the moral strength of the new position they are asked to support. But we cannot forget that the economic interests at play in the civil movement were those of a few major Southern landowners and – even at that time – people of colour were not perceived as a threat to white people's jobs or prospects. The situation for ecologically-based governance is altogether different.

In our case, ecological concerns are perceived (correctly in the context of present economic arrangements) as conflicting with economic growth, understood as "business as usual". The wealthy, more than likely, would find a way to continue to prosper, even when some of their most harmful activities might be curbed by new regulatory regimes. Note that most of the Big Tobacco MNCs, moved on to new markets (Asia and developing countries), but also to new harmful products, laden with fats and sugar, when the Tobacco Convention was enacted in 2005.

Thus it will be the poor and the blue collar workers who depend on some of the industries who will suffer, and possibly pay with their jobs, until the industries might be retooled to offer new employment. Hence the faith in the power of democracy to be transformed even by the best, most thorough, up-to-date information is under attack in two separate ways, at least in the North American continent and its supporters. First, the US's powerful media with its roots in corporate America, has sold ideas, myths, preferences and choices to all citizens, in direct conflict with ecological reality, regardless of the real harms imposed.[58]

Second, and originating to a great extent from the first problem cited, citizens appear to have lost their capacity to use their own ability for critical thought, as they have become used to accept uncritically media/corporate/government messages as truth, a single reflection of reality, rather than the self-interested "social myths" that they are. In addition, again in North America, especially in the US, the government/corporate "mafia" has succeeded for the most part in criminalizing dissent.

The criminalization of dissent

> By framing the issue of injustice in a new way with the slogan "99%" the movement had tapped into a wide and deep alienation and anger over the inequalities, injustice and corruption of the current economic and political system.[59]

Since peaceful legal avenues are blocked, the only way forward that seems to emerge is to rebel and protest, as dissent is the right of citizens in democratic countries; in fact, peaceful dissent is one of the duties of citizenship.[60] For instance dissent was basic to the evolution of African American rights in the US starting with peaceful and not so peaceful dissent in the 1960s. The transformation of civil societies in Eastern Europe in the post-communist era was foundational and an expression of "socialist legality".[61]

Recently, starting with the events of the Arab Spring in 2012 and its terrible though inspiring examples of self-immolation, protests based on forceful resistance, captured the attention first of the media, then of the world itself.

Beyond Arab countries and their brave revolts against exploitive tyrants, many other European countries also had to face forceful and loud resistance form the "Indignados" of Spain, the "Indignati" of Italy, and many others in Greece, England and beyond.

In all those countries citizens united in protests intended to demonstrate that injustice and inequality would no longer be accepted in silence and simply tolerated. In all cases it was economic and corporate power that was (and is) the main target of anger. Yet neither the oppressed people of the Arab Spring, nor the various versions of the "Indignati" of Europe, represented fully original movements.

In some sense the Lords of Davos already knew those forceful protest and that anger well. From Seattle, to Quebec, from Genoa to Toronto and many other places, G8 and G20 meetings have been provoking anger and resistance for years. In all those cases, economic and corporate power as well as their relation to governance were the source of an anger so profound that, increasingly, riot squads and endless police and army forces were needed to control it.

Perhaps there is a global commonality that unites all these disparate movements, with their different ethnicities, situations, religious beliefs and geographical locations: it is the focus of the anger of each of these protests. It is the injustice of unequal treatment, poor living conditions, unquestioned economic power, with no redress for the oppressed, those without work, even without hope: the victims. These protesters appear to discharge their collective obligations, at least to yell loud and clear to pinpoint the cause of all the harms they have suffered.

Even if they demonstrate for themselves and for their families, perhaps for the communities, still, because the sources of the problem are so intimately connected, in the final analysis they are fighting for the collective.

Perhaps not all of us can be in the "trenches", the tents, or stand in front of the police brutality facing every form of resistance, from Egypt to New York. But even those who are not strong enough, free enough, or young enough to meet their obligation in that way, the obligation to state clearly our dissent remains. Acquiescence and silence have been viewed as culpable by such disparate thinkers as Thomas Aquinas, Martin Luther King Jr., and Thomas Jefferson. Dissent itself has become even more difficult today, than it was when those thinkers declared it to represent our common duty as we attempt to achieve justice.

> It is important to note that government measures limiting organized dissent have become increasingly common in our society since the terrorist attacks of 2001. These assaults upon and criminalization of dissent – from the surveillance of activist to the federalization of local law enforcement, to the labeling of activists as "terrorists" – dismantle piece by piece a core right considered essential to meaningful democracy.[62]

So explains the well-supported recent work of Michael and Margaret Ratner. It seems ridiculous to claim that today's dissent and civil disobedience are becoming increasingly harder to sustain than they were in older times, before human rights and democracy gained sway in the world. It is no coincidence that the most terrifying aspects of the repression of dissent occur in North America, principally in the United States (or in countries subject to its influence) although Canada, under its former government was attempting to follow in the steps of its powerful "partner".

The US Constitution guarantees the right to dissent, through free speech, also the right to lobby government officials "for the redress of grievances".[63] But, after 9/11, the success of civil disobedience in the south of the 1960s and 1970s has been forgotten and the US has enacted "special laws that treat acts of civil disobedience as terrorism, and single out environmentalists for especially harsh sentences".[64]

In contrast, there have been a number of laws enacted to attack dissent in all its forms, in order to protect government and corporate interests, which appear to be totally intertwined.[65] Some of the strongest Acts intent upon dismantling what is left of the US democracy, such as the Antiterrorism and Effective Death Penalty Act of 1966, the USA Patriot Act of 2001, and the Animal Enterprise Terrorism Act of 2006,[66] are far from addressing acts of terrorism. The last Act is particularly inappropriate as a characterization of distributing pamphlets, speaking and other activities that are intended to disrupt "the business companies that exploit animals".

Increasingly, the new FBI guidelines allow spying and surveillance, thus establishing branches of a "political police".[67] Hence the basis for the dissent of Occupy movements is clearly justified: corporate and government interests are protected as one, and such benign groups as peaceful environmental resistance associations or societies for the protection of animals, for instance PETA, are simply treated as "terrorism".

The defence of integrity and ecological governance

> The world's economy is continuing to grow at 3–4 percent per year, meaning a doubling over twenty years or so. There are already huge pressures on the world's ecosystems, climate and oceans. We have not yet found a way to reconcile that continuing growth with environmental sustainability.[68]

In the previous section we noted the grave problems besetting democracy. This does not mean, of course, that democracy is to be discarded as a form of governance or ignored: it simply means that at a time when urgent ecological action is required and global governance must be co-opted to protect integrity, hence the survival of life, it seems wrong to make this goal conditional upon a prior reform, that of democracy, that is very difficult and even debated. Thus, it might be best to view Earth democracy as a second step, giving it time to remedy the present problems and flaws in democratic practice, perhaps resorting first to various means of informing citizens of the immediate ongoing hazards they face.

In the meantime, as Biermann, Bosselmann and many others including myself have suggested, we need a centralized global governance that is not prey to commenrcial interests and to political power: a tall order indeed! Aside from the eminently desirable formation of a United Nations Environmental Organization (UNEO), a World Environmental Organization (WEO), or even a UN Trusteeship Council as reviewed or proposed by Klaus Bosselmann,[69] we must face the fact that even the United Nations is controlled to some extent by Western political and economic interests or, at least, that it is unable to support fully its own resolutions[70] and to implement its own principles; we might turn instead to the one of its organs which is not as highly politicized or otherwise controlled: the World Health Organization (WHO). The WHO presents some advantages as an initial basis for global governance, but the WHO is still an organ of the UN, so subject to some of the same pressures at least in part, and it is a "stage" supported by countries both richer and poorer, as well as being an independent actor.

This political reality lends credence to the belief that the first "enemy" which must be removed in order to establish an "eco-kingdom of freedom", is the present globalized economic system.[71] Richard Westra adds:

> there will never be the heroic showdown between capitalism and socialism because capitalism in any *substantive* sense is *gone* … yes, significant residues of capital persist, particularly in the realm of the superstructure. These include the ideological fixation on abstract quantitative mercantile wealth expansion as the social goal along political policy exhortations to wring quantitative "growth" at any cost to society and the earth's biosphere from a decayed and depleted economic and resource superstructure … And, the lingering superstructure manifestations of capital, including the view that capitalism is forever, are now the greatest danger to humanity.[72]

The main points that emerge from our perspective are two: one is that the superstructure of globalization, according to Westra, *includes* the UN and all its institutions. The second is that from this perspective, the main question remains: if the present Earth situation is both grave and urgent, it seems that the major goal of public policy, globally, is to remove all the present global superstructure, in order to give primacy to a new form of economy. This new economy is an organized/state/bureaucratic structure, one that is delinked from the economic superstructure that prevails through globalization (an example might be the position of Greece after the referendum that gave their government 70 per cent of votes in favour of leaving the EU in 2015).

The details of Richard Westra's proposal for this form of regional governance are far more specific than those that emerge from the superficially similar regionalism proposed by William Rees; as well, Rees does not give "delinking" from the globalized economy as a condition of the renewed ecologically informed public policy. However, as noted above the same urgency is present in this case that to which we have appealed when discussing democracy and its reliance on informing/transforming citizens as a first step necessary prior to the achievement of Earth democracy, or "commoning".

The present situation, including unliveable conditions in many parts of the world, attacks on the basic rights of humanity based on disintegrity everywhere, from the Arctic to sub-Saharan Africa, is not such that the solutions proposed can be realized first, before the Earth emergency can truly be addressed.

Essentially, all the proposals and strategies we have been discussing, have various degrees of merit, in fact some may even coexist, as we shall show below. But what they all share is problematic, as they appear to be pursued as a "second step" after some otherwise primal condition has been met. In each case, the primary requirement, be it the transforming of citizens' consciousness, the desire of enough citizens to engage in meetings involving "deliberations", demands a complex, multifaceted and radical change from the present available public.

But the first thing to note is that, whatever our ultimate goal, the present situation is so dire, that we need immediately some reasonable change, reasonable in the sense that it must be based on currently existing institutions, legal regimes and accepted practices. The first step then must be to decide what would be possible, even probable to achieve, while we are waiting for a great transformation of public consciousness, or the delinking of states and whole regions from the present predatory globalized economic controls.

But although the economic conditions imposed by globalization are the main reason for all the biological and ecological ills that beset the Earth and its inhabitants great and small, we cannot throw away the baby with the bath water: corrupt and "lawless" though it is now, because of the imperialism of the great powers, we cannot simply dispose of the whole international legal structure at the same time, even if such an extreme action would be possible.

Indeed, the UN and all its organs and institutions originated from the states who won WWII, essentially the same powers that control globalization today. But the law, both domestic and internationally is, paradoxically, both the enabler of the development of globalization and of all the regulatory regimes that culminate in the WTO, a tribunal without due process, without transparency, and, on the other hand, it is the source of the regimes and institutions that may give us reason to hope.

For example, both the UNESCO and the WHO are also part of the same international law structures. The law is intended to exist for the protection of human rights, and – to some extent – there are also conventions for the protection of the environment and even the climate, weak and almost powerless though they are. Hence it seems wrong to insist that the whole international UN system must be eliminated together with the economic superstructure it has spawned or at least enabled. Richard Westra believes that the UN system cannot be reformed, but must be condemned together with globalization.

However, it would seem impossible to expect a series of delinked, separate regional enclaves and their citizens to concern themselves with the reality of global problems while their main concern had been to abandon the global for the local. Hence it seems we have reached a dead end, a "solution" that demands an almost infinite postponement of what we intend to establish, that is, ecologically based global governance. Yet this "blockage" at least serves to show the parameters within which we must remain in order to be able to progress: they must include and be based upon what is achievable in a reasonable length of time, at least temporarily and as a start. As well, international laws are the only basis for real and lasting change.

Before returning to what might be possible now, we should clarify once again that, as things stand now, we have no absolute certainly in the protection of the law: the law today is part of the politics of plunder.

The politics of plunder

> The construction of a neo-colonial scheme is quite simple: rather than warships and an openly discriminatory legal system, it is the mirage of efficiency.[73]

Before we venture further along this route, we should understand the basic meaning of "plunder" in this context. Mattei and Nader cite the American Heritage Dictionary's definition: "to rob of goods by force, especially in times of war; 'pillage', and 'plunder' (the noun) a 'property stolen by fraud or force'".[74]

The removal of others' property "by fraud or force" fits well the project of Western hegemony, especially if we include in "fraud", public misinformation campaigns, and the deliberate promotion of national interests, as attempts to implement the "public good". But economic activity is by no means the whole story of their motivation, not even the greatest part of it.

In addition, while I concur fully with Mattei and Nader's evaluation of neo-liberalism, the subtitle of their work goes further than I would: "when the rule of law is illegal" describes well the neoliberal policies, the promotion of the market and the "self-enforcing" logic of the World Trade Organization (WTO), and strong economic and political realization that meets any attempt to "close the market", but it ignores counter forces present in international *erga omnes* obligations and existence of *jus cogens* norms.[75]

The authors correctly note the "highly simplistic but highly interventionist legal formulations" that lead to the constitutionalization of the neo-liberal order", by claiming "sovereignty over local politics".[76] Thus, by privileging the market over local needs, Western powers impose the preference of Western financial institutions and Western multinational bodies, over the needs and choices of local (poorer) populations. They do so, Mattei and Nader explain, by promoting the intrusion into the governance of weaker, local communities, using the law itself to support the plunder, through "structural adjustment programs" and the thrust to "comprehensive development".[77]

> Neo-liberalism is thus an aggregate of social, political, economic, legal and ideological practices, carried out by a variety of actors that respond to what we consider the formidable logic of plunder. The reduction of the public sphere, and the large extension of the private sector, to the exclusive advantage of the stronger, and the corporate actors, is the thrust of such policy.[78]

Yet, despite the accuracy of most aspects of this position, and the accurate recognition of the superiority of the WTO, for instance, there are some components of the international law regimes, such as natural law principles, principles of justice and of moral fairness, that are resistant to the overwhelming wave of neoliberalism that we face today. These universal principles are strongly opposed to neoliberalism, and they are upheld by many and diverse legal scholars, philosophers, economists, and political scientists too numerous to list. Legal scholars such as Hersch Lauterpacht, Richard Falk, Margot Salomon, Maurizio Ragazzi, Dwight Newman and Upendra Baxi, as well as Christian Tomuschat, for instance; or philosophers and political scientists such as Will Kymlicka, Arne Naess, Richard Westra; economists such as Herman Daly and William Rees, to name but a few, clearly see and indict the present global situation, and defend principles and policies in direct conflict with the "rule of plunder" Mattei and Nader describe.[79]

It would be naïve to say that these forces can prevail, let alone that they surely will, any more than it would be impossible to predict that the world-wide protests we have seen since Seattle in 1999 will make a difference, other than to render meetings of the G8 a travesty:

> beginning in Seattle in 1999 … there have been no meetings of the so-called "free world" leaders … that did not happen behind an iron curtain of police aimed at excluding participation, silencing opposition, and repressing protests.[80]

But it is worthy of note that whole legal school programs, and numerous scholarly writings and publishing today defend the "legal" rule of law, and strongly oppose the neoliberal paradigm.

The defence of integrity and ecological governance: the World Health Organization

> In its first decades, the WHO functioned as the singular global health authority that its constitution envisioned, with countries relying on its technical advice and normative leadership.[81]

Before we consider the problems endemic to the current functioning of the WHO, we should acknowledge the problems that the WHO shares with other law-based strategies, that is the more or less open influence of corporations, indirectly or through the "expert witness" they hire to testify in courts of law or directly, through the influence they still possess on the very processes of the WHO and the World Health Assembly (WHA). This influence manifests itself through lobbies and other means. However, this is one area through which it might be possible to move forward, I submit, without a previous time-consuming, complex change of governance, or even a global transformation of consciousness.

The WHO/WHA are still UN institutions, hence they are potentially open to the same problems that neoliberal "plunder" imposes on the rest of the legal order. However, they share a positive trait with some of the other strategies we have discussed: they are based on the scientific expertise of highly qualified teams, not open to the decision of popular voting, or the dictates of neoliberal economists. In contrast, the WTO, which includes neither ecologists nor health/medical specialists in its decision-making team, yet presumes to adjudicate matters of environmental/public health concern, as Gostin puts it:

> The World Health Organization is the global health leader endowed with a progressive constitution and international legitimacy. There is no substitute for the WHO, with its incomparable normative powers and influence.[82]

However, for several reasons, it does not, at this time, fully live up to its potential. Like many other UN institutions, it was founded in 1945, after the Second World War: on 16 June 1946, the Magna Charta for world health was signed by sixty-one delegates.[83]

Today the WHO has 194 member states and two associate members. Its governing structure includes the WHA, the Executive Board (EB), and the "regional offices".[84] The history of the WHO shows that, at first, the WHO focused on fighting infectious diseases, from tuberculosis to smallpox (eradicated in 1980), even attempting to eradicate malaria. Polio was targeted in 1988. Nevertheless, the WHO wanted to go beyond "disease specific programs" and their new approach to "health systems and health education", led them to the 1978 Alma-Ata Declaration on "Health for All by 2000":

> The landmark 1978 Alma-Ata Declaration on Primary Health Care called for Primary Health Care (PHC) setting the target of attaining for "all peoples of the world by the year 2000 … a level of health that will permit them to lead a socially and economically productive life".[85]

What is most significant from our point of view, is the need that is present to go beyond the WHO's scientific and technical expertise. Normativity may be found in the WHO's Constitution, where Article 1 states its mission as "the attainment by all peoples of the highest possible level of health" which demonstrates the "extraordinary powers" of this institution.[86] Further, the WHO has been creating "soft global health norms", but its normative activities are supported not only by scientific expertise but also by ethics and a concern for human rights.[87] As well: "Article 23 of the WHO Constitution grants the WHA 'the authority to make recommendations to members'."[88]

Some of its most prominent successes are "the International Code of Marketing of Breast Milk Substitutes" (1981) and "the Global Code of Practice of the International Recruitment of Health Personnel" (2010),[89] and it promoted numerous global strategies. Article 19 of the constitution allows the WHA to "adopt conventions and agreements", but it was not until 2003 that the WHO actually negotiated a health convention, which was adopted by the assembly: "The Framework Convention on Tobacco Control".[90]

In general, and for the most part, "the WHO has eschewed norm setting preferring scientific and technical solutions to deep-seated problems of global health".[91] In 2012 the WHA defined the reforms they intended to pursue:

1 improved health outcomes;
2 greater coherence in global health; and
3 pursuing excellence.[92]

What we need is for the WHO to go beyond their medical response ability, invaluable though it is, to assume the global leadership that is potentially theirs. The WHO employs scientists, physicians, epidemiologists and nurses, the WHA also uses lawyers, but they also need ecologists and human rights specialists. It must avoid conflicts of interest, but among all the available institutions in the UN, it demonstrates itself eminently suitable to take the leadership role, which emerges already from some of the recent reports it has produced, such as its report on the conditions present in Palestine under Israel's occupation (2008), and recently, its 2012 Report on Endocrine Disruptors,[93] documents which should have had clear immediate consequences in law and policy.

From the standpoint of the environment, it would need to use the strength and power it employed for the Tobacco Convention, to start by banning hazardous chemicals, pesticides and other industrial chemicals, beyond the simple acknowledgment of one substance at a time as carcinogenic (as per their recent declaration on glyphosate). The WHO is the only power that is somewhat (though not fully) independent, although it is still financially dependent on member states: "There is little doubt that the WHO will never reach its potential unless members ensure that financing is predictable, sustainable and scalable for global health needs."[94]

Gostin auspicates a strong influence for the WHO, beyond human health, but he also acknowledges the presence of several problems that beset the organization: it is a "servant to member states"; it has a "short term horizon" that forces it to prioritize health emergencies over "enduring health needs"; its resources are far too limited for the role it could and should play globally; its funding is restricted and often "earmarked" rather than being free to be directed to areas of greatest need; it is too decentralized in its structure, rather than possessing "global implementation capacities".[95]

From the standpoint of the protection/implementation of ecological and biological integrity, however, the WHO/WHA is ideally suited to be the first organization to lead globally at least temporarily, until a separate UN organization can be established. In fact, to review its qualifications:

1 it has the UN mandated ability to negotiate conventions and other binding instruments through the WHA;
2 it is ideally positioned to protect both ecological and biological integrity, that is, both habitats and organisms, as its many relevant reports attest;
3 it needs not extend its mandate inappropriately, that is too far beyond its mandate, as it is already staffed by scientists and others whose realm of expertise overlaps or coincides with our concerns;
4 it is highly respected worldwide already, it is heard and listened to globally;
5 it is not, at this time, totally controlled by industry, and – in fact – it is the only institution that dares to criticize industry openly, albeit too cautiously at this time;
6 it does not depend on votes and election media campaigns: its decisions on what is harmful and what needs to be done depend on the real decisions of expert teams, more than those of any other UN organization.

Further, if we consider the other strategies discussed in this work, its operation is fully compatible with both domestic and international policies based on Nature Trusts of other forms of trusteeship, and it is also compatible with future decisions reached in common by citizens in various regions, provided these decisions complement its mandates. Clearly the role of its legal experts will need to adjust to its future role, particularly regarding international human rights, but essentially it is not a revolutionary proposal as the basis and foundation for its development is already present.

As well, this proposal is not incompatible with the defence of the natural commons and the information and education of citizens: it would simply make the message even more compelling by linking it inescapably with everyone's survival, as we advocate. However, perhaps one further aspect of this proposal could be added in order to expand and complete its reach and efficiency: the added consideration of the CH, for which we argued above.

Ecological integrity and the common heritage principle again

> Nor is it convincing to argue that international law disregards the intrinsic value of the environment, including natural ecosystems and non-human species. This much is demonstrated by treaties concerned with the Antarctica, the 1972 World Heritage Convention on the Conservation of European Wildlife and Natural Habitat, the 1973 Convention on International Trade in Endangered Species and the 1992 Biological Diversity Convention, as well as the World Charter for Nature.[96]

Despite the existence of this list of international law instruments intended to protect the environment and natural ecosystems within it, provided by recognized authorities in the field, today we can see how ineffective these regulatory regimes have been, and many more besides, regarding the climate, the seas and beyond. We have explored just how conflicted any attempt to establish the primacy of integrity is and has been, from the first time the concept emerged in the law,[97] and the subsequent enactment of the instruments listed above has not helped in any way, thus far.

Hence, the main problems we have discussed start with non-implementation, combined with weak and non-specific language. Both non-implementation and confusing, non-binding language originate from the input of industrial and other corporate interests. These interests affect equally the public everywhere, that is, the citizens of countries who *might* be able to change the ineffective structures, who *might* vote out of office the domestic regulatory agencies that do not seriously defend their mandate, if the economic interests did not continue to thwart all efforts to stop the corporate control of environmental agencies, and to use the media to disinform the public and to elect their preferred candidates, especially in North America.

Therefore our effort has been to find the best candidate as a government institution that would not act according to corporate controls. We sought an organization that had the potential for leadership, had general acceptance and respect worldwide, whose decisions were based on team-findings that included doctors, epidemiologists, toxicologists and other scientists, but did not depend on economists. The WHA also employs lawyers.

Still there are other aspects of integrity that go beyond public health and the supporting ecology within states: these may be protected by the CH. The CH principle is not intended primarily to protect biological or ecological integrity as such, rather, its aim is the protection of the deep-sea and other areas beyond state borders from the industrial exploitation originating from powerful Western countries. Although it is not as powerful as the WHO, both are not subject to propaganda campaigns for their decisions, but depend on scholarly teams. As well, they may also function well together with the eventual establishment of an institution designed for world Governance, as they remain particularly close to the concept of trusteeship, the importance of which we have noted in the proposals of M. C. Wood and Bosselmann.

The CH complements our proposal, which may be a temporary measure, given that most of the characteristics we seek for a central organization for integrity are present in the WHO/WHA. Thus this strategy may offer a quicker possibility of ecological success or at least clear improvement until a more elaborate organization may be formed and implemented. The combination of the WHO and the CH principle may well remain as foundational in any new organization eventually founded for ecological governance, as they reach together all natural areas of the world, providing both their scientific and traditional/cultural basis, necessary to inform and direct legal and administrative aspects. The interface between biodiversity – if not integrity – is established also by the Preamble of that document which states, unequivocally, the "conservation of biodiversity is a common concern of humankind".[98] Three states have not ratified it to date: the US, Somalia and Iraq. The US's main concern was the fact that the final text of the Convention "threatened to retard biotechnology and undermine the protection of ideas".[99] Hence, while neither the CBD nor the CH demonstrate an identity of goals with the principle of integrity we are supporting, both appear, at least, compatible with it.

Beyond scholarly support for the protection of ecological integrity: normativity and legality

> A crucial question is whether an oppressed people is legally permitted to take some sort of action to enforce the right to self-determination. In the past, many Third World countries and socialist bloc in the United Nations took the view that peoples entitled to self-determination were authorized to use force to secure self-determination. To render this consistent under the Charter system, those countries argued that the use of force by colonial people was warranted as a form of self defense against the armed aggression constituted by colonial domination.[100]

Given the present and ongoing destruction of the Earth, it seems that the normative element for our position cannot be in doubt. One needs not speak as a religious leader to understand the folly of eliminating one after the other the many organisms and natural aspects of a functioning Earth (the "Creation" to which Pope Francis refers), without a full understanding of their functions, their respective roles, or their connection to the survival of life on Earth.

The economic interests that effectively govern the world put their faith in their power and in the power of their technologies: after all climate and other disasters serve to augment the GDP of the country where they occur. In contrast, our discussion in the earlier chapters has shown beyond a doubt that all clever new technologies represent further attacks on ecological or biological integrity instead, as they are not assessed from the standpoint of health and ecology. Hence their way is contrary not only to prudence and good governance, but also to any form of morality that prescribes respect for humanity, or simply even respect for life, be it proposed by Thomas Aquinas, Immanuel Kant or another philosopher.

This work's goal is the quest for the best possible form of ecogovernance *now*, as we acknowledge with many other scholars the urgency of the situation. Thus we need to go beyond the normativity all feel is required: climate change, continued attacks on nature and populations, rampant immorality and illegality in all dealings among states and peoples, unpunished for the most part, support this contention. What is immediately required is to identify legal regimes that may defend integrity at the biological level of single organisms, and at the ecological level of natural systems. In both cases, established legal instruments defend the right to life, the respect for minorities proscribe the infliction of cruel and unusual punishment, at least on paper, all of which could be used to defend the rights of peoples through the protection of integrity, but thus far, no effort has been made to extend the meaning of several rights in this direction, including the right to health.

In order to correct this oversight supported by the overwhelming power of state/corporate control, we could start by acknowledging the multiple harms we face and invoke another well-established principle: the right to self-defence. Clearly self-determination regarding other states and actions attempting to occupy a territory should no longer be an issue, given the UN prohibition of colonization and occupation, although at least one ongoing example to the contrary exists, in Israel as the colonizing and occupying power in Palestine.

In addition, the imperialistic practices that alter permanently the land, water and air, causing unavoidable harm to citizens, also persists with impunity. Thus we can consider the governments that allow this to happen guilty – at least – of complicity with the industries that profit from this state of affairs.[101] This situation should spur us to seek radical change in our legal system, as Capra and Mattei state:

> a legal system based on principles that are the polar opposite of the careless extractive transformation of commons into capital that we have celebrated over the past three hundred years.[102]

The legal system we are seeking must incorporate precisely the principles that are understood to be the main principles governing "civilized people". If self-determination to which we referred is not that of a community or nation seeking to separate from the country within which it is embedded, or a country attempting to affirm its independence, then its seems that perhaps internal self-determination is at issue, which Cassese terms a "customary rule":

> Internal self-determination means the right to authentic self-government that is the right for a people really and freely to choose its own political and economic regime – which is much more than choosing among what is on offer perhaps from one political or economic position only. It is an ongoing right.[103]

This right has been viewed as due primarily to "people of a territory … geographically distinct and ethnically or culturally diverse from the remainder of the territory of the state administering it".[104] However, the right entails also "equal access to the government which they are entitled, not equal rights", as "the existence of a government which tramples upon its citizens' basic rights and fundamental freedoms does not give rise to a right of internal self-determination".[105]

Therefore, it is yet another case of an existing law, legal regime or institution, which perhaps could be expanded to remedy the present urgent situation, although it needs expansion, re-interpretation or review to better apply to the situation where peoples are routinely victimized through environmental crimes, with no recourse. As well, even if the law regarding self-determination of peoples is not as good a fit for what we are searching, the principle of self-defence cannot be disputed, once the source of the harms and the ecoviolence that prevails has been identified.[106] This would seem to be a reasonable interpretation of that principle, as harms inflicted by a form of governance that is neither *from* nor *for* the people.

Human rights violations that ought to have been eliminated at the source, through due diligence of legal actors and through government controls, now still persist. In addition, there are no environmental tribunals to adjudicate the breaches that occur regularly, without even considering the basic issues discussed here:

> A further factor inhibiting the creation of environmental tribunals may be the fact that most environmental harm is directly caused by private actors and not by the actions of state or its agents. State responsibility is usually based instead on the State's failure to act with due diligence to prevent or to remedy injury, for acts by private entities under its control, often but not always in violation of domestic law.[107]

The inaction of States permits the ongoing destruction of integrity and it includes the disregard for the biological integrity of individuals, hence the breaches of the basic rights of humanity. Hence, "despite the reluctance of some states to create international environmental monitoring bodies",[108] human rights bodies should hear environmental human rights cases, in fact, strong monitoring bodies should be added to present legal regimes. However, the only cases heard with any hopes of favourable results, have been those pertaining to Indigenous peoples.[109]

In contrast, most of the legal regimes in existence focus on the right to information and public participation, without any direct action on substantive issues instead.

Thus our effort to re-integrate the defence of all life beyond facile appeals to moral duty, which, although accepted and adopted by the "converts", fall upon the closed ears of the majority, especially those in power. We cannot join in "commoning" simply dismissing all that must be excised simply as something we will slowly cut away, a regional pocket or community at a time, as we continue to transform our consciousness, learn to dismiss our social myths almost by fiat.

It would seem better to respect our belief in radical future change, both bottom-up and top-down, with renewed organizations, practices and institutions, but without closing our mind to the immediate need for action demanded by the overwhelming ecological crises that are already present. To that effect, we have proposed a temporary/permanent reconsideration and expansion of those institutions and instruments that already appear to be – for the most part – beyond the control of trade and economic organizations, as they are already committed to support the actions demanded by *jus cogens* norms, already existing.

In the cases and the organizations we have proposed, the basis we require is already present, including the openness to new scientific findings, the respect for life, humanity and the natural world, as these principles are already embedded in their respective mandates. Further their connection with, yet their independence from, the flawed UN system lends them the legitimacy that we need. This strategy seems like a plausible, even achievable, short-term goal on which to focus for immediate changes, while still maintaining an ongoing dialogue with all citizens for a radically altered future solution.

Concluding thoughts

The task I undertook was admittedly a very ambitious one: to take a concept that had barely emerged in international and domestic law, before almost sinking into oblivion, ignored, misunderstood and generally barely acknowledged – and attempt to make it basic to a world-wide campaign to achieve global ecological governance. The first chapters emphasized the causality, direct though not always immediate, between the condition of disintegrity and the resulting human rights violations, which affect our habitat and all within it, public health in several ways (Chapter 2), forced migrations (Chapter 3), food, water deprivations and climate change (Chapter 4).

All these effects are first engendered then supported by the economic/trade interests of globalization (Chapter 5). Those who understand the importance of integrity, however, are not the only ones who acknowledge the presence of these issues, hence the relation between governance, public policy and environmental harms. Hence Chapter 6 reviewed and discussed each of the main recent proposals for ecological governance. Chapter 7 contrasts our proposal for a new strategy to those who have been presented and discussed, starting with the new, powerful analysis of our failed governance and environmental problems by Pope Francis in his *Laudato Si'* encyclical.

Finally, rather than deciding that one or another of the proposed strategies appears to be the better one, I suggest that all of them have merit and may work eventually. Yet they all share a major problem: most need a lengthy period of preparatory work in order to have a chance of being accepted, let alone adopted in practice. Thus our final proposal suggests a "halfway" strategy, something that meets the criterion of being easier to achieve perhaps, than the other proposals we have reviewed.

It is not so novel or perhaps as radical as the other suggestions reviewed in Chapter 6. Yet, while some or all of those strategies suggest a radical system change before becoming operational, the changes here proposed pertain to some of the existing institutions and regimes and may be easier to implement in order to mitigate or remove the multiple ongoing threats we are facing *now*. The changes I propose appear to be possible and faster to achieve; as well, they are such that they are compatible with other proposals, and can eventually remain to complement other, more extensive future changes.

Notes

1 Pope Francis, 24 May 2015, "Encyclical Letter *Laudato Si'* of the Holy Father Francis On Care for Our Common Home", available at http://w2.vatican.va/content/francesco/en/encyclicals/documents/papa-francesco_20150524_enciclica-laudato-si.html, para. 8, quoting Patriarch Bartholomew's Address in Santa Barbara, California, on 8 November 1997. Subsequent quotations in the text giving paragraph numbers refer to the same encyclical letter, hereafter referred to as "*Laudato Si'*".

2 Laura Westra, 2004, *Ecoviolence and the Law*, Transnational Publishers/Brill, Leyden, The Netherlands.

3 Laura Westra, 1995, "The Ethics of Integrity", in Si Balch (ed.), *The Land Ethic: Meeting Human Needs for the Land and Its Resources*, Society of American Foresters, Bethesda, MD, pp. 31–44, here p. 35.

4 Thomas W. Pogge (ed.), 2001, *Global Justice*, Blackwell Publishers, Oxford; Amedeo Postiglione, 2001, *Giustizia e Ambiente Globale*, Giuffrè Editore, Milan; Robert Bullard, *Dumping in Dixie*, Westview Press, Boulder, CO; Laura Westra and Bill Lawson, 2001, *Faces of State Terrorism*, 2nd edn, Rowman Littlefield, Lanham, MD; and too many other works to mention.

5 Hans Jonas, 1984, *The Imperative of Responsibility*, University of Chicago Press, Chicago, IL.

6 Ibid., p. 32.

7 Jeffrey D. Sachs, 2015, *The Age of Sustainable Development*, Columbia University Press, New York, p. 452.

8 Laura Westra, 2011, *Human Rights: The "Commons" and the Collective*, University of British Columbia Press, Vancouver, BC.

9 Burns H. Weston and David Bollier, 2013, *Green Governance: Ecological Survival, Human Rights and the Law of the Commons*, Cambridge University Press, New York.

10 Klaus Bosselmann, 2015, *Earth Governance*, Edward Elgar, Cheltenham, p. 53.

11 Ibid., p. 54.

12 Ibid., p. 186.

13 The Canadian Constitution, §s.35(1) (documents available at http://laws.justice.gc.ca/eng/Const/Const_index.html).
14 Laura Westra, 2012, "Health and Environment: The Denied Connection", in Laura Westra, Colin Soskolne and Donald Spady (eds), *Human Health and Ecological Integrity*, Earthscan, London, pp. 7–19.
15 Mary Christina Wood, 2014, *Nature's Trust*, Cambridge University Press, New York, p. 218.
16 Ibid., p. 219.
17 Ibid.
18 Recommended on 23 January 2015, by the Ad Hoc Informal Working Group, by consensus, to the United Nations as a possible future Third UNCLOS Implementation Agreement; see Tullio Scovazzi, 2015, "The Conservation and Sustainable Use of Marine Biodiversity, Including Genetic Resources, in Areas beyond National Jurisdiction: A Legal Perspective", available at www.un.org/Depts/los/consultative_process/ICP12_Presentations/Scovazzi_Presentation.pdf.
19 Olivia Woolley, 2013, *Ecological Governance*, Cambridge University Press, Cambridge.
20 George Monbiot, 2015, *Feral*, University of Chicago Press, Chicago, IL.
21 Aristotle, *The Politics*, tr. E. Barker, 1973, Oxford University Press, Oxford, p. 173.
22 Saskia Sassen, 2006, *Territory Authority Rights: From Medieval to Global Assemblages*, Princeton University Press, Princeton, NJ.
23 Klaus Bosselmann, 2010, "Earth Democracy: Institutionalizing Sustainability and Ecological Integrity", in J. Ron Engel, Laura Westra and Klaus Bosselmann (eds), *Democracy, Ecological Integrity and International Law*, Cambridge Scholars Publications, Newcastle upon Tyne.
24 Wood, *Nature's Trust*.
25 Secretary-General Boutros Boutros-Ghali, Statement at Security Council Summit Meeting, SC/5360/Rev. 1, 31 January 1992.
26 Thomas M. Franck, 1995, *Fairness in International Law and Institutions*, Oxford University Press, Oxford, pp. 218–244, here pp. 245–283; Susan Lamb, 1999, "Legal Limits to United Nations Security Council Powers", in Guy S. Goodwin-Gill and Stefan Talmon (eds), *The Reality of International Law: Essays in Honour of Ian Brownlie*, Clarendon Press, Oxford, pp. 361–388.
27 Lamb, "Legal Limits to United Nations Security Council Powers", p. 363; no. 10 adds, from the *travaux préparatoires*, "Proposals made during the drafting of the Charter to place the ultimate authority to interpret the Charter in the International Court of Justice were not accepted … As anticipated in 1945, therefore, each organ must, in the first place at least, determine its own jurisdiction" (ICJ Rep. 1962, 151 at 168).
28 *Prosecutor v. Dusko Tadic* (Jurisdiction) 1995.
29 Lamb, "Legal Limits to United Nations Security Council Powers", p. 366; D. Bowett, 1982, *The Law of International Institutions*, 4th edn, Sweet and Maxwell, London, p. 33.
30 Lamb, "Legal Limits to United Nations Security Council Powers", p. 368.
31 Ian Brownlie, 1995, "International Law at the Fiftieth Anniversary of the United Nations: General Course on Public International Law", *Recueil des Cours* 255, pp. 9–228, here pp. 216–217.
32 Lamb, "Legal Limits to United Nations Security Council Powers", pp. 375–376.
33 Ibid., p. 377.
34 SC Res. S/RES/827 (1993); Res. S/RES/808 (1993).
35 G. G. Fitzmaurice, 1950, "The Law & Procedure of the International Court of Justice: General Principles and Substantive Law," *The British Yearbook of International Law* 1950, pp. 1–70.
36 Lamb, "Legal Limits to United Nations Security Council Powers", p. 387.

37 Ibid.; Brownlie, "International Law at the Fiftieth Anniversary of the United Nations", p. 26.
38 Lawrence Gostin, 2014, "Law and Ethics in Population Health", *Australia and New Zealand Journal of Public Health* 28, pp. 3–4.
39 Karin Mickelson and Rees, William, 2003, "The Environment: Ecological and Ethical Dimensions", in E. Hughes, A. R. Lucas, and W. A. Tilleman (eds), *Environmental Law and Policy*, 3rd edn, Edmond Montgomery Publications, Toronto, pp. 1–40, here p. 10.
40 William E. Rees, 2014, *Avoiding Collapse: An Agenda for Sustainable Degrowth and Relocalizing the Economy*, Climate Justice Projects, Canadian Centre for Policy Alternatives, British Colombia.
41 Woolley, *Ecological Governance*, p. 198.
42 Ibid., p. 199.
43 Ibid., p. 209.
44 Wood, *Nature's Trust*, p. 74.
45 Ibid., p. 114.
46 Ibid., p. 115.
47 Ibid., p. 116.
48 Ibid., p. 117.
49 Ibid., p. 336, citing petition for original jurisdiction at 16, *Barhaugh v. Mont.*, No. OP 11-0258, 4 May 2011, quoting Ansel Adams.
50 Charles L. Black, Jr., 1960, "The Lawfulness of the Segregation Decisions," Faculty Scholarship Series, Paper 2586, http://digitalcommons.law.yale.edu/fss_papers/2586; see also Ira Michael Heyman, 1961, "The Chief Justice, Racial Segregation, and the Friendly Critics", *California Law Review* 49, p. 104.
51 Anders Walker, 2009, "'Neutral' Principles: Re-thinking the Legal History of Civil Rights, 1934–1964", *Loyola University of Chicago Law Journal* 40(3), pp. 385–436, here p. 396; see *Gitlow v. New York*, 268 US 652(1925)7; David M. Rabban, 1997, *Free Speech in its Forgotten Years*, Cambridge Historical Studies in American Law and Society, Cambridge University Press, Cambridge.
52 Terrorist Act, US 2006; see also Laura Westra, 2013, *The Supranational Corporation*, Brill, Leyden, The Netherlands.
53 Kenneth Mack, 2009, "Bringing the Law Back into the History of the Civil Rights Movement", *Law and History Review* 27, pp. 657–669.
54 Ibid.; see also Aldon D. Morris, 1984, *The Origins of the Civil Rights Movement: Black Communities Organizing for Change*, Free Press, New York, pp. 35–37; but also work focused on the North, where "explicit legal segregation" did not exist, such as Thomas J. Sugue, 2008, *Sweet Land of Liberty: The Forgotten Struggle for Civil Rights in the North*, Random House, New York.
55 Gerald N. Rosenberg, 1991, *The Hollow Hope: Can Courts bring About Social Change*, University of Chicago Press, Chicago, IL, pp. 157–169, 336–342.
56 Nancy MacLean, 2005, *Freedom is not Enough: The Opening of the American Workplace*, Harvard University Press, Cambridge, MA.
57 Ibid.
58 Mickelson and Rees, "The Environment: Ecological and Ethical Dimensions".
59 Sheila Collins, 2011, "Occupy Wall Street", unpublished paper on file with the author.
60 Bruce D'Arcus, 2004, "Dissent, Public Space and Citizenship", *Space and Polity* 8(3), pp. 355–370.
61 Jiri Priban, 2005, "Political Dissent, Human Rights, and Legal Transformations: Communist and Post-Communist Experiences", *East European Politics and Societies* 19(4), pp. 553–572, here p. 556.
62 Michael Ratner and Margaret Ratner Kunstler, 2001, *Hell No: Your Right to Dissent in Twenty-first Century America*, The New Press, New York, p. 2.
63 Ibid., p. 4.

64 Ibid., p. 5.
65 Ibid.
66 Ibid., pp. 8–9.
67 Ibid., p. 16.
68 Sachs, *The Age of Sustainable Development*, p. 447.
69 Bosselmann, *Earth Governance*, pp. 257–258, see also ibid., n. 128 on p. 258 for a thorough list of such proposals.
70 Laura Westra, 2011, *Globalization, Violence and World Governance*, Brill, Leyden, The Netherlands, ch. 6.
71 Richard Westra, 2015, *Exit from Globalization*, Routledge, London, p. 182.
72 Ibid., pp. 181–182.
73 Ugo Mattei and Laura Nader, 2008, *Plunder: When the Rule of Law is Illegal*, Blackwell, Oxford, p. 25.
74 Ibid., p. 11.
75 Ibid., p. 50.
76 Ibid., p. 51.
77 Ibid., p. 53.
78 Ibid.
79 Just some examples: Margot Salomon, 2007, *Global Responsibility for Human Rights*, Oxford University Press, Oxford; Maurizio Ragazzi, 1998, *The Concept of Obligations Erga Omnes*, Clarendon Press, Oxford; Dwight G. Newman, 2004, "Collective Interests and Collective Rights", *American Journal of Jurisprudence* 49, pp. 127–163; Upendra Baxi, 1999, "Voices of Suffering and the Future of Human Rights", *Transnational Law and Contemporary Problems* 8, pp. 125–169; Richard Westra, 2009, *Political Economy and Globalization*, Routledge, Abingdon; Will Kymlicka, 1997, *Multicultural Citizenship*, Clarendon Press, Oxford.
80 Mattei and Nader, *Plunder*, p. 52.
81 Gostin, "Law and Ethics in Population Health", p. 131.
82 Ibid., p. 89.
83 Ibid., p. 91.
84 Ibid., p. 92.
85 Ibid., p. 97; *Declaration of Alma Ata* (1978)
86 Gostin, "Law and Ethics in Population Health", p. 103.
87 Ibid., p. 104.
88 Ibid.
89 Ibid., p. 104.
90 Ibid., p. 110.
91 Ibid., p. 113.
92 Ibid., p. 114.
93 WHO and UNEP, 2013, *State of the Science of Endocrine Disrupting Chemicals – 2012*, an assessment of the state of the science of endocrine disruptors prepared by a group of experts for the United Nations Environment Programme (UNEP) and World Health Organization (WHO), edited by Åke Bergman, Jerrold J. Heindel, Susan Jobling, Karen A. Kidd and R. Thomas Zoeller, available at www.who.int/ceh/publications/endocrine/en.
94 Gostin, "Law and Ethics in Population Health", p. 125.
95 Ibid., pp. 127–128.
96 Patricia Birnie, Alan Boyle and Catherine Redgwell, 2009, *International Law and the Environment*, Oxford University Press, Oxford, p. 280.
97 Clean Water Act 1972, available at www.epa.gov/laws-regulations/summary-clean-water-act.
98 Section VIII, Handbook of the Convention of Biological Diversity, 3rd edn, Montreal, 2005, "Preamble"; the Convention entered into force 29 December 1993, and it has been ratified by 191 parties.

99 Statement by President Bush, US, to the UNCED, 12 June 1992; see also discussion in Birnie et al., *International Law and the Environment.*
100 Antonio Cassese, 1995, *Self-Determination of Peoples*, Cambridge University Press, Cambridge, pp. 150–151.
101 Westra, *Ecoviolence and the Law*.
102 Fritjhof Capra and Ugo Mattei, 2015, *The Ecology of Law*, Berrett-Koehler Publishers, San Francisco, CA, p.179
103 Cassese, *Self-Determination of Peoples*, p. 101
104 Ibid., p. 115.
105 Ibid., p. 114.
106 Westra, *Ecoviolence and the Law*.
107 Dinah Shelton, 2015, "Legitimate and Necessary: Adjudicating Human Rights Violations Related to Activities Causing Environmental Harm or Risk", *Journal of Human Rights and the Environment* 6(2), pp. 139–155, here p. 142.
108 Ibid., p. 143.
109 See, for example, *Mayagna (Sumo) Awas Tingni Community v. Nicaragua* (Merits, Reparations and Costs), Judgment IACtHR (Ser. C) No. 79, 31 August 2001; *Maya Indigenous Communities of the Toledo Dist. v. Belize*, case 12.053, IACommHR, Report No. 40/04, OEA/Ser.L/V/II.122 doc. 5, rev. l; *Yakye Axa v. Paraguay* (Merits, Reparations and Costs), 17 June 2005 (Ser. C), No. 125; *Kichwa Indigenous Peoples of Sarayaku v. Ecuador*, 245 IACtHR (Ser. C) (27 June 2012). Although there is no global treaty on Indigenous rights, the General Assembly did adopt the 2007 UN Declaration on Rights of Indigenous Peoples A/RES/61/205: see particularly Preamble, articles 29(1) and 32(3).

Index

Entries in *italics* denote figures.